The Governance of
Ethnic
Communities

Recent Titles in
Contributions in Ethnic Studies

The Governance of Ethnic Communities

POLITICAL STRUCTURES AND PROCESSES IN CANADA

Raymond Breton

CONTRIBUTIONS IN ETHNIC STUDIES, NUMBER 26
Leonard W. Doob, *Series Editor*

Greenwood Press
NEW YORK • WESTPORT, CONNECTICUT • LONDON

Library of Congress Cataloging-in-Publication Data

Breton, Raymond.
    The governance of ethnic communities : political structures and
processes in Canada / Raymond Breton.
        p.   cm.—(Contributions in ethnic studies, ISSN 0196–7088 ;
no. 26)
    Includes bibliographical references and index.
    ISBN 0–313–27417–7 (alk. paper)
    1. Minorities—Canada.   2. Political leadership—Canada.
    3. Canada—Politics and government—1980–   I. Title.   II. Series.
F1035.A1B7   1991
305.8′00971—dc20   90–38423

British Library Cataloguing in Publication Data is available.

Library of Congress Catalog Card Number: 90–38423
ISBN: 0–313–27417–7
ISSN: 0196–7088

First published in 1991

Greenwood Press, 88 Post Road West, Westport, CT   06881
An imprint of Greenwood Publishing Group, Inc.

Printed in the United States of America

The paper used in this book complies with the
Permanent Paper Standard issued by the National
Information Standards Organization (Z39.48–1984).

10 9 8 7 6 5 4 3 2 1

To Lily
For her warm and continuing support

Contents

Illustrations

Series Foreword

The Contributions in Ethnic Studies series focuses upon the problems that arise when people with different cultures and goals come together and interact productively or tragically. The modes of adjustment or conflict are varied, but usually one group dominates or attempts to dominate the other. Eventually, some accommodation is reached, but the process is likely to be long and, for the weaker group, painful. No one scholarly discipline monopolizes the research necessary to comprehend these intergroup relations. This analysis, consequently, is inevitably of interest to historians, sociologists, psychologists, and psychiatrists.

Here attention is concentrated upon Chinese, German, Italian, Spanish, Portuguese, Ukrainian, and West Indian communities in Canada. Occasional references are also made to other ethnic communities in that country, including "native peoples," and to groups in the United States. The diverse cultural and historical backgrounds of these groups as well as their status within the dominating society provide rich and varied data and the bases for scholarly generalizations.

Two sources are skillfully tapped. One is the impressive number of systematic studies and less formal arguments and opinions that are available and that are culled not only to portray the challenging difficulties confronting such communities but also to extract practical and theoretical propositions of enduring interest. Theories from social science that transcend North America are relevantly cited. The other source is a survey of respondents sampled in the above-mentioned ethnic communities in Toronto.

Frequently, ethnicity in modern societies is viewed by social scientists, journalists, the general population, and ethnic groups themselves in terms of the relation between ethnic individuals and the dominant group in a society. We wonder whether prejudice is increasing or decreasing, whether stereotypes persist or are justified, whether those people with a distinguish-

ing language or color are suffering as a result of segregation or discrimination. In this book, refreshing focus is placed, as the author states, upon
the ethnic community as "a political entity." Within their own communities,
ethnic groups are confronted with significant governance as well as rules
and regulations concerning the engulfing society. They have their own leaders, formally or informally they follow policies that perpetuate and change
their own culture and society, and they adjust or fail to adjust to external
pressures and temptations. Such self-governance affects their "collective
identity" and enables them to remain more or less distinctive, without necessarily eliminating the differences among themselves that give rise to serious
internal debates and controversies.

The author concentrates upon governances. He searches for and proposes
common tendencies among the ethnic communities in spite of their diversity.
He emerges with a set of political configurations that best describes the
political processes. In this context, other social and economic factors are
not neglected.

Readers can, will, and must find in this book a splendid summary of the
current research concentrating on the ethnic communities in North America.
That summary, because it is oriented toward significant variables and principles, can be utilized now and in the future to comprehend and investigate
ethnic groups, whether they remain active or melt away. As we grasp how
other peoples strive to govern themselves, we may possibly learn to govern
ourselves, whoever we are, more wisely and to obtain keener insight into
the political and other forces forever functioning in our midst.

                                                            Leonard W. Doob

Acknowledgments

I wish to express my sincere appreciation to Professors Jeffrey Reitz, Harold Troper, Donald Avery, and Daiva Stasiulis and to anonymous readers for their valuable comments on an earlier version of this manuscript.

I am also grateful to the Connaught Fund of the University of Toronto for greatly facilitating the completion of this project.

1

Introduction: The Ethnic Community as a Polity

The ethnic community is a multidimensional phenomenon. It can be viewed as a network of interpersonal relations and of mutual assistance; as a set of institutions to meet the various needs of group members; as a system of social classes; as a microeconomy with enterprises, a labor market, a clientele for commodities and services, and sources of capital. It can also be approached as a cultural entity that provides a framework for individual identities, means for cultural expression and development, and mechanisms for the transmission of the group's cultural heritage.

In this book, the ethnic community is seen as a political entity: how ethnic communities govern themselves is the basic question that the book addresses. A central dimension of "community" is the existence of a public life beyond the private lives of the individuals, families, and small groups that constitute a community. Another central dimension is that communities conduct their public affairs through more or less institutionalized structures, mechanisms, and practices. These constitute their "government" or system of governance.

This book is based on the idea that an understanding of ethnic communities is virtually impossible or will be very limited if adequate consideration is not given to the political dimension. Of course, this is not an entirely new perspective on ethnic communities, but it is one that is relatively underdeveloped. As will be seen throughout the analysis, several studies on particular political institutions, mechanisms, or relationships in ethnic communities can be found in the literature. The most systematic treatment of ethnic communities as polities is perhaps Elazar's (1976) study of American Jewish communities. The political structures and processes of ethnic communities have not, however, received the attention they deserve.

A concern with the political functioning of ethnic communities is important not only for the understanding of these communities as important social realities in themselves (Breton, 1983). It is also particularly critical given the political importance placed on ethnic communities in recent years by government policies and programs and, as a result, by other societal institutions such as the schools and the media (Rothschild, 1981). Of course, ethnic communities have always had significance in the institutional arenas of the larger society; today, however, their existence and role in society are becoming increasingly institutionalized. Ethnic communities are becoming explicitly incorporated as such into the institutional fabric of society (Stasiulis, 1980; Jenkins, 1988). This may not generally be the case, but it seems to be happening in Canadian society.

The following analysis is not intended to apply to "territorial minorities," especially if the minority constitutes a political majority in a region of a country and as a result is incorporated in the constitutionally established state institutions of the society. Thus, it is not meant to apply to, for example, the French community of Quebec, which, because it controls the provincial government of the province, has an officially recognized government. It is restricted to ethnic groups with "unofficial governments."

THE ETHNIC COMMUNITY AS A POLITICAL COMMUNITY

In his analysis of North American Chinatowns, Lyman (1968:53) observes that the elites of the community organizations "conduct an unofficial government, legislating, executing, and adjudicating matters for their constituents." Thus, what has been said about urban neighborhoods is largely applicable to ethnic communities: that they are "in origin and continuity a political unit" (Kotler, 1969:8). "Like the communities that Tocqueville observed, today's urban neighborhoods frequently have their own unofficial arrangements for performing certain essential functions—a capacity to form and express a collective interest, the executive power to produce collective or public goods. What is usually missing is the distinctively political means for conducting this political business—legitimate physical force" (Crenson, 1983:12).

The public affairs of a community involve such phenomena as collective decisions, community events and activities, public ceremonies and rituals, debates and controversies over issues, fund-raising for community projects, the selection of community leaders, and the exercise of influence and power. The political process involves action and events pertaining to "the determination and implementation of public goals and/or the differential distribution and use of power within the group or groups concerned with the goals being considered" (Swartz, 1968:1).

Thus, to ask how ethnic communities govern themselves is to enquire about the processes of collective decision-making, the ways in which participation and resources are mobilized for collective projects, the relationship between elites and members, the differences of interests and ideologies, the management of conflicts, and the exercise of power in the management of community affairs. It is also to enquire about the network of organizations through which community governance takes place. Indeed, political processes occur through relationships among individuals, groups, and organizations that may be more or less structured and that may involve more or less formally defined roles. That is, the structural forms in which politics occur can vary considerably, and, as Swartz points out, policies or political action should not be associated with a particular form as a matter of definition.

In particular, politics and government should not be tied exclusively with the state and its various institutions. There are stateless polities that govern themselves. This is the case with ethnic communities. They have no *state* institutions, but they have *public* ones. Physical force cannot be used legitimately (which, of course, does not mean that no coercive practices can be observed in ethnic communities), but the exercise of power and influence is common in the conduct of their public affairs. No community can operate without politics, but communities can operate politically without a state apparatus. "Western contact with African and Asian cultures as well as the surviving tribal cultures of the Americas has brought a renewed cognizance of the existence of polities that are not states" (Elazar, 1976:5).[1] "There is rough parallel, in fact, between the task of finding the political system in an urban neighborhood and the business of discovering politics in a tribal society that has no distinct government or formally designated rulers.[2] In both settings one is likely to encounter examples of 'diffused government' " (Crenson, 1983:11).

Ethnic polities, however, are "encapsulated political systems" (Bailey, 1970). They are embedded in a larger sociopolitical framework that includes state and other public institutions. Accordingly, their public affairs include relationships with their social and institutional environments. Thus, like regional and national entities, ethnic political communities have "external" as well as "domestic" affairs.

Internally, their public affairs and institutions pertain to matters such as aid to new immigrants, welfare services, facilities for the aged, cultural maintenance and development, education, the celebration of heroes and historical events, recreational activities, and the dissemination of news and opinions. Externally, the matters requiring action can be the experience of prejudice and discrimination, immigration legislation and its implementation, the organization or content of public education, civil rights legislation and the activities of related agencies, relations with the country of origin and its representatives, multiculturalism policies and programs, and relations with various institutions of the larger society (e.g., media, government, police, schools, employers, labor unions).

Ethnic communities are socially differentiated or segmented in terms of factors such as social class, age, gender, income, education, religion, generation, political ideology, and regional identification (Boissevain, 1970;

Nagata, 1979; Jansen, 1981). Thus, within each domain of domestic or external activity, many interests and points of view can interact and come into cooperation or conflict with each other. Given the multiplicity of fields of political action and of interest groups, it is inappropriate to define an ethnic community as an interest group. It is more accurate to refer to it as a polity. It is, of course, possible that in certain circumstances an ethnic community will act in relation to a governmental body or agency as a single interest group. However, frequently, it is a particular interest group within the ethnic polity that relates to the external agency for its own particular purposes, one of which can be to frustrate or overcome its rivals within the ethnic community.

Political action involves two types of relationships: competitive or conflictual, on the one hand, and concerted or cooperative, on the other. To the extent that participants in the public affairs of the community have different interests and ideologies, they will promote or support more or less contradictory policies and programs. Accordingly, they are likely to compete for the acquisition of power and for the control of community resources so as to assure that their own material, ideological, or symbolic interests prevail. Viewed from this angle, the ethnic community is an arena in which rival groups may confront each other over economic interests, political philosophy, organizational prerogatives, social status, and whatever resources the collectivity has to offer or that can be generated through it.

This view, it should be emphasized, is radically opposed to the idea that "community" necessarily involves cohesion or unity; it is in contradiction with what is essentially an apolitical conception of community. Instead of adopting the notion that as long as there are divisions and conflict there is really no community, the view adopted here is that community necessarily involves social and economic differentiation and, consequently, different and more or less divergent interests. When there are no controversies and debates over the state of affairs and possible courses of action, that is, when there are no public issues, little is happening in the community. The community does not have much of a public life; in effect, there is not much of a community. What exists, rather, is a collectivity sharing a "symbolic ethnicity" (Gans, 1979) or simply an aggregate of people of a particular ethnic origin.

Social cleavages and opposition, instead of being considered obstacles to or destroyers of community, should be regarded as essential ingredients of the public affairs of any community. It is the ways in which people deal with contradictory interests or their failure to deal with these interests that can be destructive of social cohesion, not the interests' existence as such. "Ironically," writes O'Brien (1975:83–84), "it is the apolitical orientation of community development which is so instrumental in promoting rancorous conflicts" since it is an orientation that ignores the "possibility of creating organizational structures and strategies which might institutionalize the conflict."

It is misleading to think in terms of a single community interest either in the community at large or in a particular domain of activity and, when failing to find it, to conclude that the community is weak or lacks cohesiveness. It may be that, in certain circumstances, a consensus does emerge with regard to a particular problem or condition. Such an occurrence, however, should not detract attention from the process, frequently conflictual, through which that consensus came about. Indeed, even when there is a clearly identifiable external threat or internal problem, there usually is some disagreement among individuals and subgroups about the cause of the problem and/or about the best way to cope with it.

As Warren (1974) has argued and as will be examined in more detail later, the "single community interest" is frequently a political assumption made by those who claim to represent the community and who claim that there are no competing groups or organizations with different views in the community. Promoting the idea of a single community interest can also be an ideological or tactical tool used by officials of mainstream organizations for the purpose of strengthening particular organizations in the ethnic community by arguing that they are more representative of the community than other organizations.

THE COMPONENTS OF POLITIES SELECTED FOR ANALYSIS

This book is about the organization and functioning of ethnic communities as polities. It is about the structures and processes through which they conduct their domestic and external affairs. It is, more specifically, about the variations in the organization and functioning of ethnic communities. Indeed, ethnic collectivities may not show equal levels of political organization; their governance may be more or less formally organized as an institutionally distinct function; and their governance organizations may vary considerably in form or structure.

Political systems include a large number of components, all of which could be analyzed. Some components pertain to the structure of the system: the organizational apparatus through which political action takes place and features such as the system's size, form, differentiation, and complexity. Other components have to do with governance processes, for instance, the exercise of leadership, power, and authority and political participation.

Clearly, not all aspects of ethnic polities can be considered in a single book. The analysis must inevitably be selective and focus on variations of dimensions of governance that are arguably central in the functioning of an ethnic political community. Thus, the following have been selected as the major components of the study: the organization of governance; two sets of processes that governance entails, namely, the exercise of leadership or power and policy-making (or the definition of collective goals); and two dimensions of the construction and maintenance of the community: participation in the public affairs of the community and the definition, maintenance, and transformation of the collective identity.

The Organization of Governance

At one extreme, the organization through which a community governs itself can simply consist of a network of interpersonal relationships; at the other, governance may take place through a complex, formally structured system of organizations. Considerable variation can exist between the two extremes. In addition, variation can also be observed among the collectivities in which some sort of formally organized system has been established. That is to say, the type of organizational arrangement may not be the same across communities with the same level of organization.

The Exercise of Leadership, Power, and Authority

Leadership, power, and authority are essential ingredients in the functioning of any political system. Several questions can be raised in connection with this dimension of polities. For example. What is the distribution of power among the various segments of the community? Who becomes a leader in the community and who fails to do so? How can the existing distribution of power and leadership be accounted for? What strategies are used to gain power and to hold on to positions of power?

Policy-Making, or the Definition of Collective Goals

This book is concerned not with the substance of issues that constitute the public affairs of ethnic communities but rather with the processes involved in policy-making in ethnic communities.

Participation in the Political Process

The ethnic political community can include a more or less important fraction of the collectivity. Some of the potential participants may remain permanently at the margin of its public affairs. For them, their ethnicity is entirely private or leads them exclusively toward cultural activities. Other people may get involved, but only in certain domains of activity and the issues that emerge in those domains. Thus they participate when, for example, questions of immigration arise, but remain indifferent with regard to other matters. In short, as far as involvement in public affairs is concerned, the ethnic community does not differ from other types of political communities: participation varies widely in degree depending on the position of individuals in the social structure and on the domain of activity.

The Definition and Maintenance of the Collective Identity

The analysis of the ethnic polity cannot assume the existence of an ethnic community. Indeed, the community is itself a sociopolitical construction. The political process entails the creation of an ethnic consciousness among individuals belonging to a given collectivity, that is those who have an awareness of belonging to an ethnic category (McKay and Lewins, 1978). Creating an ethnic consciousness is one of the basic tasks to be accomplished if an ethnic polity is to be established and maintained, let alone function effectively. The boundaries of ethnic communities are not defined legally or territorially. The definition of the collective identity, of the social and symbolic boundaries of the community, is, accordingly, a central dimension of the formation and functioning of the ethnic polity (Barth, 1969; Kallen, 1977; Cohen, 1985). Moreover, this identity is not formed once and for all: its formation is continuous.

THE FRAMEWORK OF ANALYSIS

Ethnic communities have been described and analyzed from a number of perspectives. Two of these stand out, at least as far as the purposes of the present book are concerned. The following brief description presents these perspectives as distinct approaches. The work of researchers, however, usually draws from both perspectives, although not necessarily to the same extent. In one perspective, community organization is basically seen as a response to expressed needs on the part of members of a collectivity—needs experienced in the process of coping with their social environment. In the other perspective, community organization is the outcome of entrepreneurial activity on the part of individuals who have access to the resources required for "community building."

In the "social demand" approach, the ethnic collectivity or some of its fragments are organized in order to meet a demand for commodities, services, social support, protection, or cultural expression. That is to say, the demand can be for instrumental needs such as housing, jobs, and language training; for expressive purposes such as cultural activities or the transmission of values and ways of life to the next generation; for solidarity needs; or for defense against discrimination and hostility.

Thus, the degree and type of community organization that emerges is a function of the characteristics of the members (that is, of the potential clientele and their expressed needs) and of the features of the social environment with which the collectivity has to cope. In this approach, communities would differ in their sociopolitical organization or a given

Figure 1.1
Community Organization as a Function of Social Demand

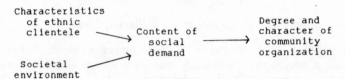

community would change over time because of differences or changes in social composition and accordingly in needs and interests. These differences or changes can pertain to factors such as the community's size, the class composition of the collectivity, the relative size of the generations that constitute it, and the age structure of the membership. Accordingly, the demand for services will differ across communities or will change over time, variations that will tend to be reflected in the community organization.

The level and content of sociopolitical demand may also be determined by environmental circumstances and their transformations. In other words, problems and the corresponding needs they generate can have causes outside of the community. For instance, discrimination is generally recognized as one of the main reasons that ethnic social networks and organizations are form. Thus, community organization is a response to a need, namely, the need to combat hostility and resist oppression and discrimination (Baureiss, 1982).

In addition to discrimination, government policies and programs as well as significant events on the international scene can have a critical impact on the demand for community organization among members of an ethnic minority. Features of the contemporary bureaucratic and technological society have also been hypothesized as being an impetus for ethnic community organization. Isajiw (1977) suggests that because of the isolation, anomie, and meaninglessness that many individuals experience in such environments, they feel the need to rediscover their sociocultural roots, to establish or consolidate a basis of social integration, and, in the process, to anchor their own personal identity in a community that has meaning in their personal history. Thus they constitute a potential clientele for various kinds of ethnic organizations, particularly organizations with a significant social and cultural component.

Figure 1.1 illustrates basic propositions of the social demand approach.

In the second approach, the "social supply" approach, the ethnic collectivity is conceived of as an arena of entrepreneurial activity. The basic idea is that ethnic collectivities become organized to the extent that they provide possibilities of action and gain to potential entrepreneurs. The opportunities they afford can be in fields of economic, political, or cultural activity (or any combination of these). In this approach, community organization does not depend primarily on the expressed needs of members but rather on the

Figure 1.2
Community Organization as a Function of Entrepreneurial Activity

range of opportunities available for entrepreneurial activity and on the fields in which they occur, whether or not these are related to needs or problems experienced by members of the collectivity.

The resources and related interests of potential organizers play a central role in this perspective. They constitute the driving force underlying organizational formation and activity in the community. That is to say, the aspirations and decisions of entrepreneurs, actual or aspiring, are a function of the resources at their disposal. These resources can be economic or material (real estate, land) or "human capital" such as experience, managerial skills, and connections with important mainstream individuals. They can also be organizational, a type of resource that can be particularly important in mobilizing and combining "the factors of material, symbolic or socioemotional production" (Collins, 1975:56–61).

In this approach, community formation and functioning is examined from the perspective of individuals who see opportunities for their own gain in terms of power, prestige, income, or ideological commitments. What is perceived as an opportunity is in turn a function of the particular assets that entrepreneurs control. For instance, people in religious roles control symbolic and socioemotional resources. They will accordingly attempt to build organizations and pursue activities that involve that type of resources. Those with legal skills will focus on matters that can be dealt with through litigation or legislative changes, those with political skills will address issues that can be politicized, and so on (Brettel, 1980; Lavigne, 1980; Rothschild, 1981). Figure 1.2 summarizes the basic proposition of this approach.

It can be noted, parenthetically, that debates over government intervention in the ethnocultural field (e.g., the multiculturalism policy of the Canadian government) consist to a significant extent in two approaches just discussed. Essentially, critics of such intervention argue that by institutionalizing ethnicity, governments provide a set of opportunities for potential ethnic entrepreneurs; that they increase the profitability of social and political action on an ethnic basis rather than through mainstream channels. It is suggested that such policies either artificially create circumstances for ethnic organizational activities or detract attention from the "true" needs and problems of the community. The impetus for action comes from above, so to speak, rather than from the grass roots of the community.

Those in favor of government intervention and support argue, in contrast, that ethnic leaders and their organizations are attempting to deal with real community needs and problems. They view the leaders as genuine representatives of the community who are aware of its needs and problems and are the most able to deal with them. Accordingly, government programs are needed to assist in the formation and maintenance of organizations that can carry out activities in relation to the needs and problems of ethnic collectivities.

An important difference between the two approaches pertains to conflict. In the social demand approach, conflict is a problem: it is a phenomenon that prevents groups from dealing effectively with the issues that confront them. The focus, then, is on strategies to prevent the emergence of conflict and, if it does occur, to limit its impact. Embedded in this approach is the apolitical view of community previously mentioned: that if there is division and conflict, there is no community.

In the social supply approach, conflict or at least competition is expected and almost inevitable. If community life is such that it offers a wide range of opportunities for action, several entrepreneurs are likely to appear on the scene. There will be competition among them and their supporters for the control of community organizations or of the resources necessary to pursue particular types of activities. They are likely to oppose each other over the allocation of community resources. They will tend to use different ideologies to justify their plans of action. In this approach, the absence of competition means that there is not much going on in the community. In fact, while in the first approach conflict means the absence of community; in this one, it is the absence of opposition that signifies that a community has ceased to exist, since there is nothing left that is worthwhile fighting about or over which to compete.

The two approaches can be used as a basis for the analysis of the political dimension of community organization and functioning since they both deal with the exercise of power. Indeed, the social demand approach corresponds largely (although not exactly) to what Gamson (1968) has referred to as the "social control" perspective on the exercise of power. In this perspective, the focus is on the power of the collectivity as an organized system—its power to mobilize and use resources to deal with collective problems or to attain collective goals. The accumulation of power is a collective phenomenon; power is accumulated for the entire collectivity in order to enable it to cope with its external environment and with internal needs and issues.

In contrast, the social supply approach tends to fit Gamson's "influence" perspective on the use of power. This perspective focuses on the individuals and groups in the system, on their interests, and on the strategies they deploy to win in the competition against each other. In this perspective, the community consists of a multiplicity of actors (entrepreneurs and groups) with competing interests. Power is accumulated for individual or sectarian purposes; each subgroup and its leaders attempts to acquire as much power as possible in order to bolster or improve its position in the community or to attain specific objectives.

The temptation can be strong to label either the social control/demand or influence/entrepreneurial approach as the best. It would be possible to argue for a long time over the merits and shortcomings of each, labelling the first as "functionalist" and the other as based on a "conflict" view of the sociopolitical order. This would be a futile and even misleading exercise for the reason that both set of processes occur in all communities. They may not occur to the same extent and in all circumstances, but both can be observed in organized collectivities. The two sets of processes identified by Gamson correspond to two aspects of the exercise of power and thus to two basic dimensions of the political functioning of communities.

Thus to analyze how ethnic communities govern themselves is to enquire about these two sets of processes within ethnic communities. Organizational structures can be established and sociopolitical processes be set in motion in order to cope with problems experienced by members of the collectivity. But this does not imply that individuals and groups are not in competition with each other for access to and control of the resources that the community has to offer. The two sets of processes are far from being mutually exclusive. In other words, community politics involve both concerted action and competition for resources and power among subgroups with divergent interests and ideologies.

In addition, since the ethnic polity is encapsulated within a larger political structure, the possible impact of external interventions needs to be considered. Indeed, the initiative to deal with issues and problems can come either from within or from outside of the ethnic collectivity. That is, the needs and problems of a community may be perceived as requiring intervention by individuals in the larger society as well as in the ethnic collectivity itself. The leadership of the early phase of the civil rights movement in the United States and the "red power" movement among native people in Canada was at least partly external. Several whites helped activities within the black and the native communities in order to bring about reforms that would be beneficial for the minority.

Individuals in the larger society can also act as entrepreneurs in ethnic communities for themselves and their organizations. For example, church leaders compete to reach ethnic clientele. Some have occasionally succeeded in recruiting members or in establishing some control over ethnic religious organizations even though they are not themselves members of the community. Mainstream labor leaders and politicians have also attempted to and sometimes succeeded in playing entrepreneurial roles within ethnic communities.

The framework for the analysis of the organization of governance, leadership, policy-making, political participation, and the definition of collective identity is designed in terms of concepts drawn from the social demand and social supply perspectives, taking into account the encapsulated condition of the ethnic polity. Specifically, the five components are examined as the result of two broad classes of forces: those stemming from the sociopolitical environment and those deriving from political competition among subgroups within the ethnic collectivity.

Environmental Circumstances and External Interventions

Ethnic communities experience events and circumstances that occur either within or outside of their boundaries. These can be perceived as beneficial, harmful, or neutral. The term *governance* refers to the capacity to cope with these environmental problems and opportunities.[3] *Political action* refers to the determination and implementation of public goals in relation to environmental conditions. In so far as the community responds to its environment, the environment is a factor in shaping the community's structures and practices.

The sociopolitical environment, however, should not be seen exclusively as a set of possible problems and opportunities. It also includes organizations whose agents may have an interest in the public affairs of the ethnic polity and as a result intervene in these affairs, directly or indirectly. What happens in the ethnic polity may be perceived by authorities of societal institutions as of some significance for their own political interests and objectives. This may lead them to intervene directly in the affairs of the ethnic polity, either to shape its political structures, to affect the relative power of its subgroups, or to orient its political action (Stasiulis, 1980; Savas, 1987; Breton, 1988).

On the other hand, organizations and groups in government, business, labor unions, churches, and political parties may adopt policies and carry out activities that have implications for ethnic groups and their members. Such policies and programs provide some of the parameters within which members of ethnic groups function (Stasiulis, 1980). As a result, these external bodies indirectly shape structures and processes in ethnic polities.

Political Competition

The ethnic community is socially differentiated and, as a result, is likely to include groups with more or less contradictory interests and/or ideologies with regard to particular events, circumstances, and courses of action. Because policies and their implementation can affect subgroups positively or negatively, subgroups will use the resources at their disposal to orient action in their favor. Governance, in this context, has to do with the differential use of power by the groups potentially affected by the outcome of public decisions. Competition and conflict are the dynamic forces in the political arena, and they help to shape the governance structures and practices.

A critical factor in the evolution of the competitive process is the distribution of power resources among the subgroups in the ethnic polity. If the distribution is fairly even, the main questions concern the conditions under which an accommodation among competing groups is likely to be worked out and its modalities. However, if power is distributed unequally among competing subgroups, the main questions concern the processes whereby political ascendancy is established and maintained by one group and the implications of this ascendancy for the functioning of the system of governance.

SOURCES OF DOCUMENTATION AND OUTLINE

The objectives of this book are to articulate a "governance" perspective on ethnic communities and to integrate a number of relevant concepts, propositions, and empirical findings found in the sociological literature. It is not an hypothesis-testing work. Empirical data are presented in order to document or give substance to the analysis. In that sense, their role is more one of illustration than rigorous testing.

In addition, although the book uses documentation on specific ethnic groups, its purpose is not to analyze the governance structures that exist and the political processes that operate in particular groups. Empirical materials are drawn from two sources. First, the empirical literature on specific ethnic groups (primarily in Canada, but also in the United States and the United Kingdom) provides more or less detailed documentation on a number of aspects of community governance.

Second, data from the Ethnic Pluralism Study is used when appropriate. This survey of 2,388 respondents was carried out in 1978 and 1979 in Toronto.[4] It allows comparisons between a number of ethnic groups: Chinese, German, Italian, Jewish, Portuguese, Ukrainian, and West Indian. These groups were selected so that the study would include variations along three dimensions: the size and socioeconomic standing of groups and the racial background of their members.[5] Information was obtained from the respondents on various aspects of their ethnic identity, their occupational situation, their social mobility, their neighborhood experience, their community participation, and their perception of community problems and of the ways in which the affairs of the community were managed by leaders.

The sample was designed in such a way that statistically valid statements could be made for each of the groups. In other words, a sample was drawn for each of the groups separately. The samples include persons eighteen to sixty-five years old who were in the labor force or were students. The interviews, which on the average lasted one hour and a half, were carried with the use of a schedule. The technical aspects of the sample design and selection and fieldwork were carried out by the York University Survey Research Center on the basis of specifications described.

The first part of the book deals with variations in the organization of governance. The second part includes an analysis of two sets of governance processes: those pertaining to the exercise of leadership and to policy-making in ethnic polities. The construction and maintenance of the sociopolitical community constitutes the object of the third part. This includes the definition and evolution of ethnic collective identity and the participation of community members in the public affairs of the community. The analysis attempts to describe some of the possible variations in each of the areas and to identify factors and processes that could account for the emergence of particular patterns.

The factors and processes considered are drawn from the approaches mentioned above. The sociopolitical environment affects the ethnic collectivity and its members either through favorable or unfavorable configurations of circumstances or through direct or indirect interventions by organizations in the larger societal context. Subgroups or factions with divergent material, political or symbolic interests compete politically. When each of the competing subgroups has a viable base of power, the groups are concerned with the conditions and processes of political accommodation; when one faction is significantly more powerful, the groups are concerned with political ascendancy.

NOTES

1. On this point, see also Balandier (1969), Swartz (1968), MacKenzie (1967), Bailey (1970), and Crenson (1983).

2. And in an ethnic collectivity.

3. Weick (1969) stresses the fact that individual and collective actors not only react to their environment but also "enact" it. That is to say, they interpret it creatively and they attempt to shape it according to their own values and goals.

4. Additional details are provided in Breton et al., 1990.

5. Since generation is an important source of variation in ethnic identity and behavior, it was also incorporated in the study design. Some of the groups include primarily one generation because significant immigration to Toronto occurred only recently (West Indians, Portuguese, and Chinese) while the others include important proportions of different generations.

2

Political Competition and the Structures of Governance

Political competition occurs because subgroups in the community have divergent or contradictory interests with regard to various issues. But, competing groups may also have interests in common and, accordingly, may find collaboration or coordination mutually beneficial. Indeed, they may be affected in some way by the same external conditions or by the action of groups and agencies outside their community. Problems or circumstances within the community may have potential implications for all of them. Thus, leaders may feel the need to pool their resources and coordinate their activities for the realization of common projects.

Some groups and organizations focus primarily on their interdependence with other groups and the ventures that they could pursue with others. Other groups are more concerned with their vulnerability vis-a-vis competitors. They tend to be preoccupied with the hostility that other groups direct or could direct against them. In the first situation, the degree of political polarization is relatively low: groups have divergent interests, but important commonalities as well. In the second, polarization is high: the subgroups have little in common or what they do have in common is given little weight in comparison to what divides them.

The analysis of political competition and of its institutional implications should also consider the distribution of power among the competing groups. Pronounced power differences and a certain equality of power among groups represent two types of political contexts. In the first, a subgroup or a coalition of subgroups is able to eliminate or politically neutralize competitors or to absorb them into its own circle. Having gained ascendancy, the dominant faction aims at structuring the governance institutions, directing the decision-making process, and shaping the policies in such a way as to maintain its dominance. In such situations, the political order is an "imposed order" in which the ascendant organization or coalition not only assumes the governance of the community but shapes its institutions as well.

In contrast control of resources and of their allocation may be spread among several subgroups. Inequalities may exist among the various groups or factions and their organizations but not to the extent that one group can impose itself on the others or ignore them in decisions and activities. Because each faction has a resource base of its own, it can retain some degree of independence and some capacity to influence the course of community affairs. Thus, an accommodation may be worked out among groups—an accommodation that would be reflected in the governance structure and processes of the community. Competition, then, is institutionalized and regulated. It persists, but within established organizational forms and practices and under a regime of mutually accepted norms. The political regime is a "negotiated order" (Strauss, 1973).

If the opposition among subgroups is intense, however, negotiations are not likely to take place nor are the less-powerful factions likely to be integrated into a hierarchically interorganizational system. Rather, a fragmented polity is the likely outcome. If the competing subgroups each have a significant power base of their own, they are likely to carve out a particular political domain for themselves. Such polities could be characterized as segmented or factionalized. If power inequalities are pronounced, however, the politically weak factions are likely to be relegated to the periphery of the public affairs of the community. Such polities could be said to be truncated: the marginalized group has essentially been dismissed; it has no significant connections with the dominant one.

The dimensions of polarization and distribution of power yield four political configurations (Table 2.1). These constitute the object of this chapter. Shifts from one to another will also be considered. Indeed, none of these configurations has a permanent character. Changes can be more or less pronounced and can occur in any direction. A fragmented community may, for example, progressively create an integrated system based on political compromises. A well-functioning overarching structure may split into factions having little to do with each other; a subgroup may be marginalized but later reemerge as an important political force; a group in a position of dominance may be challenged and compelled to accept a structure in which it shares power with other groups; and a group willing to negotiate with political competitors may exclude them if it comes to wield sufficient power to dominate the governance institutions.

ACCOMMODATION

Competition within a community is a source of uncertainty and potential instability for the subgroups involved. Subgroup leaders may "attempt to establish linkages to access resources, to stabilize outcomes, and to avert

Table 2.1
Typology of Political Configurations

Distribution of power

		Fairly equal		Unequal
		A.	.	B.
	High	Segmentation	.	Truncation
		(fragmented orders)	.	
Polarization		....		
		C.	.	D.
	Low	Accommodation (negotiated order)	.	Ascendancy (imposed order)

environmental control" (Pfeffer and Salancik, 1978:144). They may also prompt the subgroups to find ways to regulate each other's behavior. The literature on government regulation of business and other organized groups, for example, suggests that regulation is, in part, a response to demands and pressures from the parties themselves. Through the sanctioning power of the government, groups seek to control each other's competitive behavior so as to reduce uncertainty and promote stability in particular domains of operation.[1]

The perception of interdependence constitutes an impetus for the establishment of enduring interorganizational linkages even in situations of competition. The attempts by organizations to weaken (or even eliminate) each other may not, in practice, be entirely incompatible with the search for mutual regulation and even collaboration. Indeed, if the distribution of power among groups is fairly equal, they may not have any choice but to cooperate.

Organizational leaders and their supporters are likely to feel most vulnerable during the formative years of an ethnic community. Indeed, this is a period during which several entrepreneurs may be attempting to organize the community as a whole or certain of its fields of activity. Such attempts usually involve the mobilization of as much of the community's resources as possible and the monopolizing of its potential for organizational formation and growth. As time goes on and as the costs of intense competition become increasingly heavy, the competing parties may come to feel that it is in their interest to negotiate some interorganizational accommodation.

Groups may seek to cooperate for more reasons than simply to avoid the heavy social and material costs of competition. Mutually beneficial projects within the community or in relation to the external environment may be impossible without some pooling of resources. In addition, leaders of the competing organizations may be pressured by members to set aside their antagonisms for a community-wide cause.

One likely result of accommodation is that each organization acquires a certain degree of security. The interorganizational system becomes progressively structured, each organization having a recognized niche in it. Indeed, a central characteristic of such systems is that they allow organizations to engage in joint ventures while retaining a substantial degree of autonomy.

The security each group obtains allows each to turn its attention to the advantages rather than to the threats that its interdependence with other organizations represents. Thus, if the forces in the direction of coordination and mutual regulation outweigh those toward competition and antagonism, a coordinated rather than a segmented system of governance is likely to emerge in the community.

There are, for instance, integrative arrangements that bring the various community organizations into an "interorganizational field" or network characterized by the existence of (1) "more or less routinized and agreed-upon notions of their respective domains," (2) notions governing acceptable behavior either in situations of cooperation or in those in which different and incompatible outcomes are desired, and (3) a common institutionalized thought structure (Warren, 1974:19).[2] The coordination and exchange can occur through a variety of mechanisms[3] that can be classified along two dimensions: temporariness/permanence and formal/informal (Tropman, 1974).

Informal mechanisms such as occasional meetings and consultations are frequently insufficient for the management of either competitive or facilitative interdependence among community groups and organizations. As the number of organizations increases, for instance, formalized interorganizational mechanisms are also needed for communication, planning, coordination, and the protection of organizational domains (Phillips, 1960; Litwak and Hylton, 1962).

One such mechanism is the ad hoc committee or organization. It is established when organizational leaders do not perceive the need for continuous coordination of effort. A committee is usually formed to deal with a particular event or a particular action of government, the media, or a group in the larger community. Typical examples of such committees are those established to commemorate a political event, to organize an athletic competition, or to coordinate relief activities during a war or a natural disaster in the country of origin. Previous interorganizational rivalries and acrimonies subside during the crisis but frequently resume when it is over (Marunchak, 1970; Radecki, 1979).

Overarching structures constitute another type of coordinating mechanism. A critical feature of such structures is the extent to which each member-organization retains autonomy in its field of activity or renounces part of its autonomy in favor of the overarching structure. It is useful to think of overarching structures as located along a continuum. At one pole, the overarching structure is invested with considerable powers: adjudication, coordination, resource mobilization and allocation among member organizations, and external representation. Next on the continuum is the structure established to provide services for member associations such as collecting and disseminating information, planning projects for members' approval, and coordinating activities in the execution of approved plans. Alliances for a specific purpose or project would come next on the continuum. Such alliances usually dissolve once the desired objective has been attained. Finally, an overarching structure may be given little or no autonomous power. It may be established to allow leaders to exchange information on problems, programs, government legislation and activities, and other matters of common interest. The Federation of Italian Canadian Associations and Clubs is an example of such an arrangement. It was incorporated in 1970 and by 1973 consisted of sixty organizations. One of its aims is "the uniting fraternally of all corporations, associations and other legal entities with an Italian character" (Jansen, 1978:321).

The fact that an overarching body is given little or no formal authority does not mean that it has no influence on the conduct of community affairs. Whatever authority it has, however, is built on its effectiveness in dealing with practical problems and in performing services for affiliated organizations. Harrison (1959:64–69) analyzed such a structure in the context of the American Baptist Church. Although the context is not ethnic, the church's regional or national structures—the conventions—provide an interesting empirical illustration of the phenomenon. The convention "is a temporary institutional means pragmatically conceived for the achievement of a higher purpose." According to Baptist doctrine, the professional executives of these organizations do not possess legitimate ecclesiastical authority. Nevertheless, they "do exercise a form of rational authority.... It is not rational-legal but rational-pragmatic authority," an authority justified by the attainment of its assigned goals.

This also seems to be the situation for several coordinating organizations in ethnic communities, for example, the Canadian Jewish Congress. Waller (1974:32) notes that "as an umbrella organization, one might expect the role of the CJC to be somewhat limited. But an unusually able staff, a veritable 'Jewish civil service,' has enabled Congress to operate as much more."

Wherever the overarching structure has constitutionally established rational-legal authority or rational-pragmatic authority acquired through the competence and strategic position of its "civil service," the arrangement could be considered as federative since both organizational levels have a certain degree of legitimate authority even if the basis of legitimacy is different.[4] The federative arrangement, which can take different forms, is usually adopted to accommodate segments or groups with partly opposing or incompatible interests while, at the same time, being interdependent in some regards. The divergence of interests may be based on ideology, domain jurisdiction, access to financial resources, or power over particular geographical areas. A federation legitimizes a distribution of control at different levels of the interorganizational system and thus a certain degree of competition; but it also allows concerted action with regard to shared interests and permits the regulation of competitive practices.

In several instances, federations are explicitly established for such purposes. For example, in New York's Chinatown before 1930, one level of community organization consisted of family and district associations.[5] Their functions were the regulation of different interests and community representation vis-a-vis the outside world. But because of chronic rivalry, they were unable to achieve these objectives. "There were attempts to set up 'spheres of influence'—each association staking out a particular 'territory' or a certain type of trade guild—but because Chinatown was small and crowded, any minor shift in jurisdiction altered the power balance. It was to minimize this problem that a federation of family and district associations was founded. Not only did [it] act as mediator for intra-association conflicts, but it became the external representative for all Chinatown, known to outsiders as its 'city hall' " (Kwong, 1979:40–42).

Modell (1977:80) describes the Central Japanese Association in the United States "as an amalgam of the locals, with its officers chosen from among officers of the constituent local Associations.... Yet, the executives of the Central had a good deal of leeway, partly because of infrequent general meetings, but partly because of the relatively distinct sphere of action it maintained." It was organized as "a quasi-government to oversee the condition of the Japanese in its jurisdiction, while the locals had grown more spontaneously as expressions of solidary communal and neighborly resistance to white hostility."

The political organization of the Jewish community in North America is another example of the federative arrangement. According to Waller (1981:152), Jewish politics is based on two basic principles: (1) political systems are viewed in terms of groups formed by consensus through compacts or agreements, and (2) bargaining is the central method of decision-making. These beliefs have "led to the establishment of federal models of organization whereby disparate groups can affirm common interests and goals without relinquishing their own identities." As will be seen later in this chapter, such an arrangement has not always existed in the Canadian Jewish community. The present arrangement, however, is clearly based on federative principles.

Frequently, political accommodations are the outcome of a long process that can extend over several years. Typically, in such instances, a politically segmented community progressively constructs an integrated organizational system. Several illustrations can be found in the literature of shifts from segmentation to structures incorporating a variety of competing subgroups. A few instances are examined in the following section.

SEGMENTATION

In segmented political orders, parallel subsystems exist in more or less intense opposition to each other, each governing a particular segment of the community. Although Gilbert (1968:143) refers to such polities as "multi-pyramidal structures," they tend to include only two segments. In other words, the community has a single, but profound, social, economic, or ideological division, with clusters of actors at opposing poles. The system follows a "double-pyramid" (Nix, 1969:508) or a "unidimensional oppositional model, with recurrently opposed collective actors" (Laumann and Marsden, 1979:720).

Such a segmented political order is usually the result of negotiations that failed or of the outright refusal on the part of at least one subgroup and its leaders to negotiate a common arrangement. The greater the number of overlapping divisions in a community and the longer the political and institutional history of the antagonisms, the more arduous the process of building an overarching structure.

Segmentation frequently characterizes the early years or decades of community development, during which different groups are in intense competition for political power. Each group tries to gain legitimacy and recognition in the community; mobilize support for its survival and effective operation; increase its importance in the community, that is, occupy as much of the sociopolitical space as possible; resist the attempts of rivals to weaken its organization and decrease the visibility of its activities; and prevent rivals from gaining too much ground.

The New York Puerto Rican community illustrates such an institutionalized pattern of political competition. Three elite groups compete in the community: the traditional, the mid, and the opposition elites. Each (1) "controlled a specific power domain comprised of resources, such as service agencies or community organizations, ... information, access to jobs, connections to the administrative and political structure of New York City"; (2) "employed different mechanism to deliver resources in order to mobilize support"; (3) "had a specific set of ties with the administrative and political structures of the national society"; and (4) "had a different ideology on both the nature of the relationship between the larger society and the ethnic population and its role in the context of such relationships" (Herbstein, 1983:40).

Weiss (1974) suggests that a tripartite model is also the most useful for understanding segmented Chinese communities. She identifies three organizational subsystems that resemble in many ways those described by Herbstein: the traditionalist, the modernist, and the activist. The split between radical leftist and accommodationists represents another line of institutionalized opposition observed in ethnic communities.

In short, the political cleavages in a community can prevent the formation of a community-wide governance organization, at least during certain periods of the group's history. In such situations, the political competition is institutionalized without any coordinating and regulating center. It is as if the community was carved into two or more segments, each with its sociopolitical space defined in terms of territory or functions. The more or less antagonistic political subcommunities manage their own public affairs. Although functioning independently of each other, they are nevertheless watchful of each other's behavior to prevent encroachments on their domain and to take advantage of opportunities for political gains.

As indicated earlier, segmentation can progressively evolve toward a structure of accommodation. The evolution of the Polish polity in Canada provides an illustration. Radecki (1979:69) shows that with new waves of immigration, the community became more socially and organizationally differentiated. It appears that the clerical/lay and then the communist/noncommunist divisions were the first bases of interorganizational competition. "Throughout the 1920–1939 period, the Polish clergy were frequently uncooperative, hostile or opposed to various independent lay organizations." Although the nonsocialist lay and clerical organizations shared, with differences in priorities, the same overall goals, they were competing for leadership, preeminence in the community, and control of particular spheres of activity. Both, however, condemned the leftist radical organizations.

In the late 1930s, the leaders of Polish lay organizations attempted to form a Canada-wide federation encompassing all types of organizations. They failed. The clergy refused to participate; it established its own Alliance of Polish Priests. Also, the official Polish government representatives counterproposed a federation under different auspices. "None of the factions were willing to compromise, each insisting that their proposals should be accepted fully, and no common ground was found" (Radecki, 1979:70–71).

A segmentary organization characterized that period: the Polish Alliance was formed in the 1930s with several branches in different parts of Ontario; the Federation of Polish Societies in Canada was established in Montreal in 1931 under the guidance of the Polish consuls; the radical leftist organizations founded their own federation in the late 1920s; the Polish clergy formed its federation in 1933; another Ontario-based Federation was formed in 1938. All federations were hostile toward the Communist group, but there also were "conflicts, struggles, and rivalries for new members and for greater influence among all factions" (Radecki, 1979:72–74).

This segmented governance system progressively evolved in the direction of some interorganizational coordination. The situation in Poland immediately before and during World War II led to a certain unity; an organization was formed mobilizing all Polish federations and independent organizations, including the communists, in a common war relief effort. The fate of Poland and the war itself with its pains and anxieties reduced the salience of internal divisions.

This mobilization showed that it was possible for the different subgroups to engage in joint activities, and in 1944 an umbrella organization, the Canadian Polish Congress, was formed. It can be described as a "loose alliance of organizations designed basically as a representative, coordinative and planning body. . . . The affiliate members were to adhere to the stipulated ideology and aims, but were free to pursue interests and goals of their own, if they did not conflict with those of the congress" (Radecki, 1979:80). Its role seems to be primarily that of a facilitator for autonomous affiliates. It was, however, given powers with regard to the external affairs of the community in relationships with the Canadian government and with Polish organizations in other countries.

The equilibrium that the congress represented was, however, disturbed by the postwar arrival of exiles and refugees. The expectation in the community was that the established organizations would be able to accommodate the newcomers with their political interests and ideologies. But this did not turn out to be possible. A separate network of associations and auxiliaries was established to oppose the Polish government in Poland and support the exiled Polish government in London. The congress remained concerned primarily with the Polish people in Canada. The Cold War that followed, however, changed the focus of the postwar immigrants' organization and set the stage for an accommodation. The group became an affiliate of the congress.

But this was not entirely a reconciliation. A number of member-organizations saw the postwar immigrants as "having gained control in the executive branches of the Congress . . . [and as having] imposed their ideology . . . on all the affiliated member organizations" (Radecki, 1979:149). As a result, some members withdrew from the Congress in the early 1970s.

Another example of evolution from segmentation to accommodation is provided by the Montreal Jewish community at the beginning of the century. In this case, the segmentation was along class lines corresponding to two waves of immigration. A relatively small group of families who had come to Canada in the middle of the nineteenth century moved to Montreal a few decades later. Since they had already been in Canada for some twenty

years, they had learned English well and could take advantage of the opportunities that industrialization offered. They were economically very successful and "they moved to Westmount and took up residence in great
mansions alongside the Scottish fur barons" (Paris, 1980:28).

Later, at the turn of the century, thousands of Yiddish-speaking immigrants from eastern Europe came to Canada. Most of them were destitute
and settled in the poor sections of Montreal. The "uptowners," as the
wealthy established Jews came to be called, were deeply committed to Jewish
life and community and believed they had a duty with regard to the settlement of the new immigrants (the "downtowners"). "The wealthy anglicized
Jews were never disloyal to their self-appointed task of aiding immigrants
and refugees. They occasionally dispensed their help and advice with a
condescension not untypical of Victorian society, but they dispensed it all
the same" (Paris, 1980:30).

Given the differences in class positions, a profound split between the two
groups was inevitable.[6] They formed separate communities and institutions
in different parts of the city. Although there were linkages between the two
groups, the collectivity was highly segmented (Rosenberg, 1971; Paris,
1980). Differences in class positions corresponded to different ideological
orientations and attitudes. These were expressed, for instance, in the newspapers of the two subcommunities. The uptowners' newspaper "promoted
'Canadianization' and the ways of the British Empire. It looked for leadership to Jewish notables in Britain and to the chief rabbi of France.... (It)
was emphatically *not* interested in promoting the interests of the Yiddish
'masses,' who were seething with new ideas and left-wing ideology." The
downtowners had their own paper that "maintained a steady opposition to
the assimilationist tendencies of ... the Uptowners, and promoted a deliberate strengthening of Yiddish language and culture in the new land" (Paris,
1980:30–31).[7]

The formation of a community-wide organization did not come without
considerable difficulty and required a fairly long period of time. An initial
impetus to form such an organization was the fate of the Jews caught in
the war zones during World War I. A combined fund-raising effort was
organized in Montreal, but there were disagreements between the uptowners
and the downtowners over the distribution of the sums collected. Distribution
was controlled by the former, and the latter resented being left out of the decision-making process. They decided to invite all organizations "on their side" to
unite. They aspired to a united Jewish voice at the peace talks at the end of the
war, but one cast in their political orientation. The result was a new coalition:
the Canadian Jewish Alliance. It included Labour Zionists, left-wing socialists,
and Jewish nationalists (Paris, 1980).

Given the existing sociopolitical segmentation, it was to be expected that
the alliance would meet considerable opposition. And it did. "The Canadian
Zionist Federation refused to cooperate—for political reasons. The Feder-

ation considered itself the national Jewish voice and believed that it alone should represent Canadian Jewry at an eventual peace conference". The federation called a counterconference. "They were joined by wealthy uptown Jews who objected to the idea that Jews within Canada constituted a national group, by Orthodox Jews who objected to the irreligious attitudes of many of the labour-dominated Alliance, and by Reform Jews who considered Judaism as a religion only and also rejected Jewish ethnic nationalism" (Paris, 1980:37).

It seems that rather than leading to a united congress, the issues raised by the war accentuated the interorganizational competition. But as the international situation did not change, the Jewish community continued to feel the need for a common front, but the social and ideological gap remained wide. The formation of a Jewish congress in the United States appears to have been a critical event in that it persuaded the Canadian antagonists that an overarching structure was possible. The two factions joined in a single congress in 1919, a move that entailed several compromises.

There was no delegation of Jews when the Treaty of Versailles was signed. The views of Canadian Jews were presented by the American delegation. In the absence of an active role and because the immediate issues that had been the object of common action had been dealt with, the Congress became inactive in the early 1920s. Members of the community "were often too preoccupied adjusting to the new environment, or else, if active in the community, involved primarily with their own small groups and organizations" (Rosenberg, 1971:42).

The rise of German Nazism in the 1930s led to the reorganization of the congress. For several years, it functioned as a representative communal organization concerned with the internal and external affairs of the community. It defines itself as the "Parliament of Canadian Jewry." Its members are not individuals but organizations, each retaining a certain autonomy and independence. It is a federal organization incorporating both regional (Pacific, western, central, and eastern) and functional (i.e., type of activity) differentiation.

With time, the size and internal differentiation of the community increased considerably, partly as a result of the large (relative to the size of the community) number of war refugees and postwar immigrants.[8] The range of organizational activities and the need for funds and specialized skills to carry them out also increased. Accordingly, new organizations were created or existing ones transformed. For instance, in Montreal, the Combined Jewish Appeal was established in 1941 as the fund-raising arm of the Federation of Jewish Philanthropies (which had been founded in 1916). Later, in 1965, the Allied Jewish Community Services (AJCS) replaced the federation (Waller, 1974).

Progressively, because of the extensive control they had over the collection and allocation of funds, these new organizations became very powerful in the community. The AJCS had a leading, if not the dominant, role. Inevitably, conflict occurred between the AJCS and the congress, frequently over questions of jurisdiction (Waller, 1974). Demographic and socioeconomic changes increased the importance of other community organizations. Thus a central problem of the congress as a community-wide organization was a threat to its authority: its major problem was the competition from other bodies with independent power bases.

The same interorganizational competition occurred in Toronto between the congress and the United Jewish Welfare Fund, which eventually acquired a position of dominance in the community (Glickman, 1976:242–144). The dominance of the fund increased the community's efficacy as it permitted more money to be raised and more programs to be launched. But that dominance generated problems. On the one hand, "the resistance of the other organizations to relinquish their grasp on various functions that are now dominated by the Welfare Fund, notably education, resulted in large duplication and waste of resources and funds." On the other hand, "whereas the legitimacy of the Congress continued to be vested in its democratic tradition, both in philosophy and practice, the Welfare Fund had no broad constituent base to rely on, a fact that many of its leaders were keenly aware of" (Glickman, 1976:244).

In short, the community experienced several problems of governance: the position of the congress as the central representative and organizing community organization was threatened; the autonomy of a number of other organizations was reduced; the legitimacy of the dominant organization was perceived as not being in accord with its power; and resources were perceived as being wasted or not used as efficiently as they could be. As a result, considerable pressure for cooperation was applied on the two main rival organizations (Glickman, 1976).

Eventually, the two organizations merged and the congress was reestablished as the central representative organization of the community. This entailed several compromises. Also, "the constitutional arrangements set forth during the transition to the new community structure resulted in a de facto co-optation of practically the entire leadership into the same positions of power" (Glickman, 1976:260).[9]

POLITICAL ASCENDANCY

The institutionalization of political competition may not be the outcome of political struggles in a community. As already noted, a group or a coalition may be sufficiently powerful to acquire virtually complete control of the governance institutions. Groups in a position of dominance may be challenged, and their ascendancy depends on their ability to contain or neutralize the opposition.

Price (1959:281) writes that "where migrants of somewhat different backgrounds decide to set up a common school, church or similar institution, this institution may take control of the situation and impose a policy which is not necessarily a compromise between the various backgrounds concerned but something of its own." In the mid-nineteenth century, the Lutheran pastors of the various Norwegian district groups (in an area of Wisconsin) "insisted on orthodox ritual, frowned upon the lay-preaching (usually in dialect) hitherto prevailing, encouraged parochial schools with plenty of religious instruction in literary Norwegian, and supported the early Norwegian press." In the process, the various district, dialectical, and theological differences were replaced by uniformity.

An organization or a set of organizations may acquire a position of dominance simply because they were the first to be established in the immigrant settlement. Certain types of organizations such as religious ones, have the advantage of being able to transplant an organizational system, the country of origin providing not only the model but frequently trained leaders and financial assistance as well. By the time other groups arrive, they have to deal with a system already in place. As already noted, this can be a source of conflict when they attempt to establish their own organizations, especially if successive waves of immigration are characterized by differences in ideological orientation, political background, and social-class composition.

The advantage of the founding leaders was observed by Tryggvason (1971:97–98) in an unidentified Vancouver ethnic community. He writes that "the traditional leaders who took the initiative in establishing these associations acquired, more or less automatically, what became the key positions in the developing leadership structure. Furthermore, they continued to occupy these positions and generally appropriated exclusive control over policy-making."

A position of dominance, however, is frequently not the result of historical circumstances but rather the result of strategic uses of power to weaken or eliminate competitors or prevent potential competitors to enter the political arena. Control of the governance apparatus is systematically defended by the dominant group.

Alliances may be formed for the acquisition of power. Leaders will tend to form alliances if they believe that they cannot achieve their political ambitions alone. But since alliances entail the sharing of power, they pose an enormous risk for the power-seekers. Indeed, alliances may be a strategy used by a group for the successive elimination of political opponents: Once an alliance of organizations has gained control, conflict may break out among them. The new power struggle leads to a suballiance; when it is won, a new conflict breaks out. Eventually, one faction dominates, all opponents having been successively subdued or eliminated.

This appears to have been the situation for the Ukrainian Canadian Committee (UCC) during a fairly long period after its creation. Its policy has been that "of a non-elective executive body and re-partition of powers among the founding organizations.... New organizations joined the Committee for the sake of solidarity... but newcomers were given no opportunity to play a leading role in the work of the executive." Some, however, refused to join partly because of the undemocratic, centralized structure (Woycenko, 1967:211–12; see also Gerus, 1976, 1982).

There were national congresses that "until recently exerted little tangible influence on the UCC.... Three-day sessions once every three years gave delegates no real opportunity to make their presence felt. Though many public commissions to parallel the assembly were introduced, the chairmen were selected in advance by the UCC executive. With a prearranged congress agenda, the executive has always been firmly in control" (Gerus, 1982:204–205).

Eventually, pressures toward decentralization were applied by strong locals who resented the absence of elections and the constitutional provisions giving permanent positions on the executive to representatives of a limited number of organizations (Woycenko, 1967). "The executive monopoly of power and its tendency to stress backroom politics have been the two main forces behind the move for a democratically elected executive" (Gerus, 1982:205).

Traditional Chinese communities also tended to be dominated by a particular subgroup. Generally, it was the small merchant class. Most Chinese immigrants were initially of low socioeconomic status. Because of discrimination and their low level of skills, advancement for these immigrants in the larger society was very limited, if not entirely absent. Within their community, a small merchant elite emerged "that provided informal leadership but was primarily defending its own interests." Subsequently a number of formal organizations were established and through them "members of the merchant elite were able to legitimize their power structure, and informal leadership was institutionalized" (Baureiss, 1982:75).[10]

The social organization of Chinese communities in North America was very complex. It included family name, district and village associations, fongs, and clans. According to Kwong (1979:41), the social and political structure of all the Chinatowns (in the United States) consisted of two tiers: the fongs and village associations at the bottom and the family and district associations at the top. The former dealt with matters of immediate concerns to individual members and the latter "arose out of the necessity for regulating different interests within Chinatown as well as for providing community representation vis-a-vis the outside world." The underlying organizational model was essentially feudal. The traditional associations were run on strict hierarchical lines. Unquestioning obedience was demanded. "Membership was mandatory.... No business transaction was considered legal without recognition from, and registration with, an association."

The power of the merchant class who controlled this organizational structure was not maintained only because it was in conformity with a cultural tradition. Exclusion from channels of mobility in the larger society made most community members highly dependent on their own elites who controlled the opportunity structure within the community (Baureiss, 1982; Light, 1972; Kwong, 1979; Lyman, 1968). "Business class leaders were usually in a position to squash serious dissenters by depriving those who made trouble of employment opportunities. Purges of radicals and trade unionists were fairly common. . . . Even a self-employed businessman needed the goodwill of powerful leaders to stay in business. This dependency was particularly strong among the Chinese whose very title to property depended on licenses obtainable only from the Six Companies and district associations" (Light, 1972:175).[11] Needless to say, this structure of dominance was eventually challenged by contending groups and elites (see Chapter 4).

Unitary political power usually involves attempts to acquire control over the various community functions that, in one way or another, are critical for governance and the associated exercise of power. These include fundraising (or "informal taxation"), the ethnic media, service delivery, and relations with government and other societal institutions. The expression *vertical integration* could be used in this context since it refers to "a method of extending organizational control over exchanges vital to its operation" (Pfeffer and Salancik, 1978:114).

The extension of political power can also take place through "horizontal integration," which "represents a method of attaining dominance to increase the organization's power in exchange relationships and to reduce uncertainty generated from competition" (Pfeffer and Salancik, 1978:114). This is achieved through the merging of two or more organizations. Frequently, the rhetoric justifying mergers or the fusion of organizations consists of arguments about the need to avoid the duplication of efforts and to deal with the fact that the different organizations are working at cross-purposes. The validity of the arguments, however, is frequently secondary in the dynamics of the situation. The main objective is to reduce or eliminate competition, "duplication" and "cross-purposes" being convenient euphemisms for competition in the pursuit of this aim.

The extension of power in the community also involves controlling the access to external sources of funding and sociopolitical validation. Dominant leaders, for example, will try to convince institutional authorities in the larger society to consult them before establishing contact and doing business with any other group or association in the community.

The dominant elite will also seek to approve the appointment of people to the leadership positions of the various community organizations. People who depart from the official interpretation of events or who advocate ideologies or courses of action detrimental to the interests of the dominant elite expose themselves to severe social sanctions.

The successful exercise of power by a group or coalition tends to bring about a unitary system of governance that integrates virtually all organizations of any significance in the community and assigns them a domain and role and controls their access to resources. Unitary systems have a single structure of power and authority: "decision-making, as to policy and program, takes place at the top of the structure and final authority over the units rests there" (Warren, 1967:404). Such systems seem to fit Laumann and Marsden's (1979) "centrally administered model." They have also been labelled "pyramidal" in some community studies (Gilbert, 1968). The leadership structure of such systems has also been labelled "pyramidal," "focused," or "unitary" (Nix, 1969).

Unitary systems may vary in the extent to which they are organizationally differentiated and, if differentiated, in the degree to which the various units are integrated in the inclusive system. For instance, an ethnic community may be organizationally undifferentiated in the sense that the various community functions and related policies and activities are decided upon and carried out by a single, multipurpose organization. Tirado (1974:121), for example, notes that "the Mexican American traditionally has not developed highly specialized organizations for the sole purpose of political action. Rather he has preferred to establish undifferentiated multi-purpose organizations which will serve not only his political needs but also his economic, social and cultural ones as well." Accordingly, if there is any differentiation, it will be observed within the organization. Such an arrangement, however, is fairly rare especially in ethnic communities of a certain size and with a fairly long history in a particular society.

It was noted earlier that the competing groups in a fragmented polity can find it in their interest to construct accommodative arrangements in which each can function. In certain instances fragmentation may also be replaced by a unitary hierarchical system. The road to this mode of political integration can be as, if not more, chaotic than the one to accommodation, as the Ukrainian experience in Canada illustrates.

Soon after the beginning of the existence of the Ukrainian collectivity in Canada, several lines of social division became significant within its ranks: social class, religion, political allegiance and ideology, and cultural identification. As each subgroup built its own organizations, the collectivity became a series of conflicting subcommunities.

They diverged over the fate of Ukraine and the policies to be adopted with regard to the main problems it was facing in the early part of the century. They fought over the control of community institutions and the representation of the community in Canada. They differed with regard to the importance that ethnicity (the nation) and social class should have in the public affairs of the community. They opposed each other over the ethnocultural character of their religious institutions. They took different positions on the matter of their relation with the larger society and, in particular, of the hostile behavior and derogatory attitudes toward them of some of the larger society's members and institutional agents.

Although there were several lines of division and conflict, two seem to have been dominant during substantial periods of time and to have had a particularly determining role in the construction of the governance institutions of the community. These are the conflicts between religious groups and between socialists and nationalists. Not surprisingly, social-class divisions were a significant factor in the nationalist-socialist opposition. Also, divisions existed within these main factions (e.g., between clergy and laity, between those in favor of and opposed to Bolshevization among communists). "The major Ukrainian social, religious, and political currents, such as the Catholic Church and the socialists, were not only hostile to each other but were themselves torn by centrifugal forces" (Makuch, 1979:43).

From as early as 1910, calls for unity were regularly voiced in the collectivity. On several occasions collective action was organized for particular purposes (e.g., protesting some event or situation in Ukraine, fighting for the retention of bilingual schools in Manitoba, providing assistance to war victims). Attempts were occasionally made to create an overarching organization through which the collectivity could act corporately. But several years passed before some form of organizational unification took place.

The establishment of the Ukrainian Canadian Citizen's Committee (UCCC) in 1918 was one of the first significant attempts toward unification. The procommunist organizations, however, were excluded because they were considered traitors. "The rise of nativism in Canada necessitated an organizational mediator who could assure Anglo-Canadians that Ukrainian-Canadians were indeed loyal, and the end of the war made it possible to send material aid to war-torn Ukraine and to intervene at the upcoming peace conference" (Makuch, 1979:52–53). The committee functioned for a few years, one of its accomplishments being the formation of the Ukrainian Red Cross Society in 1919. But dissention soon arose within its ranks over a variety of issues, such as the representation at the post–World War I peace conference and the control of the Ukrainian Red Cross. The UCCC disintegrated in 1922.

But, in spite of unification failures, "the organizational life of Ukrainian Canadians strengthened and multiplied at the local and national levels. Thus in lieu of one superstructure, national organizations of the various factions began to emerge in the twenties and thirties. Each functioned independently, some in [an] aggressive, hostile manner" (Woycenko, 1967:207).

Another attempt to form an overarching structure took place in 1933. The organization was called the Ukrainian National Council. It also excluded Communists. Its efforts as a national coordinating agency were not successful because of the presence of several competing organizations. The Ukrainian Self-Reliance League, the Ukrainian National Federation (UNF), the Ukrainian Catholic Brotherhood, and the United Hetman Organization "did not wish to recognize this body as their overall, political authority" (Marunchak, 1970:546).

In the late thirties, the nationalist federation and the Catholic Brotherhood teamed up to form the Representative Committee of Ukrainians in Canada (RCUC), in part through the assistance of a non-Ukrainian academic.[12] This left the other national organizations in a difficult position. A superstructure appeared to be created, and they were left out. Accordingly, they formed their own "representative" structure: the Ukrainian Canadian Central Committee (UCCC), which also included the Ukrainian Workers' League—an organization that had split from the procommunist ULFTA. Another non-Ukrainian academic was instrumental in the formation of this second organization.[13] But the two professors were not successful in uniting the two feuding organizations.

The federal government intervened to unite the two organizations because it saw the lack of unity among Ukrainians as detrimental to the war effort. Ukrainians were seen as a large reservoir of recruits and of badly needed manpower. As a result, the federal government was cast into the role of arbitrator between the RCUC and the UCCC (Gerus, 1982). Thus in 1940, the Ukrainian Canadian Committee was formed. It was an ad hoc structure established to facilitate the war effort. But "despite the intervention of non-Ukrainians . . . and despite the fact that the alliance became possible through compromise, the Ukrainian Canadian community at large accepted the long awaited superstructure enthusiastically" (Woycenko, 1967:210). The committee eventually evolved into a permanent coordinating organization.

A community's governance system can, of course, change in the opposite direction, that is from a unitary hierarchical organization to fragmentation. An integrated interorganizational system can be taken apart by power struggles. This is what appears to have happened in the unidentified ethnic community studied by Tryggvason (1971:100). The centralized structure of governance of that community, briefly described earlier, was challenged by a group of "modern leaders." They had their own ideas and the "determination, as well as the ability, to carry them out." In contrast with the traditional leaders, they were mostly from the younger native-born generation, although some were new immigrants and older native-born people.

Because the supply of potential traditional leaders became very small, the modern leaders could begin to penetrate the organizational system. They did so and introduced several changes that led to serious disagreements between themselves and the traditional leaders not only over the substance of policies but over the decision-making process itself. Thus, they soon realized that the full implementation of their ideas required the removal from office of the traditional leaders (Tryggvason, 1971).

They took over one of the major organizations by gaining control of its nominating process. Traditional leaders could then be kept off the slate of nominees for office. This ploy, however, "was coupled with private warnings to individual traditional leaders that if they attempted to promote their own re-election, steps would be taken to make certain potentially embarrassing errors made by them in the past a matter of public knowledge" (Tryggvason, 1971:103).

The removal of traditional leaders from office was not sufficient to assure the position of the modern leaders. They also had to prevent a coup that traditional leaders in other organizations might launch against them. They did this by gaining the public support of a leader of the organization occupying a critical position in the system—a leader who, even though he had not played a key role in decision-making, enjoyed a reputation in the community equal or superior to that of any other leader.

The modern leaders also needed members who would accept the changes they wanted to introduce. This is one reason why they sought to retain control of the major organization. The modern leaders compelled the other leaders to abandon any role in decision-making by publicly humiliating and embarrassing them so that they would withdraw from the sociopolitical scene in order to avoid further humiliation (Tryggvason, 1971).

The campaign was successful: the modern leaders were able to gain complete control of the organization. But their control did not extend to the community as a whole. They could not achieve the dominance of the interorganizational system attained by the cohesive group of traditional leaders. Through their confrontation with the traditional elite, the modern leaders had set in motion a course of events that divided the community into separate and loosely linked parts—a process they could not control.

The leadership was also divided into several distinct groups whose activities and influence was confined to the specific associations they led. Each group of leaders monitored the activities of the others and planned their own actions in part as if there were a conspiracy against them and their organizational base (Tryggvason, 1971). In short, the outcome was a shift from a centralized to a fragmented governance structure.

Changes in New York's Chinatown also represent a shift from a hierarchical system to one characterized by the coexistence of several centers of power (Kwong, 1979). Kwong concludes his study by noting several factors that have made Chinatown's traditional hierarchical structure obsolete. Drastic changes in the political structure of the community were in the making at the time of his study, but the situation was still in transition.

The power base of the traditional associations and of the local merchant elite was in rapid decline as a result of an economic boom in Chinatown that was to a considerable extent occasioned by international events. First, the friendlier relations between China and the United States decreased the Kuomintang Party's influence in the community. "At the same time, the recent wave of liberation struggles in the Far East has led many large Chinese business interests in those areas to emigrate to New York, creating financial blocs that have overwhelmed the old merchant elite.... This shift in the economic balance of power has demanded a different political structure, and the present instability in the community . . . is the result of a struggle for ascendancy among competing financial interests" (Kwong, 1979:153).

The growing importance of local, state, and city social welfare agencies, due in part to the public assistance they give to Chinatown, has also been a force of transformation of the political structure. In order to maintain or increase these benefits to the community, leaders establish contacts with government agencies and become involved in mainstream politics. The traditional system of hierarchical authority became less relevant as political power became increasingly a matter of establishing links with external agencies and of delivering social benefits to the community (Kwong, 1979).

TRUNCATED POLITIES

Another possible outcome of the political struggle is the marginalization of one of the sociopolitical segments. It is not incorporated in a negotiated order nor is it dominated by more powerful elements. In addition, it is too weak to control an important part of the collectivity and, accordingly, to constitute a serious opposition to other segments. It is, so to speak, at the periphery of the mainstream system in the ethnic community. It plays a marginal role in the affairs of the community. As a result, the polity is truncated.

Boissevain's (1970:33) study of Italians in Montreal provides an illustration of sociopolitical marginalization. The protestant minority functioned at the margin of the community. "Because they are outside the Roman Catholic Church, they are also outside the main stream of organizational activities of the Italian community which are heavily dependent upon church organization and support. It is important to remember that there is a Protestant minority of Italian origin which is never heard from quite simply because the positions of authority within the Italian community are monopolized by Roman Catholics."

Such a development also took place among Ukrainians. The organizational unity that was created with the formation of the Ukrainian Canadian Committee (UCC) completely ignored the socialists and communists (Makuch, 1979; Marunchak, 1970; Kostash, 1977).[14] For a while, nationalists and socialists had to coexist. In fact, they competed intensely to be the architects of "unity" in the community. But eventually, events favored the nationalist side.

At the beginning of the century, radicalism began to spread in urban industrial centers. Eventually, socialist groups began to organize. In 1904, the first local socialist cultural organization, the Taras Shevchenko Society, was formed in Winnipeg. In 1907, the first Ukrainian branches of the socialist party of Canada were established. A few years later, steps were taken to build a social-democratic organization that eventually was formed and named the Ukrainian Social-Democratic Party. Schools, newspapers, and fraternal societies were created. In 1918, a broad organization was formed, the Ukrainian Labour Farmer Temple Association (ULFTA). It opened a center for its activities in the following year. When the Social-Democratic party and its newspaper were banned in 1918, accused of antiwar and pro-Soviet agitation, the Ukrainian Labour-Farmer Temple Association replaced the party as the national organization disseminating socialist and Marxist ideas among Ukrainians. In 1924, it was incorporated nationally. Finally, Ukrainians were involved in the Communist party, initially called the workers party, through the ULFTA and as individual members. They indeed constituted a significant part of its membership and its success was largely due to their support and involvement (Kolasky, 1979).

The socialists and communists, however, experienced many difficulties. Their organizations suffered financial difficulties because they were relatively small in numbers and because the members were primarily industrial workers with low incomes. The opposition of Canadian authorities (e.g., the banning of the Social-Democratic party) led to a loss of members. "Other losses were due to expulsions and defections over ideological and other differences." For instance, in 1925, "the Communist international launched a campaign to 'bolshevize' all communist parties. This entailed the dissolution of the national federations and the language sections and the setting up of factory cells to achieve better contact with the workers" (Kolasky, 1979:14). This produced a revolt with the Communist party. A split also occurred between those who blindly supported the Soviet regime and those who were critical of its policies. But it also involved a conflict between supporters of two different types of organization: a federation as opposed to a centralized unitary structure.

The main opponents of the socialists and communists, however, were the nationalists. They were more numerous than these two groups and they had their own organizational system. Nationalist organizations included the Greek Catholic church, with its lay organization and a number of weekly newspapers; the Ukrainian Orthodox church, also with its lay organization and publications; a number of small lay and religious groups; and two political organizations, one consisting of post–1918 immigrants, most of whom had been involved in the struggles on behalf of Ukrainian independence in 1918–20 and another favoring an independent Ukraine as a monarchy (Kolasky, 1979).

The nationalists attempted by all possible means to delegitimize their opponents. This included appeals to the government to place restrictions on communist activities and to cancel ULFTA's charter, to close the communists' schools, to ban the communist press, and to deport party members (Kolasky, 1979).

The balance of power seemed to shift from one side to the other for several years. Eventually, circumstances, international events in particular, favored the nationalists. For instance, as a result of the German-Soviet pact in 1939, the ULFTA and the Communist party were declared illegal. Several ULFTA leaders were interned and others either left the country or went into hiding. The organization ceased to function. The Communist party, however, continued to be active. It was even successful in having a candidate elected to the House of Commons and to the Manitoba legislature.

In 1941, the situation was changed in the communists' favor by the surprise German attack on the USSR. The USSR was then transformed into an ally. A campaign was immediately launched for the release of the leaders who had been imprisoned and for the withdrawal of the ban on the socialist and communist organizations. The campaign was eventually successful, in good part because of the support from representatives of the upper strata of the larger society (Kolasky, 1979).

The cooperation of the Allied powers during the war and the power position of the USSR at the end of the war created a climate favorable to the Communist party in several parts of the world, including Canada. This was reflected in the growth in the party's organizational membership and in the revitalization of its press. The banned Ukrainian Labour-Farmer Temple Association was legitimized as the Association of United Ukrainian Canadians.

Communist leaders began to express their confidence that they would eventually vanquish their nationalist opponents. "Fully aware of the advantage they had gained over the nationalist organizations ... the communists exuded a confidence which bordered on presumption and arrogance. They proclaimed theirs 'the largest and most active Ukrainian organization,' the leader 'in the Ukrainian cultural field' and the 'victor' who 'can and should grow steadily.' In spirit of self-righteousness they described the nationalists as 'dead souls,' declared them completely bankrupt and predicted their early demise. The communists envisaged themselves to be the chief and rightful spokesmen of the Ukrainian community" (Kolasky, 1979:49).

Their nationalists opponents, however, were not weak. In spite of the communist gains, nationalists remained considerably more numerous. And, as indicated earlier, they had considerable organizational strength. In addition, they were successful in having some of their members elected to public office. They also obtained support from government officials. In order to increase its visibility (in competition with the efforts of the communists), the UCC organized a congress in 1943. More than 600 enthusiasts were present and demonstrated to all that the UCC was the leader of the Ukrainian community. Federal and provincial representatives were also present (Gerus, 1982).

What seemed to have tipped the balance in their favor was the arrival of large numbers of refugees after the war. In 1945, the nationalist Ukrainian Canadian Committee initiated a relief fund to assist refugees. The aid was channeled through their agency in London (the Central Ukrainian Relief

Bureau). Also, the UCC established a committee to discuss the settling of political refugees in Canada with the government. It pressured the government to change immigration laws in favor of Ukrainian refugees. "The Ukrainian pro-communists, on the other hand, were vehemently opposed to the admission of refugees to Canada.... When the war ended their star was in the ascendancy and they were well aware of the threat posed by the refugees" (Gerus, 1982:95). They also made representations to the Canadian government. Both sides attempted to influence public opinion. Eventually, the government decided to admit refugees, and between 1947 and 1955, over 33,000 Ukrainians were admitted into Canada.

For the communists, the refugees presented a serious difficulty. For instance, their pro-Soviet propaganda was challenged by firsthand accounts of experiences in the USSR. These accounts also intensified nationalist opposition to the USSR and slowed down the leftward trend that had taken place in the Ukrainian community because of Soviet popularity during the war, "and reestablished the nationalists as the dominant force in the Ukrainian community" (Gerus, 1982:107).

Thus the procommunist camp began its decline. External events such as the Cold War acted against them. The visit of large numbers of Ukrainian pro-communists to Ukraine disillusioned them about the Soviet regime. Khrushchev's indictment of Stalin in 1956 was another serious blow to their faith in a communist system.

There were also difficulties in Canada. For instance, the "Red Cross scandal" created problems of organizational legitimacy among communist members because of charges that money collected in the Red Cross campaign for medical aid to the USSR had been misappropriated. This hampered considerably the expansion and influence of the communists. The decline was also due to factors such as the migration of communist activists to Ukraine, the death of older communists, and the difficulty in recruiting young Canadian-born members, whose increasing standard of living during the postwar years and improved knowledge of English facilitated their integration into Canadian society.

Not only did the nationalists become the dominant force, but in the process the communists became a marginalized segment in the community. They lost virtually all legitimacy and recognition.

CONCLUSION

The sociopolitical structuring of ethnic polities and the corresponding organization of their governance institutions can take many different forms. Four general patterns were identified: accommodation, segmentation, ascendancy, and truncation. These patterns are partly the result of the relationship that subgroups in the collectivity establish with each other in the pursuit of their respective political, economic, organizational, or ideological interests. The underlying assumption is that each subgroup or segment of the collectivity will attempt to structure the governance institutions so as to be in the best position possible to pursue its own interests. In other words, the way in which governance is organized is not indifferent to the pursuit of interests by different interest groupings. It constitutes either a set of institutional potentialities or of constraints.

Critical to the relationships among subgroups, however, is the degree of divergence or commonality of their interests, which in turn is related to their social characteristics and ideological orientations. In reality, common interests and divergences tend to exist simultaneously in most collectivities. However, in a particular group during a period of time, common problems, opportunities, and strategies of action may predominate. In other words, each may have an interest in pooling resources and in coordinating political efforts. On the other hand, the opposition between certain segments of the collectivity may be very pronounced and have a long history. To the extent that such divergences outweigh commonalities, there will be a propensity for each group to attempt to govern itself independently of the others.

Equally and perhaps more critical, however, is the amount of power resources that each subgroup or faction can mobilize, either within the ethnic collectivity or from institutions of the larger society (e.g., the government, the media, churches, labor unions). The structuring of the governance institutions when power is distributed very unevenly is likely to differ significantly from the structuring when power is distributed equally. In the first situation, one faction is potentially powerful enough to capture the complete or quasi-complete control of the governance apparatus, while in the other, the different factions may have an interest in a system that will give each of them room to operate.

A segmented system of governance is one characterized by a high polarization of interests coinciding with a fairly even distribution of power among the sociopolitical segments. Commonalities are not sufficient to bring the groups to a pooling of resources and strategies, so each has a tendency to operate independently of the others. If they share similar interests, however, they will have an interest in negotiating an accommodation such that they pursue common objectives while retaining a certain degree of autonomy: a federative type of arrangement.

When power is very unequal but with little divergence of interests among the subgroups, the powerful group will tend to structure a unitary system of governance in which it will have the determining influence. The weak subgroups will tend to function within that system since the interests and political philosophy of the dominating faction are compatible with theirs. If, however, their interests and ideology differ, the weak groups will tend to become marginalized. Accordingly, the polity and its governance system will become truncated; one of its segments being defined as irrelevant in the public affairs of the community, as being, so to speak, a political non-entity.

NOTES

1. On regulation and the source of political demand for the formulation and application of regulatory norms, see Pfeffer and Salancik (1978) and Zald (1970).

2. The "institutionalized thought structure" refers to "the intricate interweaving or mutual reinforcement of what is known or believed or conceptualized, on the one hand, about certain problems... and the actual configuration of specific organizations and procedures employed in addressing them.... [It] constitutes the substance of [an] interorganizational consensus, the framework of thought and social structure through which the behaviour of those organizations takes place and within which it is interpreted." This common thought structure "defines how problems will be conceived and how they will be dealt with" (Warren, Rose and Bergunder, 1974:20).

3. See, for example, Litwak and Hylton (1962), Tropman (1974), and Pfeffer and Salancik (1978).

4. In a unitary system, these different functions are carried out by different departments or divisions of a single organizational apparatus, the geographical levels corresponding to different levels of the administrative structure of each division.

5. Another level consisted of fongs and village associations which "responded to the individual, natural needs of its members and dealt with matters of immediate concern" (Kwong, 1979:41).

6. Jedwab (1986) suggests that the uptown-downtown cleavage must not be exaggerated. First, the two factions had common interests, such as anti-Semitism. Second, not all uptowners were integrationist and all downtowners segregationists, and those with a particular orientation were not necessarily uncompromising over specific issues, such as the question of separate Jewish schools. Third, an overemphasis on that social division draws attention away from other ideological differences, such as that between reform and traditional Jews.

7. As will be seen later, the segmentation did not last. Forces toward unification began to operate and eventually brought about a degree of integration of the two subcommunities.

8. For an interesting overview of the social evolution of the community, see Glickman (1976).

9. For a description of the events leading to the merger, see Glickman (1976:244–259).

10. In this study, Baureiss discusses the situation in Calgary and Winnipeg at the beginning of the century. See also, Lyman (1968).

11. The Six Companies was an association of district associations usually formed to provide unofficial government to the community with regard to both its domestic and its external affairs (Lyman, 1968). Later, these associations came to be called Chinese Consolidated Benevolent Associations.

12. Professor Watson Kirkconnell of McMaster University.

13. Professor George Simpson of the University of Saskatchewan.

14. The socialists were also marginalized in the Polish community (Radecki, 1979).

3

Governance Institutions and the Sociopolitical Environment

The sociopolitical environment can, in addition to the forces of internal competition, impinge on the governance institutions of ethnic communities. The environment constitutes a set of opportunities available to members of ethnic groups, a set of possible problems and constraints with which they have to cope, and resources that can be mobilized to improve the condition of individual members or of community institutions. The sociopolitical environment also includes a number of groups and organizations that may have an interest in what goes on in the ethnic community and/or in the way it relates to the larger society and its institutions.

Viewed as a set of opportunities, constraints, and resources, the environment raises the question of the organizational capacity of the community to deal with problems or take advantage of opportunities. Also, the community-environment relationship is as dynamic as the evolution of institutional arrangements under the impact of competitive struggles was seen to be in the previous chapter. That is, institutions are shaped in the very process of coping with the conditions confronting the community. Viewed as a set of agents with an interest in the political organization of ethnic communities, the sociopolitical environment is a source of possible interventions into a community's public affairs. These two ways in which the environment can have an impact on the organization of governance of ethnic communities constitute the object of this chapter.

GOVERNANCE AS THE CAPACITY TO COPE WITH ENVIRONMENTAL CONDITIONS

Ethnic community formation, survival, and development require that problems and constraints faced by the community be dealt with and that opportunities—propitious events and circumstances—be sought and exploited. This, in turn, requires resources in the form of legitimacy, active social support, money, and information. Resources, problems, and opportunities constitute the main elements of the collectivity's internal and external environment. The needed resources may be controlled by groups and institutions of the larger society or may be available for mobilization from within the community. Opportunities may occur within or outside of the ethnic boundaries; sources of problems can be external (e.g., discrimination), internal (e.g., factional conflict) or both (e.g., cultural loss).

Accordingly, the central challenge of community governance is to create and maintain the capacity to take advantage of environmental conditions or to adapt to them, modify them, or overcome them. Governance involves the capacity to formulate policy in relation to opportunities and problems, to establish and administer the structures required for policy implementation, and to design strategies for the pursuit of desired objectives.[1]

As already indicated, this approach to the political community and its institutions corresponds, by and large, to what Gamson (1968) has called the "social control" perspective, in which the concern is with "the collective purposes to which power is put rather than its private purposes." A central question is how leadership operates "to achieve societal goals most efficiently while at the same time avoiding costly side effects" (11). What is at issue is the capacity of the system of governance to get results that can improve the well-being of the community.

Cottrell (1983:403) uses the notion of competence to refer to the capabilities that a community requires "to cope with the problems of its collective life." A competent community is "one in which the various component parts ... (1) are able to collaborate effectively in identifying the problems and needs of the community; (2) can achieve a working consensus on goals and priorities; (3) can agree on ways and means to implement the agreed-upon goals; and (4) can collaborate effectively in the required action."

The community-environment relationship, however, is reciprocal since the very process of attempting to deal with or change the environment contributes to shaping the governing structures and processes within the community. The organizational apparatus for community governance is partly constructed in relation to the environmental tasks that community members wish to accomplish. Similarly, dynamic interaction with the environment is likely to affect the composition of the leadership, its relationship with members, the formulation of goals, the allocation of resources, and the definition of the collective identity in the community. In other words, the nature of the problems and opportunities encountered contribute to define the tasks to be accomplished as well as the required leadership skills and organizational resources. Thus, the various features of the political system and of its organizational capacity can be seen as creative responses to environmental circumstances.

The impact of these conditions on the ethnic community's political system is not, however, one of simple determinism. A learning process occurs, whether it be through systematic research, trial and error, or an examination of the group's past experience or of the experience of other groups. Structures and activities are modified over the years in such a way as to maintain or increase perceived effectiveness in relation to changing circumstances. In addition, a selection process takes place. Leaders or potential leaders do not react to all aspects of their internal and external environment. They react to the problems, opportunities, and resources that they perceive can make a significant difference for the community.

Two points need to be made in this connection. First, political and administrative learning is a matter of degree. In some communities, it may be highly developed, even planned; in others, hardly any accumulation of organizational experience may take place. Second, the notion of learning implies that there is not necessarily a unique type of structure or pattern of activities in relation to a given set of circumstances. The character of communal institutions does not derive from a simple response or adaptation to environmental conditions. There is room for strategic choices, innovation, and chance discoveries (Child, 1972). In other words, governance institutions are constructed. It is possible that, faced with the same kinds of problems or opportunities, organizational builders in different ethnic groups will create structures that vary substantially in form.

Yet observed variations in organizational responses to circumstances are not random. To a considerable extent, they "can be accounted for as attempts to solve the problems of concerted action under different conditions, especially conditions of technological and environmental constraints and contingencies" (Thompson, 1967:74). Constraints and contingencies limit the range of choices possible or make certain organizational forms easier to establish than others. As a result, there may be a tendency for particular types of governance institutions to be associated with certain kinds of environmental conditions.

The environment of an ethnic community consists of the multiplicity of attitudes, perceptions, and behaviors of members of other groups and of institutional agents. It includes laws, practices, and regulations in industry, government, schools, and other societal institutions. It comprises the social definitions of situations diffused by the mass media. A possible analytic strategy would be to examine a range of specific environmental circumstances and the ways in which they impinge on ethnic governance institutions. Such an exercise, however, would be extremely lengthy as each group has been confronted with particular conditions at different periods of its history.

An alternate strategy is to identify certain types of environmental conditions and examine their possible impact on the organization of governance. Four dimensions of environmental variation have been selected from the organizational literature, namely, the severity of "environmental stress,"[2] the degree of complexity or heterogeneity in the environment, the extent to which the various groups and organizations in the environment are organized into a coherent system, and the environment's cultural features. The next sections consider the ways in which these dimensions shape the governance institutions of the ethnic community.[3]

Environmental Stress

Perhaps one of the most frequently noted aspects of the social environment of ethnic minorities is the extent to which the environment is tolerant or hostile. As noted earlier, some authors even argue that discrimination and prejudice are the central determinants of the emergence of any kind of organization in ethnic communities, that the central problem of ethnic governance is protection against prejudice and discrimination. They may not always be the central factors, but they are certainly important and frequent ones: they have an impact on the political cohesion of the group and on its organization for political action. The themes of prejudice, discrimination, subordination, oppression, and exploitation of ethnic minorities by more powerful groups are common in the literature on interethnic relations. So are the analyses of responses or reactions to those experiences.

The general hypothesis is that groups whose members perceive "the surrounding environment as hostile and people in it as prepared to engage in destructive or depriving actions" tend to develop a sociopolitical organization that permits the mobilization and coordination of individual efforts for collective action (Siegel, 1970:11). Siegel refers to the process as "defensive structuring." This is in continuity with Simmel (1955) who theorizes that external threats affect the identity, cohesion, and sociopolitical organization of groups. They sharpen group boundaries, accentuate prejudices and stereotypes concerning the adversary, and lead to the mobilization of individual energies and material resources.

Defensive structuring can consist of several subprocesses: the systematic reinforcement of symbols of collective identity, the control of individual behavior, the suppression of dissents within the group, the articulation and diffusion of intergroup ideologies, and the sensitization of members to the claims of superiority of the adversary (Adam and Giliomee, 1979; Smith, 1981). These processes tend to require a centralization of power and authority within the group, that is a particular form of governance structure that can induce members to act in a concerted way. Indeed, "when cultural survival is thought to be at stake, the matter of regulation cannot be left exclusively to self-control. It is buttressed formally by a relatively small number of authoritarian power holders. What is more, the legitimation of centralized authority stems from the urgent and apprehensive need for solutions to daily problems; the resource that confers power upon these offices is special knowledge" (Siegel, 1970:17). The orientation of individual behavior, the containment of social interaction within ethnic boundaries, and the fostering of shared understanding can be achieved partly through socialization. However, the persistence of these patterns would be difficult without an active role by a strong central public authority.

Of course, both external threats and the centralization of authority are matters of degree. The dangers that a group faces may be more or less intense; they can take the form of a diffuse hostility or of specific acts of aggression and discrimination. Intense hostility expressed regularly in concrete acts would be the most likely to lead to a sociopolitical organization that permits effective group mobilization.

Huel (1986), for example, describes the attempts on the part of the French minority in Saskatchewan to unify and organize in order to defend what it considered to be its linguistic and religious rights. The main issues that led to confrontations with the English-speaking majority centered on the school system. The events in other parts of Canada gave all the indications of a serious threat: English-speaking majorities seemed intent in using their power to impose the English language on the French minority and to put restrictions on the teaching of other languages. Hence the French community felt the need for unity and a centrally coordinated structure.

However, the possibility of obtaining educational and linguistic concessions was very limited as the number of French-speaking people was small and they were dispersed across the province without significant concentrations in any region (Huel, 1986). But they were not without resources: organizational and ideological resources could be deployed toward the creation of a local and province-wide structure to defend and promote their cultural interests.

The organizational resource was the Catholic parish and its leadership. The parish was to be the prime locus of mobilization and organization. "Each parish would gather its members into an association directed by the curé. The most effective local organization would be one which would encompass all the interests of a locality, thus making it difficult for divisive factors to emerge. In turn, this community of interests would facilitate communications between the parochial associations" (Huel, 1986:6). Also, since parishes are already part of a centralized structure and their leaders under the central authority of the bishop, the formation of a provincial association was greatly facilitated.

The second resource was the ideological fusion of religion and language. The preservation of the group's language was defined as the preservation of the faith; and vice versa (Huel, 1986). Thus linguistic assimilation was seen as a double threat to group survival, as both language and religion were essential elements of the collective identity. Given the link established between language and religion, it was not surprising that the importance of an organization unifying the French Catholics of the province was first perceived by the bishop and the clergy.

The existence of these resources does not mean that union and organization were automatic. The creation of local associations federated into a provincial organization required, for example, the formation of media of communication. (Huel, 1986, argues that the first attempt to organize failed in part because of the absence of a French-language press.) Conventions had to be called. The ideology had to be diffused and maintained. People had to be persuaded that the venture had some chances of success. It is interesting to note that comparisons with other groups were used: the Germans, for example, were said to owe their strength to organization. Finally, the importance of the threat was kept alive in people's minds by spreading information about events in New Brunswick, Alberta, and Manitoba— events that could be easily interpreted as a conspiracy against French Catholics (Huel, 1986).

A study by Buchignani and Indra (1980) underscores the importance of the perception of conflict as opposed to its objective existence. In a comparison of the experience of Sikhs and Asian Fijians in Vancouver, they observed that the former were much more likely to perceive themselves as victims of prejudice and discrimination than the latter, even though their actual experience did not differ markedly. This differential perception, they suggest, can be traced to their preemigration experience and sociocultural context. As a result of this background and of their interpretation of Canadian society and of their position in it, the Vancouver Fijians lack "social cohesion . . . except in a network sense" and the social mechanisms necessary for collective action. The historical experience of the Sikhs, on the other hand, has led them to be highly sensitive to external threats and to "establish all the social mechanisms necessary to generate a substantial degree of social cohesion and group response to collective threat" (Buchignani and Indra, 1980:155).

Another illustration of Siegel's analysis is provided by the Japanese-Canadian community. During World War II, external hostility reduced the salience of internal cleavages and promoted cohesion in the community. In his analysis of the Montreal community, Oiwa (1986) indicates (as Huel showed in the case of the Saskatchewan French) the important role of churches in providing organizational resources: the Christian churches provided the framework within which the *Nikkei* (overseas population of Japanese origin) began to organize. Eventually a standing committee was set up and political responsibility was vested in a small group of *Niseis* (second generation). It was the first attempt to create a central organization in the community. It will be seen in more detail later that with the decrease of external aggression after the war, the centralized character of the governance structure changed as submerged political cleavages reemerged.

In a benign environment, on the other hand, centralized coordination and control are not required. Members of the ethnic collectivity may still organize themselves for the pursuit of certain objectives or to deal with particular problems, but this organization would tend to take the form of "limited interest associations." This is a situation in which the "various interest fields operate more or less independently and in relative isolation from other interest fields" (Dasgupta, 1974:215). A community-wide coordinating structure is less likely to emerge and, if one does, it would tend to remain fairly fragmentary.[4]

Warren (1967:407) has given the label "social choice" to such community contexts. They are "exemplified by the autonomous behaviour of a number of organizations and individuals in the community as they relate themselves and their behaviour to any particular issue which concerns more than one of them. . . . They do not necessarily share any inclusive goal. . . . There is no formal inclusive structure within which the units make their decisions. . . . Authority rests at the unit level. There is no formally structured provisions for division of labour within an inclusive context."

In such situations, community affairs consist of the totality of activities carried out by the various limited interest organizations. The collectivity lacks integration and coordination in its structure of governance and leadership (Dasgupta, 1974). Each organization pursues its own goals and interests, independently responding to situations, problems, and opportunities. When this is the case for most organizations in a community, the governance system is atomized. This, of course, is a matter of degree; rarely do all organizations in the community operate independently of each other. The social choice community context is an ideal type.

In atomized settings, collective action is carried out by limited interest organizations. No goals are pursued through interorganizational action, either in particular fields or in the community at large. If benefits or disadvantages accrue to the community and its members, it is due to the "invisible hand" of Adam Smith, which aggregates the results of the activities carried out by particular organizations pursuing their own interests.

This seems to be the situation of the German collectivity in Canada and the United States. Luebke (1978:67) mentions that the Germans did not form a unified political organization because, "unlike Blacks, Chicanos, or Japanese, the Germans had no serious social or economic problems to unite them in a struggle against oppression." They had experienced humiliation during World War I, but both before and after the war, there was "no common interest strong enough to bind them together." The attempts made to unify them were not "capable of overcoming the centrifugal forces of personal and subgroup interests."

The benignity of the environment is clearly indicated by its openness: due largely to the "fact that the Germans, in their physical, linguistic and cultural characteristics, were close to Anglo-American norms, . . . it was possible for them to assimilate with astonishing ease if they so chose" (Luebke, 1978:67). Of course, the Germans have organizations or associations, but these tend to have a limited interest character. National associations, to the extent that they exist, tend to play a quite limited role and to have a weak unifying potential.

The impact of the fluidity of boundaries between the ethnic and the larger communities has also been noted among the Chinese in Canada. Baureiss's (1982:71) general hypothesis is that "when ethnic communities encounter a shift in their relation towards the host society from a very restrictive to a less restrictive or free market system, communities will modify their institutional systems. The change towards a less restrictive market system will make community control less effective because it permits community members to choose from among the various ethnic and host society's institutions and formal organizations."

Siegel's hypothesis, noted earlier, was that elite dominance and the ideological and behavioral control of individual members are necessary for a community to resist and cope with the hostility and discrimination from the larger society. Aggression requires an army-like sociopolitical structure. Baureiss, on the other hand, while not denying the defensive role of centralized control structures in ethnic communities, seems to give more importance to the limited choices available to individuals outside the boundaries of their own ethnic group because of discrimination. Being restricted to their own communities, "normative patterns that prescribe or proscribe courses of action" are more likely to be imposed on them (1982:70).[5]

Environmental Diversity and Complexity

The relevant social, economic, and political context can also vary in its diversity and complexity. This may manifest itself in the range of institutions of significance to an ethnic community. As a society becomes multicultural in an increasingly wider range of sectors (e.g., government, education, media, welfare, religion), it confronts ethnic leaders with a larger array of problems, opportunities, and targets of action. Dealing effectively with a complex environment requires the creation of organizations (or units within an organization) specialized by function or sector of activity. Thus, the wider the range of organizations and groups in the larger society that adopt policies and take actions of possible relevance to ethnic groups, the more ethnic communities are likely to have differentiated organizational systems for their governance (Enloe, 1981; Wickberg, 1979).

The internal as well as the external environment can become more diversified and complex. A number of authors have hypothesized that the number and diversity of a community's organizations are a function of the size of its population. Analyses by Wickberg (1979) and Baureiss (1980) seem to suggest that the hypothesis is applicable to the Chinese communities in Canada, although Wickberg emphasizes that additional factors are also critical and that, in certain cases, they may be more important. He is referring to factors such as discrimination and government intervention.

Roseman (1974:28) also argues that increases in the size of the American Jewish community brought about a change from a "single congregational government" to a more complex and differentiated organizational system. (His analysis is discussed in greater detail later.)

Patterns of Environmental Organization

The governance system can also be affected by the extent to which it has to deal with external groups and organizations whose actions are more or less efficiently coordinated. If external groups and agencies constitute a fairly well integrated interorganizational system, the ethnic community may increase its own interorganizational coordination in order to deal with them effectively.

In Canada, the organizational environment of ethnic communities is not well coordinated, at least not formally. The federal government does play a key role that may, through its influence, produce a sort of informal coordination among other societal institutions and groups. The government's role may generate a certain tendency toward centralization in ethnic governance institutions. There are, however, several other organizations acting fairly independently from the federal government in their relations with ethnic communities. These include other levels of government, school boards, business firms, churches, radio and television stations, newspapers, labor unions, welfare agencies, and various voluntary associations. In fact, what characterizes the actions of these various external organizations is how uncoordinated they are with each other. Such a situation may lead to a certain organizational decentralization in the governance of ethnic communities: different organizations would have the responsibility to deal with different sectors and/or levels. The existence of such a relationship may, however, depend on factors such as the size of the community.

The political-administrative environment of native peoples, however, does not conform to this pattern. Its level of coordination (through centralization) is much higher than is the case in other groups. A government department exists, with its own minister and an elaborate bureaucratic apparatus, to deal with Indian communities. For a long time, this very system had the effect (together with demographic and social factors) of hampering the emergence of an autonomous Indian political organization.

Beginning in the 1960s, a national organization was established: the National Indian Brotherhood (NIB)—now the Assembly of First Nations. Initially, emphasis was placed on internal development of the NIB and of the Indian community it sought to represent. The leadership "stressed participation and a non-hierarchical orientation, and sought to involve as many people as possible in NIB's work by delegating authority to them" (Ponting and Gibbins, 1980:201). This organization, in spite of the change it represents, still has to deal with a highly structured and coordinated environment of organizations, at least in comparison with other communities. In subsequent phases of development, greater emphasis was placed on the problems of dealing with the centralized organizational environment. Accordingly, the NIB became itself increasingly centralized.

It is perhaps not so much the extent to which the environment is organized that matters as the form that such organization takes. For example, in his discussion of the relationship between political federalism and the demands of interest groups, Kwavnick (1975:72) hypothesizes "that the distribution of power between the central and provincial governments influences the structure, cohesion and even the existence of interest groups; that is, that the strength and cohesion of interest groups will tend to mirror the strength, in their particular area of concern, of the government to which they enjoy access." Thus, interest groups with access to the provincial governments will be stronger than nationally based groups "enjoying access to the national government when the provincial governments enjoy a stronger position than the national government in areas of concern to those interest groups, and vice versa."

Juteau-Lee and Lapointe (1983:178) note a change in the social-psychological boundaries and in the organizational basis of francophones outside of Quebec during the 1950s and 1960s. Before that period, "all the French in Canada belonged to the French-Canadian nation. The changing of the francophone collectivity in Quebec meant that the Québécois excluded from their 'we' the francophones in other parts of Canada. . . . (This) process of differentiation-division . . . (was) formally recognized (in) 1969." Thus regional identities were strengthened: Franco-Ontarians, Franco-Manitobans, Fransaskois, etc. In addition, urbanization and the increase in the demand for educational facilities and public services in the population in general also manifested itself among francophones.

In addition to the new affirmation of Quebec's nationalism, there is a structural reason for this evolution: the federal division of powers in Canada. By Canada's constitution, much of the legislation and most of the services important for the functioning of a community are provincial (rather than federal). This is the case in the domains of justice, education, health, welfare, and culture. Thus, to a considerable extent, the growth in the welfare state during the 1950s and 1960s took place at the provincial level. This required a community organization and political action increasingly oriented toward provincial political and administrative structures and strengthened the regional basis of the identification and sociopolitical organization of French Canadians (Juteau-Lee and Lapointe, 1983).

Jackson (1975) also observes that the structure of the environment has a critical impact on political organization and activity. He uses the notions of vertical and horizontal patterns of organization introduced by Warren (1963). The horizontal system refers to the community's own social organization and the interrelationships among its components. The vertical system, however, has to do with the relationship between the community, its groups and organizations, and extracommunity systems. "For example, an issue over language in a local school may be mediated within the horizontal pattern drawing only a local parent's association and school board into play, or it may move into the vertical pattern bringing the provincial Department of Education into the picture" (Jackson, 1975:2). Generally, "if the horizontal pattern is weak, that is, if decisions concerning issues crucial to the community require the intervention of the vertical system, then the interest-articulating activity . . . will take place in extra-local systems" (168). Thus the political structuring within the community is partly a function of the way in which its political and administrative environment is organized and operates.

Structural and Cultural Models from the Larger Society

The environment in which ethnic communities find themselves is also a cultural context—a context within which strategic choices and organizational learning take place. The cultural heritage of the group operates through the parameters of the larger sociocultural environment, if it is only for the fact that the group has no choice but to function in it (Gordon, 1964; Yancey, Ericksen, and Juliani, 1976; Taylor, 1979).

A sort of organizational acculturation occurs. Indeed, communities structure their institutions by borrowing from the cultural practices of the larger society as well as transferring from the group's own culture and historical experience. People cope with the modalities of their social environment by using the cultural capital at their disposal (Whitten and Szwed quoted by Taylor, 1979). But this capital can be drawn both from the heritage and experience of their own group and from the cultural environment in which it is encapsulated. Thus, the emergent social and political organization is a blend of elements from the ethnic culture and from the larger cultural environment.

This was noted by Isajiw (1979) in his analysis of the American Ukrainian community. The Ukrainian church, while being a transplanted organization, had to undergo significant structural changes in the new societal context. For instance, in the social structure of the old country, "the clergy comprised a social class unto itself, or indeed a caste, in relation to which the peasant church member was clearly assigned an inferior status." But in the new context, arrangements "common to many American non-Catholic churches" were adopted (1979:84). Specifically, unlike in Ukraine, the church was completely dependent upon the support of the parishioners.

This was the case for church property and for the income of the clergy. Also, until 1924, the pastor could be fired by the parishioners.

The impact of the larger sociocultural context is particularly well illustrated by Roseman's (1974) analysis of the historical evolution of the American Jewish community. He indicates that the early Jewish communities in America were characterized by a single institution—the synagogue. This represented a transfer of what they had known in Europe, namely "a unified community, where one agency—not the synagogue, but the *kehillah* itself—administered the various communal functions centrally and exercised considerable power" (1974:26). But even though "the principle of unified communal government" was retained, it was modified "through the adoption of a characteristically American institution, the self-governing congregation" (27).

The next period of American Jewish history saw the emergence of a variety of autonomous organizations. The presence of different religious styles, for example, spawned new synagogues. A demand for services also existed among the religiously unaffiliated. Several autonomous organizations were created and competed with each other. The creation of new organizations was partly the result of an increase in size of the community (as noted earlier) and the accompanying social differentiation of the membership. But it also reflected the trends in American society. "Deism and secularism, religious voluntarism and congregational autonomy, democracy and individualism, were characteristic of the American ideal even before the Revolutionary War.... That the Jewish communal structures which emerged under these circumstances took a competitive, aggressive, and often confusing form can hardly be a surprise" (Roseman, 1974:30).

The lack of central coordination that characterized the second period became a problem for the community with the arrival of a large number of Jewish immigrants from Europe at the turn of the century. In order to cope with the new situation, federations were organized. The federal model of organization is part of the Jewish political heritage. Roseman notes, however, that this model was also "consonant with structural changes in American society, for it was during these decades that corporate cooperative enterprise began to supplant individual competitive entrepreneurship.... Jewish communal enterprise thus adapted for social service a form which was proving to be successful in the economic sphere" (1974:32).

Attempts at coordination at the national level were also made during this period, but without much success until the depression of the 1930s. The severity of the needs to be met and the scarcity of resources required the community to plan for maximum efficiency. The expertise required was frequently not available at the local level, and the pooling of expertise and resources came to be seen as a necessity. But the same challenges confronted governments in the larger American society—challenges that called for strong national leadership. Thus, Roseman underlines the fact that, once again, the structural models of the larger society tend to be adopted by the ethnic community in the structuring of its organizational framework. Thus, "that American Jews should have chosen to create a strong national organization in this era of emergent strong central government is exactly what has been predicted" (1974:36).

In short, "organizational acculturation" involves in part the adoption of models that are prevalent in the larger society and in part similar responses to similar problems and circumstances.

EXTERNAL INTERVENTION AND THE ORGANIZATION OF
ETHNIC GOVERNANCE

Ethnic communities are part of the environment of societal institutions—governmental, religious, educational, industrial, and so on. What leaders and members of ethnic communities define as important problems or issues, the policies they advocate, the courses of action they pursue, in short, their public affairs can have implications for the functioning of societal institutions and the interests of those who lead them. This is particularly the case for state institutions: ethnic affairs are likely to be part of the considerations that enter into the planning and decision-making of their executives. This is clearly indicated for instance by the activities undertaken to gather information about ethnic collectivities, their organizations, and their leaders: census data, special studies, conferences, meetings with organizational leaders, consultations with academic researchers, and the use of newspaper clipping services.

But executives or authorities of societal institutions do not limit themselves to a scanning of their relevant environments in order to be better able to react to them. Their situation would indeed be highly vulnerable if they were restricted to an adjustment of their structures, policies, and budgets in response to pressures from their organized publics. It is therefore in their interest to reduce the uncertainty and dependence inherent in such a situation. Accordingly, they are likely to attempt to control or influence the decisions and activities of relevant groups and individuals in ethnic collectivities. This can be achieved by structuring the institutions through which the ethnic community governs itself and the composition of its leadership and by being an active participant in its public affairs.

External agencies may perceive ethnic collectivities as a source of demands and expectations to which they may have to respond. They may, in certain circumstances, see them as a source of potential problems. Ethnic groups may voice discontent with aspects of their situation or articulate demands for changes in societal institutions. Thus, the authorities of these institutions may feel the necessity to channel or contain these demands and expectations (Katznelson, 1973). They may seek to establish linkages with the ethnic community. Through its "government," they can attempt to control the evolution of that segment of their political environment. This is illustrated by an observation made by Ponting and Gibbins (1980:196) concerning the National Indian Brotherhood: "Despite the conflict relationship between NIB and IIAP, IIAP has a definite need for NIB. That need revolves around the functions which NIB fulfills for IIAP, one of which is the provision of a certain amount of order, predictability, and manageability to the IIAP's conflict with Indians. Without NIB that conflict would at best have to be conducted on several different provincial fronts at once, and at worst would have to be simultaneously waged with all 573 bands across the country."[6]

The sociopolitical control intentions of an external agency are also well illustrated by the intervention of the Mussolini government in the North American Italian communities. "So although Toronto had its own *fascista di prima ora*, who were veterans of the Italian war effort, and the immigrated, and although the *colonia* had certainly been prepared by the patriotic gore of World War One and the Revisionist rhetoric of the postwar years for the coming of Fascism, when it came, it came as an intervention of the Italian government into the affairs of a Canadian ethnic group." Through the consular service, fascist Italy intended to "guide the lives, co-ordinate and encourage the activities, encourage initiation of our people in foreign lands" (Harney, 1981:54–55).

The same kind of intervention occurred in other North American cities. Boissevain (1970), for instance, notes that in Montreal, Italian fascist leaders formed a series of "national-political associations which were counterparts of those existing in Italy"—and this with the assistance of the consul general. These leaders also formed the Fronte Unico Italiano di Montreal, an organization that was to unify the Italian community. This organization, in which most associations were asked to participate, "was to provide material and moral support for the Italian government" (Boissevain, 1970:6).[7]

Modell (1977:81) writes of the role of the Japanese government through its consulate in the Los Angeles Japanese community at the beginning of the century. "The consul, who urged that 'all' Japanese 'should automatically' belong to their local Japanese Association, sat in on key Association meetings, arbitrated internal disputes, and emphasized his position through participation in a variety of Association ceremonies. . . . But his main source of authority was his ability to empower the Association to issue (at a fee) the various papers and certificates necessary to resident aliens if they wished to travel to Japan, to bring in relatives, and to remain in the good graces of the Japanese military authorities."

Ethnic communities, however, are not only a source of problems or demands for societal institutions. They can also be perceived as arenas of opportunities in relation to particular institutional objectives. In so far as they constitute a relevant public for these institutions, they can be a source of support and legitimacy. They can also provide a clientele for either general or specialized programs and activities. They offer a possibility for organizational expansion. The interest that churches, labor unions, businesses, and political parties have for ethnic collectivities as sources of clients and support is well known. One of its manifestations is the formation of affiliates or branches in the ethnic community.

The Protestant and Catholic churches have attempted and frequently succeeded in establishing themselves organizationally in ethnic communities. In several instances, however, these attempts have not been made without generating conflicts with the ethnic clergy (and other leaders) over the control of the religious organization. The conflict between Roman Catholics and the Greek Orthodox churches in the Ukrainian community provides an interesting example (Marunchak, 1970; Kostash, 1977). So does the conflict over clerical control in the New York Italian community at the end of the nineteenth and beginning of the twentieth century (Tomasi, 1975).

External agencies also need channels through which information can be obtained about ethnic groups and for communication with them. An organizational apparatus may also be needed for the delivery of services or for the execution of programs. For such purposes, the external organization may encourage the formation of an umbrella organization to represent the community. The formation of such an organization may even be stipulated as a condition for receiving assistance or official recognition. Taub et al. (1977:427) have argued that external agencies may promote or structure community organizations "not because the local residents are isolated, disorganized, or anomic... but because [the external agencies] need local 'representatives' to talk to." It is also "because resources from the wider society—city services, educational funds... are frequently distributed on a 'community basis,' [that] formal, locality-based associations can play an important role for neighborhood residents" (1977:439). This argument is made in relation to the geographical basis of urban social organization, but it can be applied to ethnic (or other) bases of social organization at least as far as certain kinds of services or functions are concerned.

Governments and other societal institutions frequently find it easier to deal with one representative organization than with a multiplicity of associations. They prefer to avoid being confronted with different definitions of needs and problems, conflicting policy demands, or competing claims for recognition or funds. They are also concerned with the possibility of antagonizing certain subgroups in the ethnic community by giving recognition or assistance to some organizations but not (or not as much) to others. An example is described by Jansen (1981:85): the Premier of British Columbia "suggested (in 1974) that if the various Italo-Canadian organizations would unite under one society, the B.C. government would be able to offer a subsidy of $333,333 for the building of a centre."

The external organization wants political competition to remain internalized in the communities. By having competition contained within the ethnic communities, the political costs such competition could have for the external agency are reduced or eliminated. The description of Calgary's Chinatown by Hoe (1976) makes it clear why the government preferred to deal with one rather than with several associations. It also illustrates how external pressures or requirements may lead to some degree of institution- alization of political competition within the community. "In view of the competing proposals on Chinatown development presented by both the United Calgary Chinese Association (U.C.C.A.) and the Sien Lok Society (S.L.S.) on behalf of the Chinese community, the three levels of government, city, provincial, and federal, have asked the Chinese to speak with a united voice and to spell out their differences" (Hoe, 1976:244).

Government pressure led to the formation of a new "united front." The two parties agreed that external relations would remain the prerogative of the S.L.S. representatives since because of their education in English, they were better able to deal with the larger society (Hoe, 1976). A majority of the U.C.C.A. members had to agree to the S.L.S. proposals. The outcome of the negotiations with external bodies had to be reported to the entire organization. The tacit agreement was communicated to the city council. The latter recognized the U.C.C.A. as the leading organization in the com- munity.

Not surprisingly, disagreements continued, in particular as to which group of leaders (those of S.L.S. or of U.C.C.A.) were the most qualified to handle Chinatown's problems. "Although the two organizations had agreed upon respective roles of concern with regard to internal and external relations, they still accused each other of 'mutual undercutting.' " Those acting as official spokesmen for the community were accused of promoting the po- sition of their own association. The accused organization "countered with the retort that the U.C.C.A. consisted of a 'bunch of old guys who know how to talk but not how to act' " (Hoe, 1976:245).

Political authorities feel the need to communicate with their publics. This in itself is not a noteworthy phenomenon. Some authors, however, argue that because of changing circumstances in recent years, the traditional chan- nels for communication have disappeared or their effectiveness has seriously decreased. Political parties, for example, are said to have lost importance, relatively speaking, as links between the electorate and the government (Meisel, 1976; Pross, 1986). The new situation requires the creation of new kinds of channels. This new situation is the "administrative state," which "denotes the phenomenon by which state institutions influence many aspects of the lives of citizens, especially those aspects which relate to the economic and social dimensions. It describes a system of governance through which public policies and programs, affecting almost all aspects of public life, are influenced by the decisions of public officials (Wilson and Dwivedi, 1982:5). According to Pross (1982:108), the growth of the administrative state "has fostered important changes in the way the public communicates with gov- ernment, so that ... the processes of policy formation have adapted themselves to the sectoral lines of communication that best serve the modern machinery of government. As they have done so, political parties have declined in policy influence, leaving behind a vacuum that has been filled only partially by the elaborate networks of interest groups which have come to serve both as communicators of policy needs and goals and as legitimizers of government action."

As a result of this development, government agencies have a "clientele orientation." Among the reasons for this is the fact that "the development of new programs must anticipate the reactions of those people most directly affected, and often interest groups are the only source of this information." Also, selling new programs to the relevant authorities requires support from the clientele groups. Finally, "the cooperation of those being regulated or served by a program" is required for its implementation (John E. Sinclair quoted by Pross, 1982:118).

Functional representation, then, becomes the basis for the organization of the administrative state. "Policy communities" are formed. Interorganizational networks play a crucial role in policy formation and its communication and legitimization (Pross, 1982). There is an increased interdependence between government bureaus and agencies and their policy communities, a "social articulation" or "dialectic interplay" (Herbstein, 1983:33) that takes place within a more or less integrated network of organizations in various sectors of activities. The outcome can be properly caled interorganizational policies and programs. As Jacobs (1981:1) points out, most public policies cannot be said to be simply implemented by the agencies that formulate or fund them. Through grants-in-aid and a variety of other devices, governments have "dramatically reduced the number of programs that may be analyzed solely in traditional terms of administrative efficiency. Rather, officials have developed a wide variety of multi-actor program arrangements that might be characterized as 'interorganizational policy.'"

To the extent that ethnic organizations and their members are potential constituents of policy communities, their recognition is likely to be perceived as useful and perhaps even necessary for the functioning of government agencies. That is, their explicit integration in that interorganizational sector would allow the functions mentioned earlier (from Sinclair) to be performed in relation to the ethnic component of the population.[8]

Savas (1987) provides a clear illustration of this phenomenon in his analysis of the special role that francophone communities outside of Quebec and the anglophone community in Quebec have acquired in the 1970s. One set of programs instituted to implement the 1969 Official Languages Policy of the federal government was aimed at "the social and cultural vitality of francophone and anglophone communities in provinces where they are minorities ... thus maintaining the presence of both official languages across the country" (Secretary of State document quoted by Savas, 1987:26). Thus through these programs, the official language minority organizations became "key policy agents" of the federal government. Government officials know that effective action would be difficult if not impossible without the collaboration of organizations instituted by the francophone and anglophone groups themselves. "Thus, the directorate sees the associations as 'our best aid' in bringing communities together to achieve the objectives" (secretary of state, quoted by Savas, 1987:27).[9]

CONCLUSION

The sociopolitical environment of ethnic communities consists of a set of resources, opportunities, and constraints. Through their dynamic relationship with their environment, ethnic communities may form organizations and systems of organizations with particular structural features. The structure is not formed through a deterministic process but rather through strategic choices that depend in part on the possibilities and limitations of the environmental context and also on the historical experience and cultural background of the group as well as on organizational learning and creativity.

Several features of the sociopolitical environment impinge on the organization of governance of ethnic communities. For instance, in order to deal with an environment posing severe problems, the leaders of the ethnic collectivity, are likely to find that a centralized hierarchical structure is the most effective for the required mobilization of resources and the coordination of efforts. On the other hand, in a benign environment, the leaders are not likely to feel such need. A benign environment, other factors being constant, will favor the coexistence of associations functioning independently of each other. In such situations, community affairs tend to consist in the totality of activities carried out by a set of limited interest organizations not integrated into an inclusive system. The ethnic polity is atomized.

Another feature of the environment is its diversity and complexity, which is related to the degree of organizational differentiation of the ethnic polity. A complex environment can be best dealt with through some degree of specialization. This is so because the problems it presents and the opportunities it offers are quite varied and require different types of skills and resources (e.g., legal, educational, political, communication). A simple (whether benign or hostile) environment, on the other hand, requires, so to speak, a unique specialization.

Ethnic polities adopt more or less spontaneously the modes of organizing and functioning of the larger society. This is partly a matter of organizational acculturation and partly a matter of functional necessity. Groups and their leaders have learned from experience that adopting organizational patterns compatible with those of the larger society is an effective way to deal with the problems the larger society presents and the opportunities it offers.

Another kind of environmental impact on the governance institutions of ethnic polities is direct interventions on the part of agents of societal institutions. The authorities of these institutions may have an interest in ethnic collectivities for control, clientele, communication, political, and policy implementation purposes. This is so to the extent that ethnic collectivities are perceived by institutional authorities as possible sources of problems or opportunities in relation to their policy objectives or to their need for legitimacy and support. This may lead these authorities to intervene in the formation and functioning of community organizations so that these operate in ways that are consistent with or favorable to the authorities own interests.

NOTES

1. On the administrative capacity of states, see Skocpol and Finegold (1982).

2. The expression is from Siegel (1970:11). It refers to environments that are hostile; the people in them are "prepared to engage in destructive or depriving actions."

3. On dimensions of environments, see for example Segal (1974), Jurkovich (1974), Pfeffer and Salancik (1978:63–68), and Thompson (1967:70–73).

4. This would be the case holding everything else constant, that is, holding constant possible variations in other environmental dimensions.

5. Baureiss is not concerned in this work with the form that community institutions take but with the degree of community closure and the extent to which participation in ethnic community affairs is mandatory. He does note, however, that rigid boundaries make it easier for ethnic groups to "transfer their respective institutional structure to the new ethnic communities" (1982:71).

6. IIAP stands for Indian/Inuit Affairs Program (of the Department of Indian Affairs and Northern Development).

7. Diggins (1972) presents an informative description of the Mussolini government's intervention in the American-Italian communities.

8. On this matter, see also Pross (1986); Laumann and Knoke (1987); Jenkins (1988); and Cheetham (1988).

9. The Official Language Communities Programme was called the Social Action Directorate in 1969 (Savas, 1987).

4

The Structure and Exercise of Leadership

Who is likely to control the governance apparatus of the ethnic polity? What kinds of issues are leaders likely to encounter and what factors can affect the ways in which they address these issues? What kinds of forces can impinge on the strategies and tactics they adopt? How are the leaders likely to define their roles? Toward what purposes do they exercise the power they have acquired or that has been given to them by the community or some of its segments?

These are among the questions examined in this chapter. Leadership composition, roles, and strategies depend in part on the environmental conditions and organizational actors with which ethnic communities have to deal and on the extent and nature of political competition among rival subgroups within the collectivity.

THE IMPACT OF THE SOCIOPOLITICAL ENVIRONMENT

As noted earlier, the impact of the environment on the ethnic communities can be direct or indirect. That is, the environment can be seen as consisting of a set of resources, opportunities, and problems for an ethnic group. But it can also include individual and organizational actors who may have an interest in who governs the ethnic polity or in the leadership practices that prevail in it. The relevance of these two components of the sociopolitical environment is considered in the next two sections.

Leadership and the Community's Corporate Capacity

In ethnic communities, organizational systems are created in order to cope with the sociopolitical environments and the form that such systems take depends in part on whether the environment is hostile or benign, socially and institutionally heterogeneous or homogeneous, and itself governed through a federal or a unitary system. As indicated, there is not necessarily a one-to-one relationship between environmental features and the structure of governance. Strategic choices are made, and their nature depends in part on the composition and structure of the leadership that emerges in the community.

Who controls, shapes, and runs the governance apparatus of the community—who constitutes its recognized authorities—is, therefore, an important question. The individuals or groups with the means to contribute to the attainment of collective purposes are the ones likely to gain power and influence in the community. It is these individuals who can make strategic choices to meet the social demand for various kinds of services. Leadership, then, is a function of the input an individual can make into the community's capacity for concerted action, into the total power of the community in relation to the problems and opportunities it encounters. In short, power and authority are distributed among interested individuals according to the significance of their contribution to the community's capacity to cope with its environment.

The needs experienced by community members can be quite varied: adaptation to socioeconomic circumstances (e.g., integration into the labor market, housing, social services, and language training); social solidarity and cultural expression; defense against discrimination, exploitation, and various forms of hostility; and control of the resources necessary for these various purposes (Baureiss, 1982). Through the contribution they make toward the solution of such problems, individuals rise to positions of leadership in the community. In addition, the personal and social characteristics of the individuals who become leaders depend on the nature of the problems that a collectivity faces in a particular context or at a particular point in its history.

Such a phenomenon has been observed in task-oriented groups: individuals given a higher social rank and a leadership role tend to be those who are expected to contribute the most to the solution of group problems. It is not that group members measure each other's contributions nor that the setting of expectation for one another's performance is a conscious one. Yet, some judgment is formed in the group as to each member's relevant abilities. Status and prestige are allocated "on the basis of inferred ability to contribute to a task solution" (Ridgeway, 1984:60).

This phenomenon has also been observed within organizations. Pfeffer and Salancik (1978:230) suggest that according to Hickson et al.'s (1971) "strategic contingencies theory of intra-organizational power,... those subunits most able to cope with the organization's critical problems acquire power in the organization. Since many of the uncertainties and contingencies faced by organizations are a product of the environment, the environmental context partially determines the distribution of power within the organi-

Table 4.1
Ratings of Ways of Becoming Leader as Most or Second Most Important, by Selected Variables

	Education	Wealth/ money	Relations with leaders	Organizing activities	Political orienta- tion	
	%	%	%	%	%	N
1. Ethnic group:						
Chinese	54	32	28	35	9	(57)
Germans	39	30	33	33	12	(178)
Jewish	33	48	33	37	11	(168)
Portuguese	75	19	33	17	5	(67)
Ukrainians	47	24	32	44	16	(89)
West Indians	62	21	33	41	11	(118)
2. Perception of democratic decision-making:						
Very little or none	52	41	41	29	10	(270)
Somewhat	60	37	29	27	14	(153)
A certain extent	48	31	32	40	11	(215)
Very much	51	28	33	42	12	(110)

Note: Respondents indicated the first and second most important factor. Therefore, the (horizontal) sum of percentages exceeds 100.

zation." For instance, when legal difficulties predominate, the legal unit and its experts will gain power and influence over organizational decisions.[1]

Kanter (1977:168) also defines leadership in this perspective. In her discussion of effective management and her review of related research, she notes that leadership style, at least by itself, seems to make little difference. What does make a difference is power, that is "the ability to get for the group, for subordinates or followers, a favorable share of the resources, opportunities, and rewards possible through the organization." Effective leadership, then, depends on the ability to contribute to the well-being of the group and its members.

In the Ethnic Pluralism Study (Breton et al., 1990), respondents were asked to indicate "the two best ways to become a leader" in their group. The ratings of five possible criteria are presented in Table 4.1 by ethnic group and for the total sample. Education is the most important, followed by wealth, good relations with people who are already leaders, and being successful in organizing activities. Political orientation is perceived as having little importance.[2]

Of course, wealth, occupation, and personal assets by themselves would not provide prestige and leadership. It is their use for community functions or for services to individual members that would yield influence. For instance, in her study of Slavic immigrant communities, Morawska (1985:229)

observed that status accrues to those who become involved in the "organizational networks developed in response to the needs of the immigrants
as they settled in a new environment." Not surprisingly, such involvement
occurred more frequently among those with a relatively high economic and
occupational standing, that is among those who possessed useful resources.
But other kinds of resources were also important: literacy, life experience
in general, and, in the new social context, wisdom and knowledge about
"things of the world," and personality traits.

Wealthy individuals who refused to identify with the community could
be respected and envied for their accomplishments and possessions, but
would also be considered as outcasts and even renegades. The resources
that individuals had acquired were seen as carrying a set of moral obligations
vis-a-vis the community and its members. Church donations were particularly important in this regard, as they were publicized from the pulpit, in
the community press, and through elaborate memorial plaques on church
walls or pews (Morawska, 1985). Assuming a role in the establishment and
functioning of community organizations also conferred a special position
in the community. So did services to individuals. Such services could be very
diversified, from credit to assistance with daily chores ("He had a horse and
a buggy so everybody needed him") (Morawska, 1985:25).

The results of the second section of Table 4.1 are consistent with this
view. This section shows the perception of the criteria for leadership by the
respondents' perception of the democratic character of the decision-making
process in the community.[3] It can be noted that the more the decision-
making is perceived as democratic, the less importance wealth is seen
as a channel to leadership in the community (a thirteen percent
difference). In other words, the perception of wealth as a way to leadership
is associated with the perception that community members are somewhat
cut off from community decision-making. On the other hand, success in
organizing activities is associated with the perception that members have
the possibility of input in the way the public affairs of the community are
run. (There is, however, no consistent pattern in the case of the other three
criteria.)

To the extent that leadership is associated with the use of an individual's
resources to deal with community problems and to provide services to
community members, it tends to be situational. For example, Kiefer
(1974:27) observed in the San Francisco Japanese community that leadership "tended to rotate among issei men who had special competence that
fit them for the task at hand. In dealing with the outside world, knowledge
of the English language and of American laws and customs was important.
For community organizing, a gift for rhetoric in Japanese was sometimes
more useful."

In a way, leadership is earned through an exchange of services. A pastor
of the Buddhist congregation in San Francisco told Kiefer (1974:26) that

upon coming "to the United States in 1930...I travelled here and there around the country. I found that there were many kinds of faiths and churches, and none of them seemed to be doing a lot of good. I came back to San Francisco and began to talk about establishing a temple (of my sect). There were five families that were interested from the first.... There was no money for the temple, but I decided to treat people (using moxa) who could not get relief from doctors. Pretty soon there were hundreds of patients, and we built a temple."

John (1969) describes a similar phenomenon among the Punjabi *Ilaqa* groups in London.[4] Some men were influential in the community due to the prominence of their family back in the Punjab. But, most acquired leadership in their *ilaqa* group through community activities. John notes three kinds of activities. First, often the leaders had been the first to settle in England. They helped those who came later to find jobs and housing and adjust to the environment. Second, although some sent part of the money accumulated to their families in the Punjab, others invested it in shops and houses in England. As landlords, they could control the votes of the bloc of immigrants. For instance, it was next to impossible to refuse to support one's landlord if he was active in the Indian Workers' Association (IWA) politics. Third, knowledge of English made it possible for some of the earlier immigrants to become friendly with English foremen in the factories. Thus, "They were often able to get jobs for their friends and to influence the allocation of overtime. This brought both wealth and influence over one's workmates" (John, 1969:51).

These observations point to another important source of status and leadership: connections with the "outside world," with foremen and supervisors, civil servants, politicians, police officers, school trustees and principals, and businessmen. These contacts were valued by members of ethnic communities because of "the promise of facilitating services to the community" (Morawska, 1985:28).

John's (1969:52) study reveals still another road to positions of influence in the community, one that involves a different kind of service to a somewhat different clientele. He observes that "for the earlier immigrants, political power was largely a byproduct of a long process of accumulating wealth or influence with white foremen." But others began as political activists, spending much time making friends, frequently speaking at public meetings, helping established leaders in collecting IWA memberships, and performing "public services such as organizing social functions or classes to teach English to the immigrants. This path of office appealed mainly to energetic young men who lived in towns where the established leaders had a firm grip on the existing associations." The service that this path to a position of influence entails is one primarily oriented to the existing organizational structure and to those who control it.

Finally, individuals who command symbolic resources may be able to gain positions of influence. Those, for example, who have a substantial knowledge of the group's national past and its heroes are bestowed with social prestige (Morawska, 1985:244). This is so because of the role they may play with regard to the definition of the group's collective identity (see Chapter 7). Their symbolic resources can also be significant with regard to the mobilization of members to deal with threats and other problems encountered by the group. Control of the "means of mental and emotional production" is critical in conflict with other groups or with societal institutions: "emotional rituals... are a vehicle by which alliances are formed in the struggle against other groups" (Collins, 1975:59).

In short, the exercise of leadership depends in part on the possession of strategic resources. These resources are a particular talent, knowledge of the host language, wealth, education, political skills, legal knowledge, and credibility due to past achievements. A network of contacts with individuals occupying positions of some importance in institutions of the larger society is also a significant resource. Individuals who do not possess such resources are severely limited in their ability to acquire and exercise leadership. Since leadership is seen as the capacity to deal with the environment, the absence of linkages with institutional agents in the larger society is a particularly important limitation. Not having access to relevant assets may be crippling even for those who manage to hold formal positions in community organizations.

It should be emphasized, however, that power accrues to individuals (and to the organizations they lead) because they use available resource for collective purposes, rather than for personal gains. With the relevant means at their disposal, leaders are expected to obtain benefits for individual members, support community projects, or promote the group's image or status. Elazar's (1976:336) expression "a trusteeship of givers and doers" seems appropriate here: leaders are those who "perceive their function to be one of managing the community's affairs in trust for its members."

Of course, being perceived as primarily self-interested is not the only factor that can destroy one's credibility; it can also be eroded by failures or by policies and activities that antagonize significant segments of the community. Credibility is both a matter of trust and competence.

Personal resources, however, are not sufficient. As indicated in the previous section, an integrated organizational system is also required—a system that is likely to involve some degree of centralization and hierarchical coordination. In addition, in order to exercise leadership effectively, individuals must occupy a central position in the social and organizational structure of the community. Personal abilities, prestige and access to resources are important assets, but their value for leadership depends in significant part on the existence of appropriate organizational channels (Hayes, Barth, and Watson, 1967).

As already indicated, a focus on the organizational capacity of the community to cope and even shape its environment suggests that a central element of leadership pertains to the relationships that are established with the structure of power in the wider system. The efficacy of leaders is partly a function of their position in relevant power networks: "Because the elite control the instruments of government, the government operates in their interests. Thus, in order to have the government act consistently in one's interests, one would have to become affiliated with the elite network" (Roy, 1981:1290).[5] This proposition could be applied to other institutional domains such as business, the media, the police, and education. In making basically the same argument, Laumann, Knoke, and Yong-Hak (1985) suggest that there are two relevant networks: the communication and the resource exchange networks. It is, accordingly, important for a leader to become centrally located with regard to the channels of information and to those for the exchange of resources critical in a particular field of activity.

Community leaders constitute a link between the ethnic community and the larger society. The importance of this role has been identified in several studies and given labels such as "broker" (Wolf, 1956; Snyder, 1976). In order to deal with problems and improve the condition of their community, they act as mediators between the ethnic enclave and the larger society. In order to perform this role, the broker or mediator must have "the ability to function in two cultures . . . and to mediate new ideas and pressures from outside the local community" (Snyder, 1976:40).

In the Ethnic Pluralism Study, the perception by community members of the political efficacy of their leaders was examined. Three items were presented to respondents: Do they perceive leaders as sufficiently well-connected in the larger society for their interventions to matter? Do they perceive those who have power in the larger society as taking their leaders seriously? And do they feel that if leaders were more active, they would get more attention from politicians. It was hypothesized that the evaluation of the community leadership in these regards will be associated with the propensity on the part of members to turn to their community organizations when confronted with instances of discrimination or when changes in immigration legislation are desired.[6] As can be seen from Table 4.2, there is considerable variation among ethnic groups in the perception of the efficacy of the leaders. The difference between the highest and lowest percentages of those who perceived low efficacy varies between seventeen and fifty-eight among the groups, depending on the item.

The three questions were also asked to leaders. The percentage of leaders who agree with the first statement ("Politicians do not take ethnic leaders seriously") is quite similar to that for the members in most of the groups. There are two exceptions: leaders appear to be somewhat more skeptical than members in the Italian and West Indian communities. Nevertheless, the rank order of the groups is about the same.

When asked if leaders would get more attention from politicians if they

The Governance of Ethnic Communities

Table 4.2
Perceived Efficacy of Community Leaders by Ethnic Group

	CHINESE %	GERMAN %	ITALIAN %	JEWISH %	PORTUGUESE %	UKRAINIAN %	WEST INDIAN %
1. Politicians do not take ethnic leaders seriously. Percent who agree:							
Among community members	42	17	28	20	37	41	54
Among community leaders	41	14	47	30	43	43	79
2. Even if more active, leaders would not get more attention from politicians. Percent who agree:							
Among community members	35	29	23	23	40	31	28
Among community leaders	18	38	20	37	14	24	22
3. Leaders do not have enough important connections. Percent who agree:							
Among community members	55	15	19	7	55	29	65
Among community leaders	68	53	47	11	86	63	71
N-weighted	(57)	(173)	(427)	(166)	(67)	(88)	(118)
Number of interviews	(152)	(321)	(351)	(348)	(161)	(353)	(150)
N-leaders	(22)	(21)	(30)	(38)	(7)	(45)	(18)

were more active, leaders are *less* likely to agree that being more active would *not* get more attention in four of the groups: Chinese, Portuguese, Ukrainian and West Indian. In other words, in those groups, leaders are somewhat less likely to think that they have exhausted their potential than members feel they have. There is no difference of importance in this regard between leaders and members among Italians. Among Jews and Germans, leaders more than members think that more activity *would not* get more attention from politicians. It should be noted, however, that the percentage of leaders and members who think that more action would not get more attention is fairly low in all groups.

It is in regard to the question of connections with important people in business and government that leaders and members differ the most. Only among Jews and West Indians is there close to consensus: that they have enough connections to get results in the first case and not enough in the second. In the other five groups, leaders tend to say that they do not have enough connections to get results for the community while members are much less likely to think that this is the case.

The perceptions of members about the political efficacy of the community leadership are related to their attitudes concerning ethnic organizational action. Those who agree that politicians and officials do not take the views of ethnic leaders seriously are less likely to favor taking cases of discrimination to a community organization or to seek changes in immigration laws and procedures through such an organization. Similarly, those who feel that the leaders of their community are poorly connected with important people in business and government are less likely to favor ethnic organizational action on such matters. This is the case for the total sample and for most group-by-group comparisons: generally, there is a relationship between a positive view of the efficacy of the community leaders and a positive orientation toward ethnically organized action (Breton et al., 1990:Ch. 5).[7]

In concluding this section, two caveats are in order. First, it should be noted that the acquisition of prominence by devoting some of one's resources to the satisfaction of community needs does not imply that the position of those in the community elite is totally accepted by the "ordinary" members. This is what some results from the Ethnic Pluralism Study suggest. To the question "How concerned do you think the leaders of the (group) community in Toronto are with the problems and interests of the ordinary members of the community?" a minority said "Very much" (twenty-six percent for the sample as a whole). But there are considerable variations across groups: from nine percent among the Chinese to thirty-nine percent among Jews (Table 4.3).

The perception of the leaders' concerns and interests does not vary across socioeconomic categories such as occupational status, education, and income. Nor does it vary by gender and generation. Age seems to make a difference, but only between those forty-six year old and older and those forty-five and younger (the eighteen to twenty-five year old group did not differ from the twenty-six to forty-five year old group).

What does make a difference in the way the leaders are perceived is the extent to which members know them and are aware of their activities as well as the degree of involvement of members in community affairs (Table 4.4). Leaders are more likely to be seen as very much or somewhat concerned with community problems and interests by those who know leaders (personally or not), who are very well or somewhat aware of their activities, who are members of ethnic associations, who participate actively at organizational meetings, and who feel strongly about their religious beliefs (and presumably are more active) than by those who do not have such community involvements and relationships with leaders. Closeness to the leaders and to community affairs seems to bring about a more positive perception of

Table 4.3
Perception of Leadership Concern with Problems and Interests of Ordinary
Members, by Ethnic Group

	Very much %	Somewhat %	A little %	Not at all %	Don't know %	N1	N2
Chinese	9	39	31	2	19	(57)	(152)
German	13	36	18	5	28	(175)	(321)
Italian	27	40	17	7	9	(428)	(351)
Jewish	39	41	11	2	6	(166)	(348)
Portuguese	16	29	31	10	14	(67)	(161)
Ukrainian	32	40	16	2	10	(88)	(353)
West Indian	32	28	16	3	22	(118)	(150)

N1-Weighted N.
N2-Number of interviews.

the concerns of leaders in relation to the community than distance from what is going on.

Table 4.5 presents the relationship between community members' perception of the leaders' concerns and their perception of how democratic the management of community affairs is. It shows a fairly strong association between the two perceptions: those people who perceive the management as involving the possibility of input by community members are much more likely to see the leaders as very much concerned with the problems and interests of ordinary members than those who see the practices as basically undemocratic (a thirty-six percent difference). Such a result is not surprising: indeed, those who see the leaders as running community affairs without much, if any, consultation with members are less likely to see them as pursuing community interests.

It should be noted that, with one exception, in none of the categories examined does the percentage of those who consider their leaders as "very much" concerned with community problems and interests constitutes a majority. It is among Jews with strong religious beliefs that it comes the closest (forty-eight percent). It should be underscored that the exception is found among those who perceive the decision-making as highly democratic (fifty-eight percent).

There is nothing particularly surprising in the fact that leaders are perceived as having interests other than those of the community. Indeed, they do not exist only as leaders. Their other interests can be related to the organizations they run, to their professional careers or business enterprises, or simply to the pursuit of status in the community or in the larger society. Because of this, however, ambivalence can be the prevailing attitude among members vis-a-vis the community leadership.[8] This was the case in the ethnic

Table 4.4
Perceived Concern of Leaders for Problems and Interests of Community, by Selected
Independent Variables

```
------------------------------------------------------------
                                        Percent who say
                                         "very much"
------------------------------------------------------------
1. Know leaders:
     Yes, personally                      34    (284)
     Yes, not personally                  31    (290)
     No                                   18    (523)

2. Awareness of activities of
     leaders:
     Very well & somewhat                 40    (281)
     Not too well                         23    (157)
     Not at all                           27    (111)

3. Membership in associations:
     Yes                                  33    (286)
     No                                   24    (813)

4. Express views at meetings:
     Frequently & occasionally            32    (291)
     Seldom or never                      24    (796)

5. Religion
     No preference                        19     (93)
     Protestant -- Strong beliefs         35     (91)
                    Weak beliefs          28     (58)
     Jewish       -- Strong beliefs       48     (91)
                    Weak beliefs          36     (51)
     Catholic     -- Strong beliefs       33    (396)
                    Weak beliefs          17    (144)
------------------------------------------------------------
```

community studied by Morawska (1985). She observed that the community
called upon its elite for a variety of internal and external functions. But at
the same time there was an element of resentment against the rich and those
in positions of high standing. The fact that leadership is acquired in part
through contributions to the community does not necessarily imply complete
consensus and the absence of tensions and conflict between those who have
power and those who do not. All that it implies is that leaders and members
are to a degree in a situation of interdependence.

There can be failures of leadership. The fact that a community faces
problems in relation to its surrounding social and political environment or
the fact that there are opportunities to do something that may improve the
condition of its members does not mean that leaders will necessarily appear
on the scene to mobilize resources and launch appropriate programs of

Table 4.5
Perception of Leaders' Concern for Problems and Interests of Members by Rating of
Degree of Democracy in Decision-Making

	Perception of decision-making as			
	Very democratic			Not at all democratic
	%	%	%	%

Leaders are concerned with problems and interests of members:				
Very much	22	26	29	58
Somewhat	39	42	57	35
Little or not at all	39	32	14	6
N	(259)	(145)	(214)	(110)

----

action. As noted earlier, governance institutions may not be established even
if there is some objective need for them. Several factors that could account
for such a situation were mentioned. An additional one can be the fact that
those who control resources do not assume an entrepreneurial role.

The absence of leaders may be due to prohibitions or constraints imposed
by the authorities of the larger society. This was clearly the situation of the
native people in Canada up until recently. The situation of complete administrative dependency in which they were placed was largely conceived
to prevent the emergence of leaders from their own ranks.[9] In the case of
the Japanese at the time of the war, individuals who were already leaders
or who were assuming such a role were arrested as "potential trouble-
makers," thus "removing much of the effective leadership from the community" (Kiefer, 1974:28).

Another external deterrent to the emergence of leadership is the virtual
impossibility of gains for the community due to the resoluteness of the
dominant group in resisting demands from the minority. In the study mentioned earlier, Henry (1981:31) imputes the organizational disarray of the
Toronto black community to the "harsh socio-political environment where
even anti-racism victories were demoralizingly partial, temporary or illusory." The Uncle Tom phenomenon once prevalent in black communities
in the South in the United States was also due to the virtual impossibility
of blacks accomplishing anything of significance due to the rigidity of the
white power structure. Uncle Toms were the result of situations in which
"white supremacists are willing to do business with Negro leaders who are

disposed to accept their 'place' in the biracial system" (Thompson, 1963:62). Such ineffectual leaders are leaders largely at the will of the powerful people in the dominant group. They are in effect almost completely powerless. In short, the existence of problems and needs is not sufficient for the emergence of leadership; the possibility to do something about the problems and needs is also a critical factor.

In other instances, the failure of leadership is not the result of direct external intervention but of a combination of group subordination and of the internal social structure and subculture. In his study of black politics in Toronto (up to the 1950s), Henry (1981:32) discusses the failure of black clergymen to provide effective community leadership, noting the "numbing" contrast between the opportunity for leadership and their performance: "They had a relatively captive following. The 1950s, moreover, were the ideal time for clergymen to assume leadership: for the emerging civil rights issues were highly appropriate to their vocation, and clergymen were particularly safe from accusations of communism.... In addition, there was in Canadian religious life a strong social gospel strain and ... an impressive tradition of clergymen, ex-clergymen, and their kin participating in reformist politics. The black clergymen were found wanting."

One reason for the failure of leadership has been described by Lewin (1948:195–7) as "leadership from the periphery." Such a phenomenon occurs frequently among ethnic minorities. As noted earlier, those who are successful tend to gain leadership in the community. At the same time, they are the individuals who tend to gain acceptance in the larger society. They are therefore placed in a "marginal situation." On the one hand, they seek to avoid having their good connections with the larger society endangered by a too close contact and identification with their own less-accepted ethnic group. On the other hand, because of their very connections with important people in the larger community, they are called upon to exercise leadership in the ethnic community. "As a result, we have the rather paradoxical phenomenon of what one might call 'the leader from the periphery.' Instead of having a group led by people who are proud of the group, who wish to stay in it and to promote it, we see minority leaders who are lukewarm toward the group, who may, under a thin cover of loyalty, be fundamentally eager to leave the group." (Lewin, 1948:193).[10]

Ethnic Leadership and External Intervention

External agents may attempt to determine or modify the composition of those who run the main ethnic community organizations. The main characteristic of ethnic leaders of concern to external agencies is their ideological orientation—their general sociopolitical philosophy or their stand on particular categories of issues. This is to be expected given the dynamics of the relationship between ethnic groups and societal institutions described earlier.

The authorities of societal institutions also have an interest in the extent and quality of the relationship that ethnic leaders maintain with their community. Indeed, ethnic leaders are structurally in a position of "intermediacy." They are located between the community and the institutions of the larger society. Chapter 3 considered the ways in which leaders attempt to deal with external agencies in relation to community-related problems and objectives. Here attention is on how external agents attempt to influence and use the ethnic leadership in the pursuit of their own objectives.

At least three kinds of strategies can be used for this purpose: affecting the composition of the leadership; generating dependence, primarily financial, on the external agency, whether it be governmental, religious, economic, or political; and incorporating the ethnic organizations in the larger institutional system.

Affecting the composition of the leadership. External agents can attempt to intervene in the selection and promotion of particular individuals to positions of leadership. This can be achieved, for example, through their appointment on official bodies (e.g., advisory councils, consultative committees, special task forces, and boards of direction). This may not automatically crown the appointed individuals as leaders. It does, however, provide them with a platform from which they can gain public visibility in their own community and status in the larger society. It constitutes an opportunity to gain leadership in the ethnic community.

Directly or indirectly, external organizations and their authorities can act as validating agencies establishing or eroding the prestige and authority of community leaders (and their organizations). Perrow (1961) mentions that the more difficult it is to establish the intrinsic value (of an organization and/or of the service or program it provides), the more external groups and individuals are needed to validate the organization's claims. Sometimes the importance or indispensability of particular leadership roles is far from obvious. In addition, the qualification of specific individuals for these roles may not be apparent to the average group member. Thus, approval from competent sources is sought and publicized.

The external legitimation and prestige may come from government officials in Canada and in the country of origin; universities and their affiliated research centers; churches; the media; and prominent writers, journalists, and other public personalities. An illustration is provided by Boissevain (1970:25), who observes that the "Consul General acts as host several times a year at receptions to introduce visiting Italian cultural, industrial, and commercial dignitaries to Montreal society. Key persons within the Italian Canadian community are invited to meet these dignitaries . . . because they are the elite. . . . An invitation by the Consul General thus validates publicly a person's claim to social importance within the community."

Painchaud and Poulin (1983:102) have noted a similar, if less direct process. They note that the Congrès national des Italo-Canadiens, région du Québec (CNIC, Q) is the dominant organization in the Montreal Italian community. Its control is in the hands of the "bourgeoisie italo-québécoise," a situation that represents a shift from an earlier control of community affairs by the clergy. The dominance of the CNIC, Q and of the bourgeoisie that controls it is buttressed by the government's policy and programs. Indeed, not only does the policy give official recognition to ethnic cultures and communities, but in the case of the Montreal Italian community, the CNIC, Q is the organization that has received almost all the grants awarded by the secretary of state. In the process, the hegemony of the controlling faction has been strengthened.

Individuals can also be prevented from gaining leadership positions. One tactic is to ignore leaders or potential leaders who do not support and may even oppose policy orientation and/or favored programs of an outside individual or group. Systematically bypassing such individuals may eventually make them appear ineffective in the eyes of community members and other leaders. As a result, their realistic claim to leadership decreases.

Related to this tactic is the negative side of the recognition given to some leaders. Such recognition indicates to other leaders or potential leaders the kind of person authorities and powerful people in the larger society are prepared to do business with and the kind of orientation and behavior that is expected of minority leaders. Recognition, in other words, sends messages as to who is and is not acceptable as a community representative (Thompson, 1963).

Another negative tactic is to quietly inform some of the leaders that particular individuals or categories of individuals are unacceptable and should not be included as leading participants in particular activities or should not be allowed to act as representatives of the community. Because of its very nature, such tactics tend to be covert and heavily camouflaged. They are accordingly very difficult to document.

"Divide and conquer" represents another tactic. It is described by Kibbe (quoted in Miller, 1975:79) as follows:

Anglo politicians in most cities having a sizeable Latin American population appear to have promulgated an effective, but unwritten, law which, while consenting to the appointment or election of Latin Americans to minor political posts, forbids and prevents their securing a top ranking post. Thus, when an ambitious and capable Latin American announces for office in opposition to an Anglo incumbent or candidate (who is in all probability the candidate of the local machine), Anglo politicians ...immediately sponsor the candidacy of another Latin American, preferably a personal enemy of the man who has previously announced and thereby split the Latin American vote and assure the election of the Anglo candidate.

In their analysis of the struggle for racial equality, Ben-Tovim, et al. (1986) indicate that government agencies in Liverpool and Wolverhampton (United Kingdom) have attempted to marginalize the antiracist forces in the community. This was attempted by emphasizing inequality between consultors and consulted (e.g., accepting or rejecting advice on the basis of a preordained agenda); by labeling antiracism as extremism; and by diverting attention away from issues of racial inequalities and the features of societal institutions that generate and/or perpetuate racial inequalities through a preference for the funding of cultural activities.

Generating dependence on the external agency. A second strategy is to make leaders dependent on the external organization for certain kinds of resources. Such a dependence may occur spontaneously simply because the leader has no independent resource base or a very meager one. Being dependent on external bodies for resources, the leader is more or less forced to comply with their wishes. Of course, the dependence is rarely complete; it is a matter of degree. And variations in degree may be related to types of leadership.

This is a proposition documented several years ago by Thompson (1963) in his study of race relations in New Orleans. Although the American South at that time represented a context with several unique features, the basic propositions that flow from his analysis have general relevance for the analysis of the impact of dominant groups on minority leadership. He identified different types of leaders: the "Uncle Tom," who depends entirely on the white elite and thus cannot make demands but rather begs for favors (62); the "racial diplomat," who favors a "diplomatic approach rather than pressure tactics" and whose primary role is "to interpret the peculiar needs of Negroes in terms of general community wellbeing" and to give advice to the white elite "on the 'best way' of promoting uplift in some specific area of life" (68); and the "race man," who shows "unwillingness to compromise the basic principles of freedom and equality ... In the most fundamental sense the race man never accepted racial segregation as a proper or workable way of life" (75).

Leadership types in the minority group correspond to certain "complementary" types in the dominant group. "Each social type of leader among white men of power will choose a complementary type of Negro leader with whom he is willing to negotiate" (Thompson, 1963:59): white segregationists and supremacists with Uncle Toms; moderates with racial diplomats; and liberals with race men. Thompson seems to suggest that there are different types of minority leaders because powerful whites, having different attitudes and race relations philosophies, *allow* their emergence. There is no doubt some validity to that statement: minority leaders are always to some degree in a situation of dependence vis-a-vis the dominant group.

Variations in minority leadership, however, also depend on the extent to which minority leaders control or can mobilize power resources on their own. Uncle Toms depend entirely on white power largely because the community that they "represent" is poor, uneducated, and unorganized. It lacks economic or political resources that, if mobilized, would represent a serious threat to the position of the dominant group and its institutional elites. Racial diplomats, on the other hand, can rely on a middle-class constituency and can therefore be less dependent on the dominant group. Their leadership does not depend entirely on the latter's preferences and decisions; it also depends, to some degree, on their own constituency. Finally, race men are the least dependent on the dominant racial group. This autonomy, which is largely a function of the socioeconomic and political development of the ethnic community, can be buttressed by constitutional provisions, special legislation, and the existence within societal institutions and in some powerful groups of a political philosophy favorable to human rights and social equality.[11] In short, circumstances in both the dominant and the minority communities affect the degree and nature of the minority's dependence and, hence, of the type of minority leadership that emerges.

The granting of financial assistance, especially for administrative and organizational maintenance costs (as opposed to grants for specific activities) can also make ethnic organizations and their leaders highly vulnerable and, consequently, more compliant (Stasiulis, 1980). This is especially the case if the funding pays a significant part of the salary of part-time or full-time personnel. The possible loss of a job is indeed a threat that can lead to a serious reconsideration of one's position on issues.

Incorporation in the larger institutional framework. The formation of "ethnic policy communities" with the emergence of the administrative state could be said to institutionalize the co-optation of ethnic leaders. To the extent that such policy communities exist, leaders and their organizations become part of an interorganizational system with a number of common interests. They become participants in a policy field in which organizations of the larger society play, in all likelihood, a leading role. To some degree, they become agents of state policies (Savas, 1987).

Co-optation is a process through which policy orientations of leaders are influenced and their organizational activities channeled. It blends the leader's interests with those of the external organization. In the process, ethnic leaders and their organizations become active in the state-run interorganizational system; they become participants in the decision-making process as advisors or committee members. By becoming somewhat of an insider, the co-opted leader is likely to identify with the organization and its objectives. The leader's point of view is shaped through the personal ties formed with the authorities and functionaries of the external organization.

Indirectly, if not directly, such incorporation influences the selection of leaders. Those who rise to significant positions in the ethnic community would tend to have views about policy objectives and strategies of action that are compatible with those of politicians and government functionaries and thus succeed in entering the policy network. Ethnic and government participants share the same "institutionalized thought structure" (Warren, 1976).[12] Otherwise, ethnic leaders remain at the periphery of the system and may act as challengers or protesters.

Ethnic communities usually include some leaders or potential leaders who are ripe for co-optation. For example, in interviews with Stasiulis (1980), black organizational leaders in Toronto have "pointed out the complementarity of the generally conservative interests of Black, middle-class professionals in Black organizations on the one hand, and government bodies, on the other" (36).

Miller (1975:79) has observed the phenomenon in a study of Mexican-Americans in Texas. Leaders are co-opted "by either appointing or supporting their election to decision making bodies. Thus, the Mexican-American community is given the illusory appearance of representation, yet its ostensible representatives are beholding to Anglo interests."

The administrative state can incorporate ethnic leaders and organizations, but it can also become a substitute for them. Indeed, if institutions of the larger society assume functions previously carried out within the ethnic community, they reduce the domain of activity and influence of ethnic leaders.[13] This is suggested by O'Brien (1975) who notes that the welfare state has reduced the range of domains for autonomous ethnic organizational development. The needs of the aged, the unemployed, the poor, the immigrant, for example, are largely taken care of by state agencies (although sometimes the services are operated through or with the assistance of ethnically run organizations). It should be noted that it is pressures from ethnic groups themselves that sometimes lead governments to assume the function previously carried out in the ethnic community. The teaching of traditional languages appears to be an illustration of such a transition.[14]

Another possible effect of government intervention, funding in particular, is the distance it can generate between leaders and members of the community. It has frequently been mentioned that an important result of government programs has been the creation of "ethnic bureaucracies" that are disconnected from the communities they claim to represent. Table 4.6 (presented later in the chapter) shows indeed that government funding decreases the amount of time that leaders allocate to communication with members in comparison to other activities such as administration.

The study by Savas (1987) is perhaps the only one that provides an empirical examination of this hypothesis. His systematic analysis of the impact of government policy and funding on the evolution of the leadership of the francophone community in British Columbia supports the hypothesis. His results show that while government assistance has contributed to the effectiveness of community organizations in relation to certain goals, it has at the same time detached the leadership from the community and the needs

of members. This occurred because the leaders became increasingly respon-
sive to the agenda of government agencies who came to supply the lion's
share of the organizational budgets. It was also due to the fact that the
operating force of the organizations shifted from the hands of volunteers
to those of an administrative and professional staff (made possible by substantial government funding).

LEADERSHIP AND POLITICAL COMPETITION

Leadership and Political Accommodation

Leadership roles and practices and the relations among leaders can be
shaped by the dynamics of interdependence and accommodation among
competing groups. For instance, the formation of interorganizational structures that incorporate different subgroups (whatever the seriousness of the
compromises that were required) may spawn a particular leadership phenomenon: a network of interorganizational leaders. Indeed, "the power to
shape significant community decisions resides in a number of organizations,
each containing *some* of the resources required to initiate influence or con-
strain decisions; when the resources of these organizations are combined,
they can be instrumental and most likely decisive in shaping decisions....
The resource networks [can] be identified through the overlapping executive
positions held by the same person in two or more organizations. The person
in the overlapping position is the link between organizations, and the mo-
bilizer of the resources of those organizations (Perrucci and Pilisuk,
1970:1053). The community is then governed by "a relatively small and
clearly identifiable group of interorganizational leaders, or persons who
hold high executive (policy decision-making) positions in 'many' organizations" and who play a critical role in the pooling of resources and coordination of the activities of different organizations (1044).

The collective influence exerted by a network of "interlocking associational officerships" has been observed in ethnic as well as in other types of
communities (Hoe, 1976). Skinner (1958:200) points out that "the functional importance of interlocking officerships is obvious. They are the main
channels of communication and influence uniting the various organizations.
It is largely because of them that groups of Chinese associations can coordinate policy and exercise unified control." Skinner used a fairly complex
method to describe and analyze the structure of leadership of the Bangkok
Chinese community. His objective was "to define exhaustively the groups
of leaders who by virtue of their interrelations in commercial enterprises
and nonprofit community organizations constitute important loci or clusters
of influence" (1953:208). He identified eight power blocs, "each bound
together by one of the key leaders, and each in turn unified through its key
leader with a structural apex in the person of one leader." Thus, if a leader

"desired to reach every leader in every power bloc with a recommendation or suggestion, for instance, he could do so most expeditiously by contacting the other key leaders." (210–212).

It was seen earlier that the overarching organizations may sometimes be established in the ethnic community at large or in one of its sectors of activity. Thus, in addition to leaders of individual organizations and to interorganizational leaders, there can also be leaders of overarching organizations. As indicated earlier, these overarching structures can be given varying amounts of authority. They may be considered as pure instruments by individual organizations in the network or they may be given full responsibility with regard to certain matters. The latter could be said to have, within the ethnic community, a sort of "rational-legal" authority (Weber, 1947).

To the extent that the overarching structure is instrumental, however, the authority of its officers has a different basis, namely the attainment of assigned goals or the achievement of certain tasks. As seen earlier, the authority of leaders of such organizations is "rational-pragmatic." It is acquired and maintained through regular provision of benefits to the affiliated organizations. This kind of authority is also enhanced if specialized knowledge is required for the performance of the tasks. Legal, technical, or political expertise may be needed to cope with matters such as financing and budgeting, legislation, judicial problems, negotiations with governmental or other agencies, relationships with the media, fund-raising, public education, and research.

Of course, the pragmatic authority of the leaders of overarching organizations is based on "an informal system of interpersonal and inter-group relations" (Harrison, 1959:62); on the professional executive's control over procurement and allocation of funds; on the voting power of the leader's own constituency; and on access to specialized information (Harrison, 1959). The "leader-expert" can have considerable influence on the political agenda of the organization and its affiliates, on the policy alternatives presented to the committees or boards responsible for making decisions, and on the implementation of these decisions.

In spite of the means of control at their disposal, leaders may have to engage in a considerable amount of public relations activities vis-a-vis member organizations. This may be necessary to persuade member organizations of the value of the policy objectives that they feel should be undertaken. In other words, even though leaders have been given a certain responsibility and even though they control expertise and information, they may still have to justify their particular plans and projects and obtain approval (from affiliated organizations) for their implementation. In short, the leaders of overarching organizations defined as instruments by member-organizations are ultimately in a vulnerable position. They have to be concerned, on a regular basis, with the legitimation of their role and with the building of an informal power base; more so than the leaders of overarching organizations with explicitly recognized powers.

Accommodation among leaders in the form of a network of interorganizational leaders may not occur. This was the case of the American Polish collectivity studied by Lopata (1964:130). She attributed the failure to two factors. The first factor is "the lack of goals sufficiently strong to appeal to large numbers of groups" and the set and, the "constant struggle between existing organizations for control of these associations. The endorsement of an interorganizational association by one faction of Polonia's groups usually meant its ultimate death because of the opposition of other factions." An eventual unifying link was the interest shared by different segments of the community in applying "pressure upon the American government for status recognition of Polish Americans."

A similar diagnosis was made by Henry (1981) in his study of the Toronto black community in the period between World War I and the 1950s. Henry attributes the lack of cohesion to factors such as the existence of internal subethnic and religious divisions; the attraction of potential leaders to metropolitan centers (such as New York City); and the "wide acceptance of a tradition of organizational chaos [which] had itself become an independent force crippling community efforts" (18).

In order to account for a similar phenomenon in the American-Italian collectivity, Vecoli (1964–65:412) referred to the sociocultural experience in the society of origin: "The marked incapacity of the south Italians for organizational activity was itself a result of the divisive attitudes which they had brought with them to America." This was partly the result of the spirit of *campanilismo*, whereby organized activities included only individuals from the same town and more often from the same parish. The sentiment of religionism also acted as an obstacle to organizational unity. "Rather than being allayed by emigration, this regional pride and jealousy was accentuated by the proximity of Abruzze, Calabrians, Geneose, Sicilians, and other groups in the city. Each regional group regarded those from other regions with their strange dialects and customs not as fellow Italians, but as distinct and inferior ethnic types" (413).

A final impediment noted by Vecoli was the fact that community associations were controlled by men concerned primarily with their personal ambitions: "The scope of their leadership was restricted to presiding despotically over the meetings, marching in full regalia at the head of the society, and gaining economic and political advantage through their influence over the members. If such a one were frustrated in his attempt to control a society, he would secede with his followers and found a new one. Thus even the townsmen were divided into opposing factions" (1964–65:413).

In contrast, Buchignani and Indra's (1981) study of the South Asian polity in British Columbia seems to illustrate that political accommodation among subgroups with divergent interests and political orientations is possible, at least during a period of time with regard to a particular collective problem. An accommodation among leaders of South Asians was facilitated by a number of social and cultural factors. Among the social resources at their disposal were a very specific common heritage—ninety percent were Sikhs who shared common ethnic, linguistic, religious, and historical roots; a tradition of techniques of political alliance and of devices to deal with internal conflict; a strong social support system in the community; and the existence of religious organizations that provided the means to bring people together.

The increased role of government in relation to ethnic communities constitutes an additional factor that affects accommodations. The government's intervention through administrative and financial assistance can destroy the cohesion of the leadership network or accentuate existing cleavages. It does so by favoring one organization or a set of organizations over others or by triggering an acrimonious debate as to whether government assistance should be accepted or not (Stasiulis, 1980; Savas, 1987).

Leadership and Political Ascendancy

Hierarchy in political organizations may be found in most polities but it is especially significant in those where a particular faction has gained ascendancy. This importance is perhaps accentuated by the perceived salience of social class cleavages in ethnic (as in other) collectivities and by the fact that leaders tend to be drawn from the upper echelons of the class hierarchy (Painchaud and Poulin, 1983).[15] The existence of hierarchy in a polity draws attention to a number of related issues concerning the exercise of leadership. Two will be considered here: the tendency toward distancing in the relationship between leaders and members and the means deployed by leaders to maintain themselves in power, including the control of the press or the means of communication generally.

Closeness or distance between leaders and members. In situations of political dominance, that is, in the absence of political competition, a fundamental characteristic of leadership is its tendency to distance itself from the constituency.[16] Such a phenomenon has frequently been observed in ethnic polities (Vecoli, 1964–65; Ware, 1958; Weiss, 1974; Tryggvason, 1971), but it is a phenomenon that has also been observed in many other kinds of contexts. As leaders become more concerned with the administrative functioning of their organization and with the expansion of its power and prestige they become less concerned with the needs of community members. They may even "pursue organizational objectives *at the expense of* the vital interests of their groups' membership or ... sacrifice those vital interests in attempting to secure organizational advantages or in realizing their organizational ambitions" (Kwavnick, 1973:582–83).

Michels (1962:70) in his classic study of the "iron law of oligarchy" attributes such a tendency to several factors.[17] One is the technical specialization that an extensive organization with its administrative, political, and informational functions requires. This "renders necessary what is called expert leadership. Consequently, the power of determination comes to be considered one of the specific attributes of leadership, and is gradually withdrawn from the masses to be concentrated in the hands of the leaders alone." When competition is institutionalized, this tendency is likely to be attenuated. In a noncompetitive unitary system, it can evolve without much resistance.

In addition, the tendency is probably more pronounced when organizations are managed by or with the assistance of full-time personnel, if only for the fact that these personnel spend more time on and consequently become more expert on the various issues. However, full-time professionals and technicians may be kept in check by volunteers. Indeed, a tension between these two categories of leaders has been observed to exist in some communities, a tension that was not necessarily counterproductive (Elazar, 1976). In short, the more bureaucratized and the less competitive the governance system, the greater the gap is likely to be between leaders and members.

The organizational leaders who were interviewed as part of the Ethnic Pluralism Study were asked about the allocation of their time to various kinds of activities, such as raising funds, recruiting members, doing administrative work, and communicating with members. The way they ranked these activities can be related to certain characteristics of their organizations. Table 4.6 shows the percentage of leaders who declare devoting most of their time to each of four activities according to whether or not the organization has a support staff, to the size of its salaried support staff, to the number of its committees other than the board of directors (or some equivalent body), and to the receipt of government funding. Each activity is ranked as first or second in terms of time allocated to it.

The presence of a support staff, three or more salaried support staff members, and government funding increase the amount of time devoted to administration; the percentage of leaders indicating administration as the most or second most important item in their allocation is larger when these elements are present than when they are not. The number of committees and the practice of elections, however, appear to make no difference as far as administrative work is concerned.

Given this result, it is not surprising to observe that support staff and government funding have a somewhat negative effect on the time devoted to communication with members (but not on fund-raising and on recruitment). The number of committees, on the other hand, seems to have a positive effect on communication with members—an expected result as committees provide a channel for such communication.

Although the differences are not very large, there is a tendency for leaders

Table 4.6
Importance of Time Devoted by Leaders to Various Activities by Selected
Organizational Characteristics

```
                                    Percent ranking
                                Activity as most or second
                                      most important:

                        Raising  Recruiting  Adminis-  Communication
                         funds    members    tration

1. Organization has support
     staff:

           Yes            24         14         50       47    (107)
           No             22         19         33       58    (108)

2. Number of salaried support
     staff

           None           26         23         39       52    ( 31)
           One or two     11          9         49       52    ( 35)
           Three or more  35         11         60       43    ( 43)

3. Number of committees

           One or two     25         10         43       47    ( 40)
           Three or more  28         11         42       63    ( 65)

4. Members of central board:

           Elected        21         19         43       53    (150)
           Appointed      37         10         40       43    ( 30)

5. Receive funds from any
     level of government:

           Yes            28         15         54       43    ( 46)
           No             22         17         38       55    (181)
```

Note: Since the table does not include all activities and ranks,
      the percentages in the table do not add up to 100.

of organizations with an electoral system to devote more time to communication and recruitment than those with a system of appointments. On the
other hand, the appointed officials devote more time to fund-raising than
the elected officials.

Another factor contributing to the leader-member gap is the fact that
"one who has for a certain time held the office of delegate ends by regarding
that office as his own property" (Michels, 1962:81). Leaders and especially
founding leaders may also come to consider the organization as *their* organization; because of the personal energies, time, and even money they
have invested in it and because of the sacrifices they see themselves having
made for it, they feel they have a right to rule as they see fit.

Oligarchic tendencies are also nurtured by the fact that leadership positions entail advantages (e.g., status, connections) that may push their incumbents to retain them as long as possible. "Once high status is secured, there is usually a pressing need to at least retain and protect it. This is particularly true if the discrepancy between the status and the position to which one must return on losing the status is very great" (Lipset et al., 1956:10). This phenomenon constitutes an antidemocratic force in the governing system. Indeed, democracy means insecurity for those in leadership positions: "The more truly democratic the governing system, the greater the insecurity" (Lipset et al., 1956:10). There may consequently be a tendency for organizational leaders to resist the introduction of democratic procedures, although this would be difficult to establish empirically.[18]

The less leaders are dependent on the constituency for funds, the greater the likelihood that the organization will tend toward oligarchy. More specifically, it is the dependence on voluntary contributions by members that is important in this regard. Of course, ethnic organizations do not have legal powers of taxation; they have to persuade members that their programs and activities are worthwhile and deserve support. When leaders can rely on external sources of funds, they can run the organizations without giving much consideration to the problems and interests of the community.

Perpetuating one's power. The individuals or groups who control the governing institutions of a community are strategically located with regard to the critical sources of power. Although by being in a position of power an individual may contribute to the solution of community problems, one of the central preoccupations of leaders in a position of dominance is to maintain themselves in it. Moreover, occupying such a position is not so much a function of contributing solutions to community problems as of one's organizational and political skills in mobilizing resources and in converting them into political power.

It is also a function of the ability to prevent one's rivals from doing the same.[19] This may be facilitated by the existence of widespread disagreements among opponents as to community goals and/or ways of pursuing them. In such circumstances, the opposition is not likely to acquire the cohesion sufficient to successfully challenge those in power. Accordingly, the dominant faction is likely to engage in divide-and-conquer strategies, encouraging discord among its potential rivals.

But circumstances can change and favor the contending elites. Previously negotiated accommodations (explicitly or tacitly), for instance, can be quite temporary. Indeed, enterprising leaders of an organization are likely to remain on the lookout for opportunities to outdo or even weaken other organizations in the field by, for example, attempting to reduce their base of support in the community or impede their access to government subsidies. Thus, it is possible that, even though political competition is institutionalized to some degree, circumstances may change or events may occur that would open the possibility for a particular subgroup and its leaders to gain ascendancy. The stability of an institutionalized accommodation among factions is always more or less precarious (unless the community disintegrates through assimilation and, therefore, there remains little over which to compete).

This is also the case for unitary hierarchical structures since the unified control that such structures entail does not imply the absence of competition or a generalized consensus. There may indeed be constant conflict, which, of course, may remain latent and be more or less serious. Since a unitary hierarchical system of governance will tend to serve primarily the interests of a particular segment or subgroup and thus to frustrate other interests (ideological, class, regional, etc.) in the community, a political tension or contradiction exists. Because of this, there is a potential challenge to the existing regime and its ruling elite.

There are, nevertheless, considerable advantages in being first in a particular domain of activity. Those who can from the start establish themselves as the controlling group because there is little or no competition are in a particularly favorable position to stave off potential rivals and to resist opposition to their rule.

Being there first provides several means for perpetuating one's power. One of the most important is control of communication systems, in particular, the selection, packaging, and diffusion of information.[20] Organizationally, this involves control of the media of communication in the community. It may also entail devising mechanisms to screen information about the public affairs of the ethnic community that reaches the media of the society at large. Such control can circulate information favorable to those in power and prevent the diffusion of information and points of view that could undermine the ideological basis of those in power.

Social control as an important role of the press has been mentioned by Kiefer (1974) and Elazar (1976). In discussing the power of the news media, Kiefer, for example, notes that "Japanese-language newspapers were widely circulated in San Francisco before the war and served as effective channels of social control. Few important achievements or community services performed by local residents or groups went unnoticed" (Kiefer, 1974:21).

As institutions directly involved in the public affairs of the ethnic community, the news media play a significant role in the formulation of the community's public policies by "determining the kinds of information... presented to different audiences, controlling its flow, and shaping the channels of information flow within the communications network as a whole" (Elazar, 1976:281). In ethnic communities as in the larger polity, the press tends to be partisan. A publication is usually the organ of a particular group (Young, 1931; Yusik, 1953; Daschko, 1982; Kalbfleisch, 1968; Patrias, 1978). Young (1931:165), for instance, notes that "even the best intentioned editor must resort to polemics and controversy, for the groups of an immigrant society are, in the nature of things, 'conflict groups,' and the editor is perforce compelled to participate in the struggle." Once a faction has gained in this struggle, it is to be expected to control the flow of information and to slant the interpretation of facts in such a way as to buttress its position of dominance.

Established elites also control the resources that can be used as selective incentives to retain members and attract new ones; they have access to an established network of contacts inside and outside the community. In short, being established in a field makes it easier to resist those who would want to challenge one's position of dominance (Moe, 1980; Pfeffer, 1981).

Such advantages provide an important clue as to the conditions under which a change in the composition of the elite is likely to occur. A necessary, although not a sufficient condition, is that the governing elite be weak relative to aspiring elites. The competitive advantages the governing elite enjoys must become eroded if challengers are to overthrow and replace them. Generally, change in the composition of the elite occurs when the sources of power change and/or when the access that various groups have to these sources change.

Challenges to the established power structure have taken place, for example, in several Chinese communities throughout North America. The events that brought about the rise of contending elites have, in many ways, been the same. In his study of the Toronto community, Thompson (1979) notes two sets of factors: legal and social changes that facilitated participation of the Chinese in Canadian society and changes in immigration legislation that permitted new immigrants to enter Canada. The first had the effect of making members of the community less dependent on the community leaders and the organizations they controlled. The result of the second was not only a substantial increase in the size of the Chinese collectivity in Toronto (from an estimated 8,000 in 1966 to nearly 70,000 in 1977) but also the introduction into the community of a new group of wealthy entrepreneurs and a new class of professionals and clerical and service workers. This "middle stratum" tends to consist of educated and bilingual individuals who can assume liaison roles between their community and the larger society. Some of them are second-generation Chinese Canadians, but a substantial proportion are immigrants who originally came to Canada as university students.

The appearance on the social scene of groups with their own economic and cultural capital and thus an independent source of power transformed the social and economic organization of the community. Of particular interest in the present context is the power struggle between the new groups seeking influence in community affairs and the entrenched traditional leaders. Part of the contest was purely economic: an intense competition existed between the new entrepreneurs and the traditional merchant-elite for the Chinese and tourist dollars (Thompson, 1979).

But the established merchant-elite also felt that their sociopolitical position in the community was threatened. They denied the newcomers any
legitimacy. They saw them as preoccupied only with their economic enterprises and as ignorant and unconcerned with the welfare of the community.
Whether or not the motivations of the traditional and new entrepreneurs
were in fact different is difficult to tell. What is clear, however, is that the
relationship of each group with the community differed in significant part
because of the type of economy each introduced.

The traditional economy (prior to 1965) was characterized by small firms
in which employment was based on kinship or friendship ties, and, accordingly, much more than economic obligations were involved in the relationships between owners and employees. Such "family firms" still exist, but
large-scale enterprises financed by newly immigrant Chinese entrepreneurs
are rapidly becoming dominant in the ethnic subeconomy (Thompson,
1979).

As a result, the nature of employer-employee relations are different in the
new businesses. The businesses provide no fringe benefits or job security.
"In a few of the larger businesses a hierarchy of managers and supervisors
is necessary for the effective management of the firm. Owners are seldom
involved in the day-to-day operations of a restaurant, further increasing the
social distance between worker and entrepreneur.... As a result, new immigrants must look elsewhere to satisfy social and cultural needs, and more
and more are turning to the recently formed social service agencies created
to help meet immigrant problems" (Thompson, 1979:313–314).[21]

These agencies have been designed and are administered by a group of
young Chinese professionals educated in Canada. These social and community workers have stressed, in their organizational and fund-raising efforts, the situation of the Chinese as an ethnic minority, a legitimate and
effective tactic to obtain governmental grants under its multiculturalism
policy and programs. These progressively institutionalized services constitute the power base of the Chinese social workers and related professionals
who possess the cultural capital required to operate them successfully.

The social workers and professionals "have entrenched themselves into
the key mediating positions between the Chinese worker and the Canadian
government" (Thompson, 1979:316). The increasing involvement, direct
or indirect, of government agencies in the activities of the Chinese community, increases the power of the Chinese social workers' in their community. Thus the growth of the welfare state appears to have been a factor
in changing the relative importance of different sources of power in ethnic
communities.

The traditional merchant-elite has not disappeared, but it has ceased to
be in a position of dominance in running the affairs of the community. It
has been effectively challenged by the new entrepreneurial and social elites.

Competition is now incorporated in the governance of structure of the community.[22]

It is quite possible, however, that attempts to challenge an established elite will not succeed. The structure of the control may be sufficiently entrenched that it cannot be modified. The dominant elite may be sufficiently resourceful and may be able to mobilize enough support to prevent a takeover or the establishment of parallel competing organizations. This is what happened at the beginning of the century in the Montreal Italian community when the old Italian *notabili* were challenged by a new entrepreneur (Antonio Cordasco) who had become Montreal's largest employment agent.[23] The *notabili* acted in the community through the Immigration Aid Society, but their opponent did not operate through a civic association but through a business network that included a large number of foremen who were also entrepreneurs (Ramirez and Del Balzo, 1981).

The two groups fought for control over the supply of labor generated by migration and for recognition as representative of the community (Harney, 1977). Being the exclusive employment agent of Italian labor for the company that probably was at the time the largest employer of immigrant labor in Canada (Canadian Pacific Railways), Cordasco rose to power very swiftly. He was thus a serious business competitor. But he also attempted to gain leadership in the community:

On one occasion he had proved to be capable of mobilizing large crowds in his support, and even defying the claims of the established *notabili* to represent the Montreal Italian colony. The parade through Montreal . . . followed by a much-publicized banquet and culminating with the crowning of Cordasco as "King of the Italian workers" was clearly a clever advertising operation aimed at his immediate constituency to assure them of his power and prestige. . . . But the event must have also been perceived by the old *notabili* and the Italian consular authorities as a show of power, all the more defiant and arrogant as Cordasco used the Italian regal symbols to enhance his status with the "army of pick and shovel." . . . Cordasco was convinced he deserved a status commensurate to his economic power." (Ramirez and Del Balzo, 1981:68)

The large number of immigrant laborers, the simultaneously high level of lengthy unemployment in Montreal, and the fears of social unrest generated by this situation made the practices of the immigrant labor agencies very suspect. A royal commission was set up to look into the situation, the existing social problems being the manifest reason for its creation. But the inquiry can also be seen as an instrument in the hands of the *notabili* in their conflict with those challenging their ascendancy. The commission may even have been established partly under the pressures applied by the *notabili* and the Italian consular authorities in Montreal. In any case, one of the commissioners was a member of the network in opposition to Cordasco.

The *notabili* had other political and institutional resources at their disposal. Indeed, the Immigration Aid Society included several *prominenti* in the community, powerful businessmen, professionals, and community leaders, such as the editor of the local Italian newspaper. They were at the top of the social hierarchy of the Italian community. They enjoyed the moral and financial support of the Italian government and their society enjoyed a prestige and recognition comparable to that of similar charity organizations in Montreal (Ramirez and Del Balzo, 1981).

The government inquiry yielded much information on the functioning of the recruitment of immigrant labor and on the role of the employment agencies in it. But it also accomplished the goals of the society's *notabili*, namely putting much of the blame for the problems on Cordasco and his associates. This political success is especially striking given the fact that many of the most important charges against Cordasco appear to have originated from the office of the society's vice-president (Ramirez and Del Balzo, 1981).

CONCLUSION

Four dimensions of leadership were examined in this chapter. First, leadership, in relation to the opportunities and problems that confront members of ethnic collectivities, is the capacity to gain access to strategic resources and to use them for community purposes. Leadership emerges and its characteristics are defined in the dynamic interaction between the collectivity and its sociopolitical environment. Leadership is largely a function of the nature of the resources that are required to deal with particular sets of circumstances.

Second, because what happens in ethnic collectivities can have implications, directly or indirectly, for agents of institutions in society at large, these agents are likely to attempt to influence the leadership, its policy orientations, and its activities. In today's society, the primary institution concerned is the state. But other institutions may well have interests with regard to the public affairs of ethnic communities: churches, political parties, labor unions, businesses, and the media. External agencies can attempt to affect the affairs of ethnic communities by shaping the composition of its leadership, by making the leadership dependent on the external body and its resources, or by incorporating the leadership in the larger institutional framework at particular policy communities or interorganizational networks.

Third, competition may exist among leaders of different factions or subgroups in the collectivity. In one type of situation, power is more or less evenly distributed among subgroups. These subgroup leaders frequently do not control the resources required for the pursuit of their particular objectives. They need access to the resources controlled by others. The central issue, then, has to do with the formation of linkages for the pooling of resources and for the coordination of action. It concerns the conditions under which effective leadership networks are formed.

In situations of unequal distribution of power, on the other hand, one set of leaders dominates the political landscape. The critical issues of leadership under such circumstances concern the tendency for a gap to emerge between leaders and members; the degree of communication between them, and the means used by those in leadership positions to maintain themselves in power.

NOTES

1. Crozier (1963), for example, argues with empirical evidence that power is held by those who can act effectively on the factors generating uncertainty for the organization. That is, people who control the resources (e.g., technical, administrative, political) needed to cope with particular problems or to take advantage of opportunities are the powerholders, informally, if not formally.

2. The ratings, however, are not the same in all groups: education is especially highly rated by the Portuguese and West Indian respondents, wealth by the Jews, success in organizing activities by Ukrainians and West Indians, and political orientation by Ukrainians. Relations with people already leaders is about equally seen in all groups as a way to leadership.

The responses were also examined by generation, education, and occupation. Education is the most highly rated by those of the first generation in comparison with those of the second and especially of the third or later generations. The reverse is the case for wealth. There is not much variation with the other three criteria. There is a negative relationship between the perception of education as an important way to leadership positions and the educational attainment and occupational status of the respondent: low education and occupational status individuals give more importance to education that do those higher on these items. The reverse is the case when wealth and success in organizing activities are considered. No relationships are observed in the case of the other two criteria.

3. The measure was constructed by combining the following two items: (1) The ordinary member of the (group) community does not have a chance to say much about how things are run in the community (responses from strongly agree to strongly disagree). (2) How much effort is made by decision-makers in the (group) community to get approval from the members of their organizations or from the community? Would you say a lot, some, a little, or none at all?

4. *Ilaqa*: "Although there is nothing so tedious as a quibble over terminology, I would prefer not to speak of 'village-kin groups,' because members of such a group come from several villages. The Punjabis often speak of members of their own village-kin groups as 'of our villages' ... and speak of other groups as being composed of men from the same *ilaqa*, area" (John, 1969:51).

5. See also Laumann and Pappi (1976) and Wellman (1983).

6. The average rank of groups on these efficacy items is as follows: the Chinese and West Indians are the least likely to perceive their leaders and organizations as efficacious; they are followed fairly closely by the Portuguese and then by Ukrainians.

The Jews are the most likely to see their leaders as having the capacity to get results; the Germans and Italians are next in the rank order.

7. There are exceptions. For example, among Jews, the perception of the leaders' efficacy appears to make little difference: organizational action is favored to the same extent, whatever the perceived relationship of leaders with the political and business elite. In some instances, the exception concerns only one of the items presented: for instance, West Indians who feel that politicians and officials *do not* take the views of their leaders seriously are *more* likely to favor the use of organizational resources than those who feel that *they do*. These few negative relationships, however, show no clear pattern.

8. In addition, the fact that in five of the groups members are more likely to think that leaders have enough external connections to get results for the community than the leaders themselves do may also be a reflection of this ambivalence concerning where the true interests of the leaders lie.

9. See, for example, Ponting and Gibbins (1980); Frideres (1974); and Tennant (1982, 1983).

10. There may also be variations among ethnic communities in the amount of collective effort made to recruit and train leaders. The amount of organizational attention given to the younger generation may be the most significant in this regard. Unfortunately, lack of data prevents intergroup comparisons on this matter.

11. The situation of the political boss in American machine politics is another illustration of dependence. See Banfield and Wilson (1963), Cornwell (1964), Rogler (1974), and Wilson (1962).

12. For the definition of "institutionalized thought structure," see chapter 2, note 2.

13. These two possibilities are not mutually exclusive. Both can occur to some degree in the same society: government (or religious, etc.) bureaucracies can replace ethnic organizations in some areas but use them as agents in others. Of course, variations can also be observed across societies. For an interesting set of studies on the situation in different countries, see Jenkins (1988).

14. The main effect of these trends, however, may not be so much to decrease the size of the administrative component of the system of governance (i.e., the provision of services) as to increase the relevance of its political dimension. Indeed, the fact that the state or other societal institutions become the operative agents for various services focuses the attention of the ethnic leadership on the policies underlying existing programs, on the monitoring of their implementation, and on the identification of needs and aspirations not yet addressed by societal institutions. In other words, it increases the representative function of ethnic governance institutions—the aggregation and articulation of interests—and decreases their role in the organization of services for their constituencies. Unfortunately, no empirical evidence could be found on this possibility.

15. From a political point of view, perceived differences may be equally if not more important than actual opposition. More specifically, it is the differences that are perceived as dividing the community that are important.

16. This phenomenon is similar to the "leadership from the periphery" discussed elsewhere in this book, but its causes are quite different.

17. Michel's study was originally published in 1911.

18. In Table 4.6, 150 out of 180 organizations elected individuals to the board of directors or to the equivalent body.

19. On the conversion of resources from one type to another, see Coleman (1969).

20. The role of the ethnic press in the relationship between leaders and members is manifold: (1) the press is an intermediary between community institutions and members, especially the new immigrants who are frequently overwhelmed and even frightened by the strange environment they must cope with; (2) it provides identifiable leadership for ethnic collectivities by publicizing the activities of leaders; (3) it formulates and diffuses an ideology about matters such as the relation with the country of origin and with the larger Canadian society and its institutions; (4) it performs an educational function by diffusing information such as technical knowledge about farming techniques; and (5) it voices the demands and complaints of individuals and groups.

21. These agencies provide a wide range of services: child care, English language instruction, interpretation and translation, legal aid, income tax preparation, senior citizen's clubs, old age homes, family therapy, political education, and citizenship classes (Thompson, 1979).

22. Similar transformations for similar reasons have been described and analyzed by Lyman (1968), Light and Wong (1975), Hoe (1976), Kwong (1979), and Baureiss (1982).

23. On Cordasco and his role in the Italian community, see Harney (1979).

5

Policy-Making, or the Formulation of Collective Goals

The governance of the public affairs of a collectivity involves the formulation of collective goals. Policy-making is a complex process closely related to the exercise of power and leadership considered in the previous chapter. It should be noted that the expression *collective goals* does not imply that the entire collectivity is involved in the goal formulation process and/or affected by its outcome. This may be the case, but the policies adopted and implemented may concern only some segments of the collectivity. They may also have implications for organizations or groups in the larger society.

The following analysis of policy-making in ethnic communities includes the same parameters as that of the previous chapters. First, the ways in which the external sociopolitical environment impinges on policy-making are considered. The environment, it will be recalled, is viewed either as a configuration of opportunities and constraints or as a set of organizations whose agents may intervene in the public affairs of the ethnic polity. The second part of this chapter deals with the impact on policy-making of political competition and, in particular, of the distribution of power within the ethnic collectivity.

THE IMPACT OF THE SOCIOPOLITICAL ENVIRONMENT ON POLICY-MAKING

Coping with Environmental Circumstances

An important component of leaders' ability to deal with environmental conditions is the capacity to diagnose problems, identify opportunities, and formulate relevant policies and programs of action. Leaders must formulate plans that can be shown, in some convincing way, to be appropriate and effective in relation to a particular problem or situation. The goals and strategies that are likely to prevail in the ethnic community as a whole or in particular fields of activity are those that are seen as the most likely to bring about the desired results. It is those plans that are seen as making the greatest contribution to the attainment of collective goals.

This section draws attention to the knowledge available to decision-makers with regard to given circumstances. Leaders will gain power and prestige to the extent that they devote their ingenuity, talents, and personal resources to the search for improved ways of dealing with particular problems, of increasing community resources, and of putting these resources to profitable uses. Leaders could hire or consult experts, commission research, and analyze the experience of other communities in dealing with similar conditions.

This dimension of governance can be referred to as the rational/technical capacity of the organizational apparatus and of its leaders. Goals and appropriate strategies of action are largely a matter of knowledge or ignorance about the nature of the community's problems and/or about ways or techniques to deal with them. The knowledge available is, in turn, a function of the "state of the art" in the field and of the means deployed by the ethnic community to collect, process, and use pertinent knowledge.

Limitations due to the state of the art can be quite serious in certain areas. For example, knowledge about the nature of prejudice and discrimination and the ways to combat them is limited. Leaders are confronted with many questions regarding this issue: What is the nature and extent of discrimination? What are its causes? Can prejudice be eliminated or reduced significantly? Can discrimination be controlled? How? What are the possibilities and limitations of legal means in this connection? Cultural maintenance is another area where knowledge limitations are serious. Leaders are faced with these questions: What determines cultural retention and loss and under what conditions? Can cultural loss be stopped or retarded? Can ethnic cultures flourish? Can they be transmitted from one generation to the next? What are the likely consequences for ethnic communities and their members and for the larger society of particular cultural maintenance goals, policies, and programs?

The existing body of knowledge does not provide easy, clear-cut answers to such questions. Limited knowledge limits leaders' ability to act and obtain significant results because of their inability to analyze problems and situations adequately and to come up with goals and strategies in relation to them. In other words, leaders may be painfully aware of a problem without knowing what to do about it.

Knowledge limitations are also caused by the group's capacity to collect, process, and use knowledge (Etzioni, 1967). Ethnic communities and organizations differ in their readiness and capacity to search their environments (both internal and external). For example, in their discussion of social mobility among Italians in New York, Glazer and Moynihan (1963:207) mention that "it is hard to know whether there is discrimination against

Table 5.1
Ethnic Organizations Carrying out Research Related to Discrimination or Cultural
Maintenance

	n	%	N
Chinese	–	–	(22)
German	3	11	(27)
Italian	10	32	(31)
Jewish	12	32	(38)
Portuguese	–	–	(7)
Ukrainian	10	22	(46)
West Indian	3	16	(19)
TOTAL	38	20	(190)

Italian Americans in the corporations, and in the country clubs and city clubs that are linked to their higher echelons. There are no Italian defense agencies and other community organizations to draw attention to such matters, even to the extent of formulating some general community opinion as to what the facts are." This situation, they note, is in contrast to the organizational capacity of other (e.g., Jewish) communities for the monitoring of how events in the larger society impinge on the lives of their members.

Table 5.1 lists the number and percentage of organizations that have engaged in research in relation to questions of discrimination and prejudice or of cultural maintenance according to the leaders interviewed in the Ethnic Pluralism Study. These data provide only a rough indicator as no information is available on the amount of research that each organization carries out. Yet, in some groups, the number of organizations that carry out research is significant—especially in view of the fact that research is a fairly specialized activity. It should also be noted that twenty-nine of the thirty-eight organizations (seventy-six percent) that have done research have paid for it themselves; only nine have had their research funded by the government.

The presence of a "civil service" in a community to support the leaders and provide the necessary information and expertise to policy-makers is likely to affect the policies adopted and the programs that are put in place to deal with perceived problems or opportunities. Both the size of the administrative arm and its character (e.g., the proportion of professionals and of volunteers) are relevant in relation to a group's capacity to act corporately. The perceived efficacy of Jewish governance institutions noted earlier is, no doubt, due in part to their professionalization. Elazar (1976:264) mentions that

the day-to-day business of the Jewish community is now almost exclusively in the hands of professionals—or at least people who are paid for their services. . . . Because these professionals are involved on a daily basis with the problems of the community, are to a greater or lesser extent committed to such involvement for the course of their adult lives, and are more or less trained to occupy the positions they hold, they exercise great influence in the policy-making processes of the community. . . . On the other hand, the number of voluntary leaders has not diminished. Parallel roles for professionals and volunteers have developed in virtually every Jewish organization and institution, allowing for extensive participation of both.

The capacity of a group to formulate policies in relation to changing environmental conditions is also affected by the level of commitment to organizational traditions: a "limitation on organizational adaptation derives from a commitment to doing things a certain way. . . . Some became superstitious, believing that what worked in the past will work forever. Most build traditions, mythologies, and rituals. More than mere psychological recalcitrance is involved in commitment. In many instances, the beliefs and successes of the past became entrenched in physical and managerial structures. When they do, they are nearly impossible to change" (Pfeffer and Salancik, 1978:82). When such commitment to tradition exists, there is no incentive for a group to keep up to date with social conditions and to search for new approaches to deal with them. On the contrary, the group is likely to engage in extensive rhetoric aimed at justifying traditional policies and practices. An aspect of the commitment to traditional diagnoses and solutions is the "thought structure" that becomes institutionalized in particular fields of activity (Warren, Rose, and Bergunder, 1974).[1]

Such a commitment to traditional objectives was observed by Tryggvason (1971:96) in a Vancouver ethnic community. The leaders considered the general and particular objectives of the organizations they led as "intrinsically worthwhile and deserving of the support of all 'good' ethnics." In addition, they did not favor any change in the activities sponsored by the associations. The range of objectives pursued by the associations were fairly restricted, at least in comparison to all possible objectives. The narrow range of objectives and activities was maintained by the leaders even if it had a negative impact on the size of the membership. The "leaders did not like to be reminded (nor do they even like to think about) the apparent discrepancy between what they feel the fellow ethnics think of those objectives and what the latter's actual rate of participation seems to imply about their attitudes towards those objectives." The leaders justified their position on the ground that a change would cause a loss of members because the current membership was perceived as equally committed to the existing state of affairs.

The existence of traditional ways of doing things and of a resistance to changing them usually becomes apparent in periods of transition due to external events or to changes in the social composition of the collectivity. In other words, commitment to tradition becomes especially apparent when new groups in the community begin to challenge the established leadership and their policies. When this happens, the traditional elites tend to be shocked that the consensus they had taken for granted is falling apart, that the policies and practices they had established are no longer generally accepted.

In the Ethnic Pluralism Study, leaders were asked about their ideas concerning discrimination, its causes, how it should be dealt with, and what should be the main targets of action. The most frequently mentioned manifestation of discrimination pertains to the social status of the group: negative attitudes about one's group (name-calling, stereotypes, individual prejudice), negative treatment of the group in the media (biased reporting, negative images), and hate literature and messages. Fifty-one percent of the leaders of organizations concerned with discrimination mention this type of manifestation. These respondents also mentioned physical harassment and abuse (one additional leader mentioned physical abuse, without mentioning negative attitudes as well).

Following social status in importance is job discrimination. It is mentioned by forty-one percent of the leaders of antidiscrimination organizations. The next most frequent manifestations are in the legal domain (police and the courts) and education, with nineteen percent and twelve percent of the leaders mentioning these areas respectively. Other areas, such as housing, immigration, and obtaining social services are mentioned less frequently as significant areas in which discrimination occurs.

There are a few intergroup differences worth noting. Job discrimination is mentioned by over two-thirds of the leaders of non-European origin organizations. Social status problems, on the other hand, tend to be more evenly perceived as a problem across groups, although more than average among South Asian and less than average among Italian leaders. Educational problems and problems with police and the courts are mentioned almost exclusively by South Asian and West Indian leaders, the later set of problems being mentioned especially frequently by West Indian leaders. The different groups, then, seem to have to cope with somewhat different sets of problems, although they all (except Italians) seem to experience problems of social status and recognition. Other types of discrimination are perceived as significant in some of the groups only.

Unfortunately, the questions pertaining to the causes of discrimination were asked only of leaders whose organizations deal primarily with discrimination. Also, a few did not respond to those questions. Of the twenty-nine who did respond, twenty-four (eighty-three percent) attribute discrimination to individual ignorance, feelings of superiority, fear of other cultures, or fear of competition over such things as jobs and housing. Eight mentioned racism institutionalized in various social settings and six refer to historical problems of exploitation of nonwhite peoples. On the basis of these limited data, it seems reasonable to hypothesize that there exists an "institutionalized thought structure," a certain consensus as to the sources of discriminatory practices: individual ignorance, beliefs, and attitudes.

Respondents were also asked if there are "any institutions which your organization regards as important in influencing or putting pressure on in order to best achieve its objective of dealing with discrimination" (Breton et al., 1990). Again, twenty-nine leaders responded. Eighteen (or sixty-two percent) of them mentioned government organizations, ministries, or agencies. These are by far the most important institutional targets. Educational institutions are mentioned by about a third of the leaders (ten), a little over a fourth (eight) mention legal institutions (courts, police, attorneys general), six mention the Ontario Human Rights Commission, and six refer to organizations within the ethnic community. Only three mention civil liberties associations.

It is not surprising that ethnic leaders feel governmental institutions are the most important to influence if the fight against discrimination is to yield results given the importance of governments in contemporary Canada and Western societies generally. This attitude is part of the welfare state syndrome, whereby governments are expected to be actively involved in providing individuals and groups with the means necessary for the pursuit of their goals (Janowitz, 1976).

What is perhaps surprising is the considerably less frequent mention of educational institutions, especially in view of the importance given to individual attitudes, beliefs, and ignorance as causes of discrimination. The leaders appear to be more confident in the possibilities of reducing discrimination by controlling individual behavior than by influencing attitudes, changing beliefs, or disseminating information. This interpretation is supported by the leaders' responses to questions about government policies and how they should be changed. Those who think changes are needed (about half) tend to mention passing stronger legislation, imposing harsher punishment on discriminating individuals and organizations, giving greater power to human rights commissions, broadening the scope of human rights and antidiscrimination legislation, and making such legislation more workable and enforceable. However, education is not thought to be irrelevant; a little over one-fourth of the leaders mentioned the need to project a positive image of minority groups through the national media and the educational system. But broader legislation more effectively enforced is seen as more important.

Job discrimination was mentioned as the second most important area in which discrimination manifests itself. Yet, employers and employment agencies are mentioned by only a few leaders as targets of action. Presumably, the expectation is that their behavior is to be changed when necessary through governmental intervention.

The existence of an institutionalized thought structure can be both an asset and a liability. It can be the latter if it serves "to ward off possible alternative approaches that would jeopardize" a consensus, which is more valued than new ideas (Warren, 1974:33). In such instances, it hinders innovation. The thought structure acts as a disincentive for leaders to search for alternative ways of defining the problem and/or of dealing with it. On the other hand, the thought structure may be an asset if the threat facing the group is serious. Indeed, the mobilization of group efforts and the coordination of action could be seriously hampered by a lack of consensus among elites. Such mobilization and coordination requires a minimal consensus around a political program to deal with problems.

The institutionalization of a system of ideas may also prevent opportunists from taking advantage in problem situations. For instance, problems and related events may be seen by certain individuals or subgroups as an opportunity to pursue their political careers. They may favor particular solutions for similar reasons. Thus, they may advocate courses of action that would be detrimental to the implementation of an overall, long-term strategy but beneficial to their own political fortunes. In short, one of the roles of the institutionalization of a system of ideas is to control dissent, either the positive dissent of innovators or the negative dissent of political opportunists. Both types of dissent, of course, can be detrimental to the pursuit of collective goals.

External Intervention in Ethnic Decision-Making

The political agenda of ethnic communities may be of concern to governments, political parties, churches, the government of the country of origin, labor unions, businesses, and other organizations. Indeed, the goals pursued by ethnic organizations can be either beneficial or detrimental to the policies and programs or to the organizational interests of these groups. A number of examples of the interest that organizations of the larger society have in ethnic group activities have been given earlier. Chapter 4 also presented ways in which external agencies intervene in the public affairs of ethnic communities, specifically by influencing or controlling the orientation and behavior of leaders.

Financial assistance for community projects and the conditions under which it is given present another important strategy used to affect the policies and programs of community organizations. At the beginning of the century, for example, Canadian political parties established and subsidized newspapers in some ethnic communities to make sure that their platforms and ideologies were transmitted to ethnic publics (Yusik, 1953; Daschko, 1982). Eventually, "after 1918, no major Canadian political party needed to establish a [Ukrainian-language] newspaper because existing papers were willing to transmit party views" (Daschko, 1982:266).

Today, it seems that intervention is somewhat less direct. Financial contributions may entail conditions or subtle directions as to what are desirable and objectionable activities, with a more or less extensive "zone of indifference" on the part of the governmental or political agency. This phenomenon has been referred to as "sociofiscal control" (Ponting and Gibbins, 1980). For example, the funding agency may threaten to discontinue funding in order to affect the ethnic organization's polices and projects. Financial assistance programs, however, have their impact primarily by providing a system of incentives or a structure of opportunities for ethnic organizations. Certain kinds of projects are more likely to be undertaken than others or certain kinds of activities will be organized in addition to the regular program of the organization because of the availability of funds.

Savas (1987) provides evidence on the impact of government funding on the priorities of ethnic community organizations. He categorized the expenditures of the Fédération des Franco-Colombiens into three broad categories: administration, community development, and federation affairs.[2] In the early period when the community contributed the majority of the funds, the leaders concentrated on federation affairs and community development about thirty-five percent of the time each. During the phase in which funding came in substantial part from private francophone organizations outside British Columbia, these proportions increased, especially the amount of time spent on community development. This finding suggests that external assistance need not necessarily lead organizations away from community preoccupations.[3]

What seems to have made the difference for this organization is the building of a permanent administrative secretariat with funds (supplied by a nongovernment organization). The result was an increase in administrative expenditures to over fifty percent of the budget. Secretary of state funding that began in the early 1970s permitted a return to spending on community development (sixty-three percent of expenditures). However, "the post– 1970 period of federal financing highlighted the growth of a professional and bureaucratic Federation. Professionals were hired, and salaries paid, for work previously performed by volunteers. Even though more money was allocated to community development than all other sectors, educated professionals in an enlarged bureaucratic structure drew a greater proportion of revenues in the form of salaries . . . salaries took an average of 59.4% of community development dollars" (Savas, 1987:185–186). In effect, it could be said that it is the administrative component of expenditures that increased dramatically.

THE RELEVANCE OF POLITICAL COMPETITION

Decision-Making and Political Accommodation

Several kinds of issues can emerge in an ethnic community. They may concern the country of origin, the internal life of the community (e.g., social services, cultural activities), or the relations of the collectivity with groups and organizations in the larger society.[4] These issues may involve government policies and programs such as those dealing with immigration, with multi-culturalism, with discrimination and the protection of individual rights, and with matters concerning the country of origin.

As in the larger polity, differences in policy orientation are likely to exist in ethnic communities. Different diagnoses of community problems and competing ideas as whether or not collective action is required and, if so, which line of action should be pursued are to be expected.

Given competing interests and views, an essential ingredient for policy-making is the willingness and ability to compromise. When subgroups have opposing interests in regard to certain matters, the definition of the problem and the forging of solutions require bargaining, and bargaining is impossible if one or both parties are not prepared to make concessions.[5] The perceived advantages of pooling of resources and of joint action in the execution of common projects may incite subgroups to make concessions. What divides groups or pits them against each other, however, may be more substantial than the interests that they have in common. The need for coordination may be felt by all parties, but they may be unable to agree on the organizational mechanism to achieve it.

As was seen earlier, this was the case among Poles and Ukrainians during a period of time of their history in Canada. This situation has also been observed in a number of Chinese communities: in Calgary, Medicine Hat, and Lethbridge until 1969 (Hoe, 1976) as well as in Toronto between 1923 and 1937 (Wickberg, 1979). "It appears that in Alberta, the 'political struggle' between the Kwomintang and the Freemasons had prevented the formation of a community organization.... In Calgary, the campaign for a community association was raised on at least three separate occasions, but due to mistrust and political rivalry . . . the issue was dropped subsequently" (Hoe, 1976:229–230).[6]

According to Anderson and Higgs (1976), this is also what happened in the Toronto Portuguese community in the late 1960s. The community began to feel the need for a central body that would "fight for the protection of Portuguese interests and the improvement of certain social and employment conditions that worked to their disadvantage. It was to serve as a 'federal' organization, bringing the other clubs together into a united front, while not infringing on their independence." But the effort broke down as "a result of personal disputes and political rancour" (157–161).

It should be noted that struggles for power may not always be crippling. Wickberg (1979:94) notes that the Winnipeg Chinese community, although "plagued by political discord, was able, after a struggle, to establish a CBA by 1923. And Vancouver and Victoria, the most complex and diverse communities, full of varying interests and political rivalries that led to spectacular violence, established CBA's early and maintained them somehow, although not without controversy."[7] Why some communities were able to overcome discord and others were not is unclear. A hypothesis, suggested by Hoe's (1976) comparison of Calgary and Edmonton is that, if there is a significant inequality of power among the rival groups, the one(s) that predominate may be able to convince the different groups to participate in a community-wide organization.

Anderson and Higgs (1976) also mention variations in the degree of organizational unity among Portuguese communities in Canada. Some are "split into church-oriented and anti-clerical factions. In others,... the Portuguese work without conflict both in the Church and in secular organizations." They suggest that the difference may be due in part to the presence or absence of "established leaders in these communities and to the arrival of large numbers of immigrants in the 1950's" (121). This hypothesis about established leaders is similar to Hoe's hypothesis concerning the predominance of a particular elite: if an elite does not feel seriously threatened by its competitors, it may be more willing to compromise in order to accommodate their interests.

Markides and Cohn (1982) have put forward an interesting analysis of this problem. Their discussion is framed in relation to external threats or conflicts, but it need not be restricted to such situations. It is applicable to any set of circumstances that confront a collectivity. They hypothesize that under certain conditions the important social actors of a group faced with contingencies that can be either beneficial or detrimental to the collectivity will reach the level of political cohesion sufficient to act in concert.

Markides and Cohn (1982:88) build on Williams's (1947) hypothesis about two such conditions: (1) "the group must be a 'going concern', i.e. there must be a minimal consensus among group members that the aggregate is a group and its preservation is worthwhile; and (2) the circumstance must be perceived to be profitable or detrimental to the group as a whole and not only to some of its segments." In ethnic communities, some problems (e.g., housing conditions, police behavior, employment practices) may be identified with certain segments such as lower-class individuals, women, young people, or new immigrants, while other problems are defined as community wide (e.g., treatment of the group by the media, cultural preservation, immigration policies). It should be noted as well that some conditions or events may be seen as positive by some people but as negative by others (e.g., acculturation, the trial of individuals accused of anti-Semitism, compensation for treatment during World War II).

Markides and Cohn (1982:95–96) add a hypothesis concerning the role of the competition that may exist among organized groups and their leaders. A particular set of circumstances—discrimination, a government policy or program, an international event, a demographic situation, a disaster in the country of origin, a national conference of political significance, a wave of new immigrants within the collectivity—may well be perceived by some groups or organizations as an opportunity to acquire power. If an event is used "to enhance political fortunes," it may increase political competition and fragmentation rather than lead to coordination and unification. Similarly, "different strategies for resolving the conflict" (dealing with the problem or taking advantage of the opportunity) "may differentially affect the fortunes of political groups." Thus, in communities with competing elites, "proposed solutions are likely to have little in common and, unless the threat is imminent and overwhelming, a higher priority will be attached to factional advantage than to forming consensual policies." In short, the situation may be such as to offer little or no incentives to compromise; on the contrary, it motivates particular groups to engage in opportunistic behaviour.

The willingness to compromise also depends on the ideological distance between the various groups involved with the issue (Bacharach and Lawler, 1981; Moore, 1958). The more that these philosophical principles are part of the basis of the organizations' and its leaders' identities, the more painful any compromise will be. It is virtually impossible to negotiate identities and fundamental principles. If doctrines and goals are in outright contradiction, the grounds on which a compromise can be forged is very limited. In such cases, the willingness to compromise is the same as the willingness to accept a fundamental conversion.

In other words, while controversies may arise in a community because groups have contradictory interests (material or symbolic) with regard to specific issues, they may also take place because groups have divergent conceptions of the sociopolitical order, of the driving forces in it, and of the strategies that are the most likely to be effective in it.

For instance, ideological orientations usually referred to as left, center, and right exist in ethnic as in other polities. They lead people to read events and circumstances differently, to give them different meaning, and to favor different courses of action. Also groups that are ideologically committed to confrontation and those who are committed to accommodation are frequently in opposition. The terms *militant* and *moderate* are sometimes used to denote these two positions.

Stasiulis (1982) observed such differences in orientation in the Toronto black community. One group of leaders favored "working closely with authorities in dealing with problems that emerged (such as tensions between the police and the black community). They also made use of the press to articulate their views and their responses to meetings with government officials . . . and to strengthen [their] position by prophesying a crisis such as widespread violence, promulgated by both the 'extremist' elements in the Black community and those on the far right." Another group of organizational leaders adopted a mass-based, confrontationist approach. They saw the use of a mediator to assist in the police-community relationships as "a convenient device for cooling down the people's rage while doing nothing" (Contrast, September 6, 1979; quoted in Stasiulis, 1982:148–49). Their view is that change can be obtained through pressure applied by public demonstrations, marches, boycotts, and other mass actions (Stasiulis, 1982).

Differences in political strategy were also observed by Wong (1977:14) in New York's Chinatown. The traditional elites favored techniques characterized by harmony, patience, and "inaction unless other measures are absolutely necessary" while the new elites "believe in the conflict approach— not conflict in the sense of physical force, but in the sense of social pressure and of militant attitudes."

A similar divergence of views was observed by John (1969) in his study of the Punjabi community in Britain. On the one hand, the Southall leaders adopted a "deliberately restrained" position. One leader succinctly expressed this view in the following terms: "For several years, there has been many incidents when the police treat immigrants badly or do not give enough protection. It has always been our policy not to complain. . . . We could send a letter [of complaint] after each incident, and that would be good, but what would we do after we sent the letter? The police would be angry with us, and we would accomplish nothing. It is better not to stir things up" (John, 1969:160). In contrast, the principle of militant action against racial discrimination was endorsed by the Birmingham branch of the community. Marches were organized, and there was support for the idea of protest strikes against discrimination in factories (John, 1969).

The moderate elite argues that militancy ignores the real possibilities of influencing government and alienates several community members and thus splits the community. The disagreement between the two groups of leaders is part of a long rivalry involving the competition for the leadership of the Punjabi community in Britain. (This competition is due to the fact that Southall and Birmingham contain the largest Punjabi communities in the country.)

Arriving at a compromise usually entails some degree of confrontation. It is a difficult process than can be emotionally painful and draining for those involved. Because of this, the leaders of the competing groups may be unwilling to address the issues that divide them. Fear of controversy may cause them to avoid the problems that joint action could resolve or the opportunities that concerted exploitation could turn into mutual benefit.

Selznick (1957:25–26) notes that this evasion of difficult or controversial questions is a "default of leadership" due, in part, to the "hard intellectual labour involved" and, in part, to the "wish to avoid conflicts." This failure of leadership may, in turn, result from the perception that a compromise is impossible, that the ideologies and positions on issues are irreconcilable.

It is not sufficient, however, that leaders of the different subgroups be willing to compromise; they must also be able to do so. A critical determinant of this ability to compromise pertains to the character of the relationship between leaders and their respective constituencies. Specifically, the subgroup leaders' ability to compromise is a function of the "degree of freedom" that they are given by their members or supporters. Deutsch (quoted by Bacharach and Lawler, 1981:130–131) has hypothesized that actual or imagined pressures from what leaders perceive to be their constituency tend to inhibit the search for alternate solutions and reduce the leaders' ability to grasp and understand the other party's point of view.

Conversely, if the subgroup's leaders perceive that they have some autonomy in their representative role, they are able to adopt a more flexible, open, and searching approach to dealing with the other parties. This autonomy may be due to their established prestige and their record of past accomplishments for the group. Being trusted, they are delegated, so to speak, to find the best solution with minimal compromises.

The relationship between "representative" and "constituency" is affected by many circumstances. First, the relevant constituency may be more or less vaguely defined. That is to say, it may not be clear who the leaders in fact represent, an ambiguity that can diminish their ability to negotiate. Second, the ties that those who occupy representative roles have with their perceived constituencies may be very tenuous and informal. Third, the representatives may behave in relation to imagined rather than actual pressures from their presumed constituencies. Fourth, the leaders' autonomy in dealing with other parties is affected by the "involvement of constituents in the negotiations: accountability of representatives to their constituents which, in turn, is a function of the constituents' information about the evolution of the negotiations and of their ability to apply sanctions on leaders if they are displeased with the compromises made." Finally, the leaders' autonomy as group representatives is related to their loyalty or commitment to the group. Loyal leaders are those who have internalized their subgroups aspirations to the point where they do not feel that any pressure is being exerted on them. They have no views on the issue that are independent of those of their constituents. They have, accordingly, very little flexibility (Bacharach and Lawler, 1981:130–136).

Pressures from constituents, however, may encourage leaders to compromise. For instance, a leader's failure to reach a satisfactory accommodation may bring strong community disapproval. Extremist leaders or would-be leaders may be ostracized because of their unwillingness to negotiate in good faith. The stand taken by certain leaders may be socially defined as self-interested and therefore of questionable legitimacy. The possible loss of prestige and influence can be a powerful incentive to compromise. Welch (1985), for example, argues that this has been the case in some instances in the Franco-Ontarian community; as the factional conflict over school issues began to be perceived as detrimental to the long-term interest of the community and its survival, the various parties began to exercise restraint and modified their positions. They responded to community pressures.

In short, there are situations in which constituents will, directly or indirectly, apply pressures on their leaders not to compromise, to make virtually no concessions. But there can also be situations in which members pressure leaders to compromise because they perceive that the welfare of the community is endangered by a protracted conflict among factions.

The involvement of a third party can facilitate compromise and accommodation between conflicting subgroups. Third parties "consist of relatively neutral persons who act as intermediaries in the conflict. They facilitate communication; they interpret to each party the other's position; they present alternative points of view and solutions; and they help to lower the emotional intensity of controversy" (Kriesberg, 1973:215–216).

Prominent members of the community and older "statesmen" are in a position to act as mediators and frequently do so. In some ethnic communities, the consul of the country of origin has frequently taken this role (Modell, 1977; Boissevain, 1970). Gerus, for instance, mentions "the pivotal role in initiating the talks played by Kushnir, who possessed that rare capacity among Ukrainian leaders, the ability to compromise. To achieve unity, he set out to reconcile political, religious, and personal antagonisms, to the frequent annoyance of the more doctrinaire element within the Ukrainian Catholic Brotherhood itself" (Gerus, 1981:196).

The willingness to compromise may spring from the perception that the opposition is more apparent than real, that a sort of symbiotic relationship can develop between the two factions. Thus moderates may see the radical groups as performing an important political function from their own perspective: "Radical political groups bring racism out in the open. They do a good job in bringing it out in the open, whereas other moderate groups start dealing with it" (an organizational leader in the black community, quoted by Stasiulis, 1982:156). Thus, confrontation may draw the attention of political authorities and relevant publics to the situation and draw from them a responsiveness that facilitates the process of communication and negotiation undertaken by more moderate elements (Stasiulis, 1982).

The willingness and ability to compromise also depends on the existence and intensity of personal rancor among leaders of different subgroups. Personal feuds may precede controversies over issues; they may also develop in the course of the conflict. But once they exist, they have a dynamic of their own: an atmosphere of suspicion and mistrust is created, affecting the leader's perception and interpretations of each other's moves, frequently giving these actions a significance much greater than actually justified. Thus, suspicion and mistrust feed on themselves (Tryggvason, 1971).

John (1969) emphasizes the fact that personal feuds frequently overlap with ideological battles. He argues that such an overlap is typical of small-community politics. In extreme cases, personal rancor is virtually the only basis of the conflict. Ideological differences in such instances render personal struggles for power socially acceptable and are themselves hardly relevant. In short, personal animosities constitute an important obstacle to compromise. They also make bargaining difficult because emotions are not negotiable.

Decision-Making in Situations of Political Dominance

In situations of political ascendancy, organizational leaders do not primarily, if at all, respond to the demands and expectations of community members. On the contrary, they tend to be the ones who define problems and opportunities. They attempt to do so in terms of their own political agenda, the political advantages they seek, and the limits imposed by the resources at their disposal. Their attempts to define the political agenda also involve the management of demands and expectations. In short, policy alternatives are assessed in terms of their bearing on the political success of the elite and on the elite's continued ascendancy, not in terms of community needs as perceived by members.

There is more to the relationship between objective conditions and goals or plans of action than the process of acquiring information about those conditions and about alternative ways of dealing with them. To begin with, problems and opportunities are what people think they are (Henshel, 1976). Becker (1967:5–6) points out that "people clearly *can* define nonexistent conditions as social problems. The inhabitants of Salem, Massachusetts believed in witches and imagined that their community was infested with them. . . . [People] can also define any condition that does exist as a social problem."

The situations selected as problems or opportunities can be defined in varied ways by different subgroups or over time. As a result, the information collected and used by groups is really about situations as defined by the people concerned. This makes setting goals and defining problems less a technical and more a cultural and ideological matter. "The definition of a problem usually contains, implicitly or explicitly, suggestions for how it may be solved." (Becker, 1967:10). As a result, the search for solutions, which may be a partly technical process, is carried out within the context of cultural and ideological definitions of problems and opportunities.

The particular aspects of situations that are defined as problems or opportunities and the ways in which they are so defined are likely to affect the chances of success of leaders and their organizations. This is the case because of the practical implications of various definitions and their implied solutions in terms of costs, manageability, organizational requirements, personnel, and so on. Leaders of organizations, then, have an interest in the ways in which community problems and opportunities for action are defined. Indeed, particular definitions tend to shape what members of the community (or segments of its) come to expect from organizational leaders. This in turn affects the ease with which organizations can gain legitimacy, the ways in which they will be evaluated, and their chances of obtaining required resources.

In this perspective, the interest of leaders is not so much to learn about existing situations faced by members of the community as it is to influence or, if possible, directly shape community members' definition of problems and/or solutions. Much of the leaders' behavior will be to resist definitions that are detrimental either to the formation, maintenance, or growth of their organization and its power. The distribution of power is reflected not in the use of ingenuity, the mobilization of expertise and tools that allow the most significant contributions to the community, but rather in the ability to shape demands and expectations so that the goals and strategies adopted are those that permit the greatest chances of organizational success. Organizations and projects are formed not in relation to objective situations that founders and leaders survey and analyze but in relations to situations that they define or help to define in ways compatible with the means and resources at their disposal.

In their study of American Chinatowns, Light and Wong (1975) found that a large number of new immigrants increased the problems of housing, health, poverty, and delinquency in the community. The responsibility to seek governmental relief funds and public housing fell upon the established leaders of the community. However, they resisted such action because in order to obtain public assistance they would have to document and make public the deteriorating social conditions in their neighborhoods. Doing so, they feared, would "decrease the visits of tourists to their own places of business." Thus, they "have initiated no studies of local social conditions ...and have done nothing to publicize unwholesome conditions in Chinatowns." Rather, they have encouraged the "district and family name associations to redouble their efforts to provide membership services." In other words, they continued to follow the traditional mode of dealing with problems, a course of action more compatible with their own class interests (1975:1356, 1357).

Similarly, on the basis of his study of the Portuguese community in Montreal, Lavigne (1980) suggests that community organizations and their policies are manifestations of the economic interests of the ethnic petty bourgeoisie. Members of the bourgeoisie attempt, for example, to maintain the ethnoculture and to organize political pressure against any governmental measure that would reduce the flow of immigrants. Such activities are pursued in order to maintain the labor force and clientele for their businesses. When they become sufficiently successful to try to penetrate the larger economy, they politicize interethnic relations through the denunciation of discrimination, attempts to control the politico-administrative structures to which they have access, and the manipulation of political issues.

Whatever the ultimate objective, once established an organization generates particular kinds of interests. "The personnel of the organization devoted to the problem tend to build their lives and careers around its continued existence. They become attached to 'their' problem, and anything that threatens to make it disappear or diminish in importance is a threat." This applies to the staff of any organization devoted to dealing with a social problem, even in fields such as race relations, housing, or education. Thus, "organizations, particularly when they are seeking funds, typically oscillate between two kinds of claims. First, they say that by reason of their efforts the problem they deal with is approaching solution. But, in the same breath, they say the problem is perhaps worse than ever... and requires renewed and increased effort to keep it under control" (Becker, 1967:13).

There are several things leaders of organizations can do to promote their social definition of community conditions and the continued existence of the organization. For instance, they can create or stimulate the demand for the service or activity provided by their organizations. In doing so, however, they run the risk of creating expectations that their organization may not be able to meet. Goals and strategies can be quite important in motivating community members to support an organization and/or participate in community projects. But they can entail a danger: they carry expectations that, if not met, can cause people to be disenchanted. It is therefore in the interest of leaders to put forward moderate proposals, moderate in the sense that they entail reasonable chances of being realized.

For similar reasons, leaders may incorporate a certain degree of ambiguity in the formulation of their goals and programs. "Whenever ambiguity exists either in the statement of criteria or in their application to a particular output, there will exist the possibility of equivocality in interpretation. . . . [Thus there will be] discretion in determining whether a demand is satisfied" (Pfeffer and Salancik, 1978:99). Of course, ambiguity also has its dangers: it may give considerable leeway to organizational leaders, but too much of it may fail to attract supporters.

Another strategy is to try to define the situation in such a way that the organization itself is not responsible for bringing about the desired results, but rather some other organization is, usually a governmental organization. The continued existence of the problem is then defined as the failure of these other organizations and the action required is therefore to apply pressure on them to reform or to undertake further action. The lack of results can then be attributed to the stubbornness of those bodies rather than to the failure of one's own organization. The plausibility of this attribution resides largely in the fact that the definition of the problem is such that it detracts attention from other definitions that could have been adopted and courses of action that could have been pursued for which the responsibility for success or failure would have more squarely rested on the organizational leaders themselves.

To achieve such control over the social definition of problems and opportunities, the accompanying demands and expectations, and, therefore, the criteria of social evaluation of performance, organizational leaders have a variety of means at their disposal. Perhaps the most significant, because its impact can be the most enduring, is the formulation and diffusion of a doctrine or ideology: "The creation of a doctrine has often been one of the very first steps along the road to power. With widely varying degrees of elaboration, the doctrine provides an explanation of what is wrong with the current state of affairs and what should be done to correct this state. We may designate such a doctrine the charter myth of a power-seeking organization" (Moore, 1958:10).

In short, community goals, strategies and decisions are, in part, determined by the actions of organizational elites in defining situations in certain ways, in shaping social demands and expectations and, as a result, in orienting community activities and projects. The extent of the leaders' efforts is a function of how they think these factors can affect their own organizational interests and pursuits. Thus, the sociopolitical orientation of the community becomes progressively identified with the orientation of the successful organizational elites.

CONCLUSION

In many ways, the analysis of policy-making in ethnic communities is an extension of the discussion of leadership in the preceding chapter. As in the previous analysis, the four sets of processes considered led to the identification of somewhat different dimensions of policy-making.

First, the capacity to collect relevant information, to diagnose adequately favorable and unfavorable circumstances, and to formulate appropriate courses of action is the central issue to be addressed if the collectivity is to cope effectively with its sociopolitical environment. There is, in other words, a rational-technical aspect to problems of discrimination, unemployment, housing, cultural maintenance, and immigration. The information and skills required to devise and carry out appropriate policies can be legal, political, organizational, managerial, and so on. The chapter has examined some of the sources of variation (possibilities and obstacles) in the extent to which ethnic collectivities develop such a rational-technical capacity.

Second, ethnic policies and actions can be of concern to external bodies. It was seen in the previous chapter that the representatives of such agencies can attempt to influence the composition and orientations of ethnic leaderships. Similarly, they can attempt to influence more or less directly the policy-making process and its substantive outcomes. Sociofiscal control or intervention through financial assistance was examined as one of the main means of intervention.

Third, in so far as policy-making is concerned, the accommodation of competing interests has to do primarily with the willingness and ability to compromise. The compromises can pertain to the policy objectives, to the strategies to be deployed in their pursuit, or both. The chapter examined some of the conditions under which leaders of different subgroups will be willing and/or able to compromise.

Situations of political ascendancy involve different sets of policy-making issues and processes. The dynamics of these situations is such that the opportunities and problems selected for political attention as well as the particular courses of action adopted tend to be defined in relation to the power interests of the elite and only secondarily and coincidentally to those of the members of the polity. The driving force underlying policy-making is to protect and preferably enhance the power position of the governing elite. Accordingly, the leaders' tendency is not so much to ascertain the interests and problems that confront the community but to manipulate the political demands that emerge from the public, to structure issues in ways that buttress the position of leaders.

NOTES

1. Warren's definition of this concept is presented in chapter 2, note 2.

2. Administration includes general office expenditures, publication costs, and the salary of the liaison officer. Community activities and development refer to such activities as committee work (education, radio broadcasts), institutional support (theater groups), French prizes, donations, banquets, and picnics. Federation affairs include meetings, delegate transportation to the annual general assembly, and delegate expenses outside the province (Savas, 1987).

3. Strictly speaking, it would be necessary to know about the specific content of activities to examine this question in a satisfactory way.

4. For interesting discussions and analyses of internal issues in an ethnic community, see Elazar (1976); Glickman (1976); Wong (1977); and Jabbra and Jabbra (1984).

5. Bacharach and Lawler (1981:113) state

Explicit bargaining is essentially what nations, corporations, and unions do when they sit at the bargaining table, that is, exchange offers and counteroffers. In such settings, the parties have relatively open lines of communication, define the relationship as a bargaining one, and consent to consider compromise. . . . Tacit bargaining, on the other hand, implies that the parties have obstructed communication lines and may not even define the relationship as a bargaining one or be conscious of the fact that they are in a bargaining relationship. . . . The give-and-take involves few explicit offers or counteroffers; instead parties attempt to outmaneuver and manipulate each other, often using subtle influence tactics or rewards and punishments.

6. Hoe (1976:230) points out, however, that "despite the absence of a community association, a community-wide committee was formed whenever there was a crisis threatening the community."

7. CBA stands for Chinese Benevolent Association.

6

Participation in Community Affairs

Closely related to policy-making and implementation is the question of the political participation of members of the collectivity. As will be seen, however, the issues that become salient are different when the goals involved concern the entire polity than when there are subgroups with more or less divergent goals and aspirations with regard to the affairs of the collectivity. The issues are also different when external agents see the level and especially the modes of participation in ethnic polities as having implications for their own policies and organizations. These are the concerns discussed in this chapter.

THE IMPACT OF ENVIRONMENTAL CONDITIONS

Participation: A Question of Resource Mobilization

The pursuit of collective goals requires financial contributions, investments of time and energy, involvement in activities, and sociopolitical support. Action oriented toward environmental problems and opportunities involves the mobilization of such resources. In other words, a critical element of the environmental capacity of ethnic governance institutions is the active participation of community members. Three categories of incentives can be used to motivate group members' participation: purposive, material, and solidaristic (Clark and Wilson, 1961; Knoke, 1988). Members can also, under certain circumstances, be constrained to participate.

Purposive incentives pertain to the policy objectives pursued. An individual's decision to become an active participant in community affairs is partly a function of what is to be accomplished and the related values. Purposive incentives to participate "derive from the stated ends of the association. . . .

[They] are to be found in the suprapersonal goals of the organization" (Clark and Wilson, 1961:135).

Goals have two components: a policy and a program. The policy identifies, at least in general terms, what is wrong with the world and what needs to be changed or improved or what state of affairs should be preserved or protected from destructive forces. It also points to the lines of action that should be pursued and to the opponents or inimical forces that have to be confronted, dealt with, or overcome. Programs of action, on the other hand, refer to specific plans for the implementation of policies. Programs operationalize goals and, as such, may be more or less faithful to the intentions that underlie the goals.

Policies and programs may or may not reinforce each other in motivating individuals to participate in or contribute to an organization. The ideal situation for the mobilization of support is that both appeal to a large number of individuals; persuading potential or actual members is then the easiest. Frequently, however, individuals may agree only with certain aspects of policies and programs. They may share the basic values but disagree with the analysis of what is wrong, the proposed lines of action, or the specific programs. Or, they may find the values and line of action quite acceptable, but reject the specific programs on the grounds that they will not bring the desired results or even that they will be detrimental. As a result, leaders may have to compromise on their ideology, reorient their theory of action, or modify their proposed programs in order to attract sufficient numbers of supporters.

Another difficulty may be the simple absence of an important element in a program. An organization may have a specific program, but one based on expediency rather than on a well-articulated theory and ideology. Alternatively, it may have a fairly coherent ideology and even a theory about the problem and its causes but only a vague program of action or none at all. Its appeal to potential or actual members may therefore generate some sympathy but not much support. An even more precarious situation is when the appeal is purely ideological: leaders propogate basic values but without being clear as to the specific nature of the problem and its causes (the "system" or the establishment is to blame) or the lines of action and the programs of activities that should be pursued. Such a situation is not very favorable for the mobilization of sustained support.

Finally, the willingness to contribute to the pursuit of collective action is also dependent on the perceived efficacy of proposed plans and strategies. Group members must see that the policies adopted by those who govern can resolve the problem in a satisfactory way (Markides and Cohn, 1982).[1]

How people perceive the efficacy of programs of action in relation to opportunities is partly affected by their system of beliefs concerning individual versus collective action. Tajfel (1974:5–6) delineates the "social mobility" and "social change" orientations to action. The first refers to the perception that one's position can be improved through one's efforts. The underlying "assumption is that the system is flexible and permeable, that it permits a fairly free movement of the individual particles of which it consists." Social change, on the other hand, refers to the belief that one is enclosed within a social group and that one's fate is tied to it. Therefore, the only way to change one's condition is together with the group.

If social mobility is a group's prevailing system of belief, they will believe it possible to improve their condition through existing structures and rules of the game, and ethnic mobilization will be difficult. This hypothesis receives some support from the Ethnic Pluralism Study data. Respondents were asked about the types of action they would consider the most effective to deal with instances of job discrimination. The actions presented to the respondent can be grouped under three headings: individual action,[2] activation of social networks,[3] and the use of organizational resources.[4]

Taking one's case to a "community agency like the Ontario Human Rights Commission" is the action that, in most groups, is the most frequently seen as the most likely to give results. Also, with few exceptions, taking one's case to the union comes as a close second-most-favored action. Generally, then, the use of organizational resources appears to be the most favored action.

However, the organizational resources favored appear to be those of the community at large not those of the ethnic community. The latter are not the least favored of all types of action, but they are thought of, on the average, as significantly less effective than societal organizations (thirty-nine percent in comparison with seventy-one percent and seventy-four percent for the other two types of organizations).[5]

Much of the literature on collective action points to the importance of organization in translating discontent, grievances, or aspirations into collective action. In social psychological terms, this means that individuals will favor the type of action that they perceive as having the best organizational apparatus and support system for its execution. This may be the reason why societal institutions like the Ontario Human Rights Commission are the most favored. This may also be why Jewish respondents are more likely to favor action through their own organizations than members of other minorities: indeed, Jewish communities tend to be among the better organized for a variety of purposes, including the fight against anti-Semitism.

Generally, most respondents do not appear inclined towards ethnically based action. They seem to believe that there are more effective means to remove barriers to mobility outside the ethnic community or that individual efforts or the use of social networks can be more effective.

Finally, the perception of the efficacy of action in relation to issues is also related to the strength of the horizontal versus the vertical system of societal organization. If the horizontal system is relatively unimportant; if, in other words, the significant arena of decisions and actions is at the level of the mainstream rather than the ethnic institutions, there will be little need for involvement of individuals at the latter level (Jackson, 1975). The involvement required will be primarily on the part of the ethnic community's politicians and functionaries who will have to deal with the extracommunity systems.

The policies and programs supplied by leaders and their organizations may mobilize a certain degree of support, but they are not likely to be sufficient. They may only motivate a relatively small proportion of the members to contribute to the collective effort.[6] It has frequently been observed that individuals who agree with certain objectives and who would even benefit personally from their attainment do not contribute to the organization necessary for their pursuit. Olson (1965) provides a powerful explanation of this phenomenon in his public goods theory of collective action or participation in interest groups.[7] Public goods are not divisible; that is, their benefits cannot be withheld from any person in the collectivity whether or not the person contributed to their costs.

If individuals have a common interest in regard to certain matters, they may not be willing to share the costs (monetary or nonmonetary) of pursuing them. Except in the case of small groups, the voluntary contribution of a single individual toward a collective good would not make a noticeable difference; the loss of one contribution will not noticeably increase the burden for any other single contributor. So, "a rational person would not believe that if he were to withdraw from an organization he would drive others to do so.... The individual member (or potential member) of the typical large organization is in a position analogous of that of ... the taxpayer in the state: his own efforts will not have a noticeable effect on the situation of his organization, and he can enjoy any improvements brought about by others whether or not he has worked in support of his organization" (Olson, 1965 :12, 16).

Consequently, an organization may not be established or, if one is established, it may not be able to sustain itself. A particular collective action may be highly desirable from the point of view of the objective interests at stake, yet it may not be undertaken as a result of the phenomenon described by Olson. Thus, persons acting in their own individual interest may bring about situations against their collective objective interests. Or, to put it differently, the collective venture will fail "simultaneously against the will and through the will of the actors" (Boudon, 1977:22).[8]

Under such circumstances, how can individuals be made to participate in organizations and contribute toward the provision of collective goods? Special means are necessary as such participation is not likely to come about spontaneously. Two general classes of devices can be used under appropriate conditions: constraints and selective incentives.

Olson (1965) argues that the purely social constraints are effective only in small groups. In large aggregates, legal means are required if individuals are to coerce each other into paying the costs of organization and of the pursuit of collective benefits. He discusses at great length the case of labor unions in the United States as an instance of the "public goods dilemma" being resolved through legal intervention (the Wagner Act passed in 1935 and defined as constitutional by the Supreme Court in 1937). An exclusive emphasis on legal means, however, may be misleading. Coercion involves the capacity to make participation or contributions compulsory through a credible (that is enforceable) threat of sanctions. Although legal mechanisms may be the most effective in this regard, other types of sanctions may be available even to fairly large aggregates of people.

In ethnic groups, legal means are rarely available; it is generally not a realistic possibility. Social and moral coercion are more frequently attempted: the spread of a bad reputation; social ostracism; the withdrawal of business patronage. The fear of such reprisals may be sufficient to induce individuals to contribute "their fair share."

The various means of social coercion, however, are in many ways the negative side of incentives that can be offered in exchange for participation. Before discussing different types of incentives and how they are used, it is important to point out that contrary to the collective goods, they are divisible. That is to say, incentives are benefits that can be made available to those who participate or contribute and withdraw from those who do not. The reverse is true with sanctions. The individual may join to obtain some benefit that they cannot receive otherwise or to avoid disadvantages or penalties that they would otherwise have to endure.

The positive side, so to speak, of social constraints is the emergence of a sense of obligation toward the group and its members. The constraint is then internalized. Community organizations frequently devote considerable effort to generating loyalty among their members—to fostering a sense of commonality between the individual's own identity and social and economic conditions and those of the group. Establishing a link between individual and collective identity and an individual's fate can lead to a commitment or obligation to the group.

An individual's participation in organizations and/or activities can be the result of a feeling of responsibility vis-a-vis the group. Moe (1980) found this to be the case for economic interest groups such as retailers, printers, and farmers: for four of the five interest groups surveyed, fifty percent or more of the respondents rated as "very important" or "of some importance" the sense of responsibility or obligation as a consideration in their decision to maintain membership.

Given the importance of the sense of obligation for participation in economic interest groups, one would expect it to be significant in ethnic groups as well. In the Ethnic Pluralism Study, respondents were asked whether or not they agreed with the statement that one "should support special needs and causes of the group" and with an item referring to a more personal

Table 6.1
Sense of Obligation to Support the Ethnic Group's Needs and Causes by Ethnic
Group

	A. General obligation			B. Personal obligation		
	Strongly agree %	Agree %	Total %	Strongly agree %	Agree %	Total %
Chinese	2	68	70	1	60	61
German	1	49	50	2	14	16
Italian	7	68	75	4	49	53
Jewish	25	68	93	24	59	83
Portuguese	16	68	84	11	69	80
Ukrainian	9	71	80	6	51	57
West Indian	13	69	82	5	63	68

sense of obligation: "I personally feel that I should support the special causes and needs of the (name of ethnic group to which respondent belongs)."

Table 6.1 presents the distribution of the sense of obligation by ethnic groups. The percentages of people who agree with the items presented vary between fifty percent and ninety-three percent, the German respondent being the least and the Jewish respondents the most likely to feel that members should support the special needs and causes of the group (a forty-three percent difference). The difference is even more pronounced when the question is formulated in terms of personal obligation: from sixteen to eighty-three percent (a sixty-seven percent difference).

The distribution against other variables appears in Table 6.2. Although there are some variations with age, education, and occupational status, these are not very pronounced. On the other hand, the sense of obligation, especially personal obligation, is related to generation (it is stronger in the first than in the third or later generation). But it is especially related to religious affiliation and, in particular, to the strength of religious beliefs. Commitment to a religious doctrine tends to manifest itself in social obligations.

The results also show that those who are active in community affairs are more likely to agree with the sense of obligation statements than those who are less active or not active (Table 6.3).[9] The relationship is even stronger when the statement refers to one's personal obligation, as opposed to a general norm: "I personally feel that I should support the special causes and needs of the (group)". This is the case when membership in associations and participation at meetings are considered as well as closeness to the center of community activities.

In addition to the purposive incentives, material and solidaristic benefits can also be used as selective incentives to induce participation. Material

Table 6.2
Sense of Obligation to Ethnic Community by Selected Independent Variables

| | % who agree with statement | |
	About general obligation	About personal obligation
A. Generation:		
First	79 (666)	64 (677)
Second	76 (279)	47 (282)
Third	70 (125)	37 (128)
B. Age		
18-25	73 (307)	46 (310)
26-45	80 (504)	63 (514)
46+	77 (259)	57 (262)
C. Religious identification and strength of belief:		
No preference	61 (120)	35 (122)
Protestant Strong	72 (113)	53 (113)
Weak	62 (74)	31 (79)
Jewish Strong	97 (94)	94 (94)
Weak	94 (54)	72 (54)
Catholic Strong	83 (433)	60 (437)
Weak	68 (152)	49 (157)
D. Occupational Status		
Low	83 (374)	62 (385)
Intermediate	73 (311)	54 (312)
High	76 (268)	53 (273)
E. Education		
10 years or less	80 (388)	63 (397)
11-13 years	75 (351)	47 (355)
14+ years	77 (330)	57 (334)

Table 6.3
Participation in Community Activities by "Sense of Obligation" Attitude

| | Sense of obligation | | | | | |
| | For group members | | | For self | | |
	Agree %	Neutral %	Disagree %	Agree %	Neutral %	Disagree %
Participation in ethnic associations	31 (829)	10 (59)	11 (182)	36 (612)	17 (107)	12 (368)
Expresses views about community affairs	31 (826)	19 (57)	14 (177)	37 (611)	19 (106)	14 (361)
Feels close to the center of community activities	46 (823)	31 (59)	25 (181)	57 (607)	37 (105)	17 (367)

incentives have a monetary value or can easily be translated into ones that have. These incentives include, of course, wages and the like; but they also include services of various sorts such as health insurance or services, financial assistance, job information, education, and language training. Material benefits may also involve protection against physical attack or against discrimination in employment and housing. Solidaristic incentives pertain in part to sociability. They derive "from the act of associating and include such rewards as socializing, congeniality, the sense of group membership and identification" (Clark and Wilson, 1961:134). These benefits are frequently independent of the specific goals of the organization.

The importance of these incentives has been recognized by many ethnic organizations. Tirado (1974:122), for example, says, "Most Mexican American community political organizations in the past have been characterized by their willingness to serve many different functions for their membership. Most successful Mexican American political organizations, for example, also seem to offer mutual aid benefits of some sort to help their members in time of financial need. They attempt to meet the social needs of their community by sponsoring dances, picnics, banquets, etc. Mexican American political organizations that ignored those various other needs of their members have often found it difficult to retain the interest and support of their membership." Solidaristic incentives can also consist in "the involvement of members' families in the activities of the organization, either through the establishment of women's and young persons' auxiliaries or through regular group social activities in which the members' families can participate" (Tirado, 1974:123).

Tirado's observations about Mexican-American political organizations could be made about those of several other ethnic groups. Cultural and folklore activities are also ways of attracting individuals to join associations and participate in them. The mobilization of participation may be one of the latent functions of government grants to ethnic organizations and this latent function is perhaps sometimes equally if not more important than the manifest one pertaining to the stated goals of the funded activity (such as cultural maintenance or the fight against discrimination).

The substantial expansion of the welfare state in recent decades may, however, have reduced the range of material incentives that ethnic organizations can offer their members. Indeed, many of the services that members of ethnic groups had previously found within their own communities can now be obtained from government agencies and departments. Or, to put it differently, the ethnic organizer "now must compete with large-scale operations in trying to provide services meaningful enough to induce persons to support collective action. . . . The monopolization of resources [by these large-scale organizations] can destroy the material bases of communities" by reducing the range of services that "political entrepreneurs [can] offer as inducements to potential interest group members" (O'Brien, 1975:189–190).

Another category of solidaristic incentives involve "the status resulting from membership . . . and the maintenance of social distinctions" (Clark and Wilson, 1961:135). Such incentives relate to sociability in the sense that group members derive gratification from the company of prominent people. Status rewards also come from the fact that organizational leaders engage in rituals of recognition vis-a-vis ordinary members (e.g., knowing their names, acknowledging their efforts, taking the time to talk with them at meetings, recognizing them on the street).

But status incentives for participation derive primarily from the authority and prestige of the corporate body itself. Authority, here, refers to the "legitimation of activities, the right and responsibility to carry out programs of a certain kind, dealing with a broad problem or focus" (Benson, 1975:232). While authority has to do with the recognized domain of jurisdiction of the ethnic organization, its prestige refers to its image among relevant publics. Indeed, organizations and other corporate entities can be "placed along a continuum from unfavorable to favorable public images" (Perrow, 1961:335). A well-established authority and a high prestige can motivate community members to participate in or contribute to the existence and functioning of the organized body.

The authority and status of an organization may be enhanced by relating its goals and activities to some ultimate value widely shared in the society at large: social justice, equality, the building of a distinctive society, and the preservative of ancestral values. Thus the organization may come to be seen not only in terms of its immediate practical accomplishments but also in terms of its societal importance.

A board of directors consisting of prominent individuals, a distinguished person as honorary president or vice-president, distinguished political personalities as keynote speakers at banquets and conferences are among the symbolic ways to confirm the authority of the organization and raise its prestige.

Leaders of ethnic communities may not focus exclusively on the prestige of their organizations; they may be concerned as well with the image of their ethnic group and with the value given to ethnicity and ethnic affiliation in the society at large. The more multiculturalism becomes a mainstream value in the society, the more participation in ethnic associations would become a mainstream activity, like participation in any other type of association. Also, if leaders can demonstrate to members of the collectivity that their group has made a significant contribution to the development of society at large or that their group is connected with a nation with a glorious history, they may render the group socially more attractive and thus encourage identification with it and participation in it.

The participation of members in community affairs and in the realization of collective projects places a burden on leaders. Indeed, they not only have to mobilize the resources necessary for programs and projects but they also have to obtain the resources to motivate participation as well. They have to work on the goals of the organization, on the reasons for its existence and, indeed, on the reasons for the continued existence of an organized ethnic community. They have to find benefits they can provide to the members of their organization, benefits of some significance that would not be available to nonmembers.

The Impact of External Intervention on Participation

An organization of the larger society may have an interest in the participation of members of ethnic collectivities in its programs. The ethnic collectivity, then, is seen as a potential public or clientele. The external organization may seek to expand its domain by integrating members of ethnic collectivities within its sphere of activity and of influence. It may also seek to integrate or assimilate them in the larger society. This has been the case of labor unions (Avery, 1979), churches (Tomasi, 1975; Isajiw, 1979; Marunchak, 1970), and political parties.

The impact of such recruitment in pulling members of ethnic collectivities away from participation in the affairs of their own community has not been examined empirically. Several studies of acculturation have included items on community participation. But to what extent increased participation in organizations of the larger society is the result of active recruitment or of general forces of integration operating over time and generations is not known.

It is not, however, only through direct mobilization of members or clients that external organizations can affect participation in ethnic community affairs. By supplying the resources necessary for organizational functioning and activities, they can free leaders from the tasks of recruiting members and soliciting funds from the community. This may lead members to feel that their contribution is not essential.

This was the situation observed by Savas (1987) in the francophone community of British Columbia. First, it seems that instead of supplementing financial contributions from the community, government funding replaced them to a significant extent. Second, as already noted, government funding permitted the growth of a paid bureaurcracy that, to some extent, has replaced volunteers who appeared less willing to become involved in a "distant" bureaucratic federation. For a few, community spirit and participation lost some of its life when the federation's professional staff replaced local volunteers. To quote one activist: "Why do volunteer work when they're paid for it at the Federation?" A former federation president "went so far as to announce the death knoll of Franco-Columbian spirit; federal government financing, he stated, was maintaining a bureaucracy which no longer had the support of the community" (Savas, 1987:179). Savas also quotes the result of a survey of francophones outside of Quebec: twenty-five percent of respondents mentioned "the danger of loosing volunteers and of killing community initiative" as a disadvantage of government funding.

These results should not lead one to conclude that neglect by government and other societal institutions (a laissez-faire policy) would have a positive or neutral effect on community participation. An extreme situation is the "defeated neighborhood" that Suttles (1972:239) describes as suffering from two sources of weakness: "First, it is unable to participate fully in its own governance ... [in part because] it is so heavily stigmatized and outcast that its residents retreat from most forms of public participation out of shame, mutual fear, and an absence of faith in each other's collective concern" and second, because it is chosen "as a site for businesses and industries which have powerful interests that are simply antithetical to the aims of any residential group."[10]

The critical variables are sociopolitical; that is, they are those that characterize the relationship between local communities and the structures of power (Kapsis, 1978:1135). Communities vary in the extent of "effective linkages to the wider society" which, in turn, depend on the nature of policies that governmental and nongovernmental agencies establish in relation to local communities. For instance, Kapsis found that such sociopolitical variables are important in accounting for variations among black residential areas in their degree of anomie, a sense of despair and perceived normlessness. It would seem then that both the presence or absence and perhaps especially the type of policy intervention can affect the level of social participation in community affairs.

PARTICIPATION AND POLITICAL COMPETITION

Participation and Political Accommodation

Members constitute a resource for community organizations. They can provide legitimacy, money, moral support, time, and effort toward the pursuit of goals within the community or in relation to institutions of the larger society. On the other hand, the number of individuals who have the resources and motivation necessary to become active participants is limited. This is especially so if the organization requires that its members adopt a very distinctive ideological orientation. Leaders of organizations are likely to be in more or less intense competition for support because of the scarcity of potential members.

Political opponents deploy various kinds of strategies and tactics in order to mobilize support for their side and/or to divert it away from their opponents. For example, a strategy frequently used by different entrepreneurs and their associates is to claim that they are the only true representatives of the community. They question the right and/or the competence of their opponents to operate in a particular field of activity or to be spokesmen for the community (Tryggvason, 1971). Claiming to be a true representative of the group is a very sensitive matter since it pertains to the group's true identity and distinctive culture. Frequently, such conflicts are related to power struggles and events in the country of origin.

A related line of attack is leaders' attempts to demonstrate that their organization and activities are likely to be the most beneficial to the community. There are two kinds of possible advantages to this exercise: besides showing that one's organization is "better" for the community, the struggle for power and influence is less likely to appear as self-serving.

Financial contributions to community projects is a related strategy. Werbner (1985:369, 373) observes that "donations, made for culturally defined communal ends, constitute highly potent symbolic acts. When made competitively, they encode differentiation and hierarchy, and serve to increase individual power and influence. Through such public generosity, members of an elite establish their credentials as men of high status, and attempt to legitimize their claims to positions of leadership.... In self-interested terms, charitable benefaction can be seen as a strategy in seeking personal influence and prestige, by surpassing a rival in generosity and thus, in Levi-Strauss' words, 'taking from him privileges, titles, rank, authority, and prestige.' "

Werbner (1985) discusses a strategy of competition for public legitimation. John (1969:52–53), on the other hand, discusses one consisting of obligating individuals through personal favors: jobs, filling out forms, passport renewal, mortgages, and help in dealing with officials, real estate agents, doctors, and lawyers. "Giving such help is known among Indians as doing 'social work.'... Doing social work without charging creates a bond between the social workers and the client, so those who did the favours without charging become influential men in the immigrant settlements. When the time came for an... election, they could visit their former clients and be fairly confident of winning their support."[11]

Political opponents also attempt to use circumstances and situations to their advantage. Molotch and Lester (1974:102) present a framework for the analysis of this process. They distinguish between occurrences that are "any cognized happening" and events that are occurrences creatively used by individuals and groups pursuing particular purposes: "occurrences *become events* according to their usefulness to an individual" or to a group. Also, "to the degree to which individuals or collectivities have differing purposes, rooted in diverse biographies, statuses, cultures, class origins, and specific situations, they will have differing and sometimes competing uses for occurrences. An issue arises when there are at least two such competing uses, involving at least two parties having access to event-creating mechanisms. For public issues, these mechanisms are the mass media.... A struggle takes place over the nature of the occurrence, and embedded in that struggle are differing interests in an outcome" (103).

The leaders of competing subgroups, factions, and organizations are involved in such competition. They attempt, through press conferences or speeches, for example, to promote an occurrence, to make it a significant event, or to define it in a way that favors their position. Each side also tends to have their newspapers or news bulletins and their readers.

In order to win, competitors can also attempt to gain support from external agencies and their representatives such as a favorable report in the media, recognition by a government agency or official, privileged access to information, promises that a rival organization will not be recognized or supported, that it will be ignored by the media or given an unfavorable coverage, and so on.

Competition among organizations and leaders can be so intense as to discourage participation in the public affairs of the community—on any side. The ideological and emotional intensity of the opposition can reach very high levels. It can accordingly express itself in irrational arguments, that is through mutual denigration, accusations, and verbal abuse. This can turn off many individuals in the community. Tryggvason (1971) for example, observed in the community that he studied that bitter public fighting among the leaders was one of the factors that irritated many members and led them to withdraw because of the raging public disputes. This seems to have been the case as well in the nineteenth-century German community in Ontario. In his study of this community, Kalbfleisch (1968) mentions that the feuds between newspapers became so acrimonious and prolonged that individuals outside the press intervened because of the disastrous effects of these feuds for the community.

If competition is not acrimonious, it can encourage participation in community affairs. Enloe (1973) suggests that intracommunal subdivisions provide wider bases of identification and involvement and thus can stimulate participation among individuals of different social backgrounds. Conversely, a unified sociopolitical structure based on a more or less imposed consensus can discourage participation and commitment. The dynamic debate of issues, when perceived as ultimately constructive (or at least not destructive) could incite individuals to get involved.

Participation and Political Dominance

In so far as the operating forces in the political process are attempts by the elite to maintain its position of political ascendancy in the community, participation is a matter of obtaining compliance and deference. Elites want group participants to subscribe to their policies, at least passively; follow their plans or at least offer no resistance to their implementation; and show acceptance of their authority. Strategies for such purposes include limiting participation, ideological indoctrination, and the use of public rituals.

When the aim is the maintenance of political dominance, apathy among members of the collectivity is usually not perceived as a problem by the ruling group. On the contrary, it is a high level of involvement in the political process that is seen as potentially threatening. The complaints occasionally voiced about members' apathy tend to be rhetorical. Little is done to activate their interest and involvement, except when absolutely necessary. Tryggvason (1971) for example, indicates that in the ethnic community he studied, organizational elites complained about the apathy displayed by ordinary members but in private, among themselves. It is as if the occasional reference to membership apathy helped to justify the leaders' hegemony over community affairs.

In fact, the apathy of members may be the very result of the structure of decision-making of the organization. Sills (1957:20–21) indicates that "when authority and functions are delegated *upward* in an association, there is a tendency for the membership to lose interest in participating in the program of the organization." Knoke (1981:142) found evidence for the hypothesis "that members' commitment and detachment from the collectivity are strongly affected by the degree to which the organizational polity facilitates social control by members."[12] He argues that the polity may facilitate or inhibit "members' ability to gain effective influence over the direction of organizational affairs. The less conducive the structural opportunities are for exercising control, the less supportive and more cut off the members feel" (154).

In the Ethnic Pluralism Study, participation is somewhat related to the perception of the way decisions are made in the community (Table 6.4). Respondents who perceive decision-making as democratic are more likely to be members of associations, to participate at meetings, to feel close to

Table 6.4
Community Participation by Perception of Decision-Making

	Perception of community decision-making as having a democratic character			
	Little or not at all %	%	%	Very much %
1. Have membership in associations	27	32	31	48
2. Closeness to center of activities:				
Close	8	17	8	10
Intermediate	38	37	32	47
Distant	54	46	60	43
3. Participation at meetings:				
Frequently and occasionally	9	15	10	20
Seldom	20	18	25	27
Never	71	68	65	53
N	(270)	(153)	(215)	(110)

---

the center of activities than those who perceive the possibility of input as small or nil.

Lipset et al. (1956:11) note that leaders will often attempt to sustain the image of their organization as an administrative agency requiring specialized technical skills in order "to prevent 'interference' with the conduct of their job." Another argument leaders use is that unity and consensus are essential if the group is to present a common front in the face of external problems or opposition. Thus, participation is discouraged if it could bring about the expression of contradictory points of view. In the same vein, an elite may exaggerate external threats in order to obtain the continued acceptance of its rule, a change in leadership being presented as a danger to the welfare of the group.

Occasionally, however, controlled participation in public rituals may be sought and organized for the sake of legitimizing the structure of political power in the community. Rituals are used for the ceremonial display of the leadership and thus emphasize its authority and central role in the community. The public assertion of authority through rituals can also undermine actual or potential opposition to those in power (Lane, 1901; Lukes, 1975; Gusfield and Michalowicz, 1984).

CONCLUSION

For the ethnic polity attempting to cope with environmental circumstances, political participation is primarily a question of the mobilization of resources (money, time, effort, and commitment) for the attainment of collective goals. For competing organizations and their leaders, participation is a scarce resource. They accordingly deploy strategies to attract support for their points of view, their causes, and their organizations.

External bodies can also be competitors attempting to mobilize participation in their direction, away from ethnic organizations in the same field of activity. Authorities of societal institutions can also be interested in the level of participation in ethnic polities as a test of the representativeness of the current leadership, as a test of the legitimacy of certain demands expressed by individuals who claim to represent the community.

From the point of view of a dominant elite preoccupied with maintaining itself in power and in carrying out its own policy objectives, political participation is primarily a problem of obtaining compliance and preventing the political articulation of "unacceptable" demands. In this regard, dominant elites may not find political apathy a significant problem. Apathy may become a problem if their representativeness is systematically challenged. But in the normal course of events, it is not likely to be a preoccupation. It may not be as worthwhile as compliance with their aspirations; but it is something they can easily live with.

NOTES

1. This question is closely related to the perceived efficacy of the leadership discussed earlier.

2. The items read to the respondent were: "Complain directly to the boss or personnel manager" and "Say nothing, but work harder than the others so as to impress the boss."

3. The items read to the respondent were: "Get together with coworkers to complain to the boss" and "Deal with the situation by contacting a friend one happens to have in the company."

4. The items read to the respondent were: "Take the case to the union or employee association, if there is one in the company," "Take the case to a community agency like to Ontario Human Rights Commission whose purpose is to handle cases of discrimination," and "Take his case to an organization in his ethnic community."

5. For more details, see Breton et al. (1990:Ch. 5).

6. For an interesting review and analysis of empirical results on this question, see Moe (1980:Ch. 8).

7. See also Moe (1980), O'Brien (1975), Wilson (1973), Boudon (1977), and Kriesberg (1973).

8. "À la fois contre la volonté et par la volonté des acteurs." Boudon refers to such phenomena as "effets pervers."

9. The question referred to the ethnic identification of the respondent.

10. See also Clairmont and Magill (1976) and Stasiulis (1980).

11. For illustrations of competitive strategies, see Ramirez and Del Balzo, 1981.

12. This hypothesis was supported by the data on members of thirty-two non-economic associations in Indianapolis.

7

The Collective Identity: Definition and Maintenance

Ethnic communities are, at one level, symbolic objects with which individuals can identify (Cohen, 1985). The identification with a social entity generates a "consciousness of kind" among individual members; a sense of a common identity. A collective identity is essential for the very existence of a group or community (as opposed to an aggregate) as most definitions of an ethnic group underscore (Isajiw, 1974; McKay and Lewins, 1978). An awareness of sharing the same history, of being similarly affected by certain social, economic, and political conditions and therefore of having a common fate is a basic ingredient in the definition of group boundaries.

One of the requirements for the organization and conduct of collective action—economic, social, or political—is the sense among potential participants that they constitute a distinct social entity and that they have certain symbolic or material interests in common (Enloe, 1973). In other words, a collective identity is basic if an ethnic polity is to exist at all and if it is to function effectively. As Cohen (1985:70) points out, sociologists and social anthropologists have traditionally "concentrated on the structures and forms of community organization," and have somewhat neglected the analysis of the cultural underpinnings of these structures and forms, that is, the meaning they have for those who function in and through them. The analysis of collective identity constitutes an important element of the symbolic as opposed to the structural construction and functioning of community.

A collective identity, however, cannot be taken as a given or as emerging entirely spontaneously. It is a social construction more or less consciously shaped in relation to a variety of social, economic, and political conditions. It is the product of forces operating on the group and its members from within and of those impinging on them from without (Epstein, 1978). In addition, these forces can be either positive or negative; that is to say, they can reinforce or weaken the symbolic boundaries of the group.

At the individual level, membership in an ethnic category may be automatic by birth from parents of a particular ethnic origin,[1] but membership in an ethnic collectivity and community entails a degree of voluntariness,[2] which, of course, does not mean that it is not subject to the social pressures and constraints and the effects of socialization.[3] In other words, identification with and participation in a community are partly a matter of choice and strategy on the part of individuals as the considerable variation in the degree of identification and participation attests.[4] The point made by Elazar (1976) and by Petryshyn (1980) with regard to the Jewish and Ukranian collectivities respectively could be applied to most ethnic groups: "The elimination of visible external social differences between Ukranians and other Canadians has relieved some of the earlier constraints of identity affecting Ukranian Canadians. However, this has also made Ukranian-Canadian cultural life more voluntary, more atomized and less certain of survival and development" (Petryshyn, 1980:xiii).[5]

Similarly, at the collective level, the ethnic category can be constructed on the basis of "objective" criteria, but the community as an object of identification and as a locus of social participation cannot be taken as a given. Its formation entails elements of choice and strategy as does individual identity and behavior. If successful, the community will have meaning for individuals and pull them within its symbolic boundaries and its interpersonal and interorganizational networks. If, on the other hand, the community loses its symbolic power, it will be difficult for individuals to identify with it in any meaningful way. Having lost its attractiveness, its social boundaries are likely to progressively shrink and may even disappear.

The symbolic boundaries of a community are not defined once and for all: their molding and remolding go on continuously, whether in a planned or spontaneous fashion. Driedger (1988:24), among others, has noted that "identity is at all times in a process of formation, dynamic (not a once-and-for-all unchanging form), and struggling to find itself in the midst of other changes. The world is a changing mass of individuals, groups, communities, nations struggling for selfhood, for stable environments, for meaningful arenas which make sense, and for important ideals and goals."

It should be emphasized that what is at stake is collective, not individual, identity. In recent years, several studies have been carried out on the social psychology of ethnic identity: the maintenance or loss of identity among members of different ethnic groups, the resurgence of ethnic identity among third-generation individuals, and changes in the character or content of ethnic identities over time and generations.[6] As Smolicz (1981:85) points out, the "socio-psychological viewpoint is the one usually adopted by most writers in discussing ethnic identity." Relatively little research has been done on ethnic identity as a collective phenomena, although, as will be seen, the subject has not been entirely neglected.

Identity refers to self-conceptions and to self-evaluations. At the individual level, it refers to "the self as the object of one's knowledge, the thoughts one has about oneself—in other words, one's self-cognitions.... [T]hese deal with attributes which describe oneself;... which are distinctive to oneself; ...and which are essential for being oneself" (Aboud, 1981:37). At the collective level, it is the group that is the object of knowledge, evaluations, and perceptions. It is, accordingly, possible to refer to the collective identity of a community as a system of collective representations: a system of ideas, beliefs, evaluations, and symbols (Durkheim, 1898). These representations are collective in the sense that they express something about a group of people and in the sense that they exist independently of any one individual in the group. The collective identity, like the institutional order, "is experienced as an objective reality. It has a history that antedates the individual's birth and is not accessible to his biographical recollection" (Berger and Luckmann, 1966:60).

In a recent work on American racial ideology, Prager (1982:102) argues that racial ideologies should be seen as collective representations, as Durkheim has used the term. He points out that in the social psychological and structural explanations of race relations behavior, prejudice and discrimination have a pivotal role. They are based on "the intentional individual actor."[7] The concept of institutional racism, he suggests, has been formulated as a response to this overemphasis on the intentional actor. However, "if this brand of investigation served to reinstate a concern for social structure as independent from individuals, there has not emerged a complementary movement to free the cultural and ideational realm from the individualistic nexus of the prejudice and discrimination schools of thought" (Prager, 1982:107). Prager's argument is applicable, *mutatis mutandis*, to the analysis of ethnic identity. It is important to avoid individualistic perspectives and to approach ethnic identity as a system of collective representations, especially when the focus is the ethnic community qua community.[8]

It should also be noted that identity is not the same as social attachment to a group, or solidarity, although the two phenomena are related. As noted, identity refers to self-conceptions and self-knowledge. Attachments, on the other hand, refer to social affiliations, to relationships with other individuals or with groups and organizations. Individuals may have a cognitively rich sense of their ethnic identity but not be integrated in a network of ethnic relations and associations. At the collective level, identity refers to a set of ideas, beliefs, and knowledge about the group while solidarity or cohesion refers to the presence of relationships that hold the collectivity together. Commonly held knowledge about the history of one's group may serve to strengthen cohesion of the group but it is not the same as the pattern of relationships that members of the group have with each other.

The next part of the chapter examines some components of ethnic collective identity. This is followed by an analysis of the emergence, maintenance, and transformation of the community as a symbolic object. The four sets of processes used in the other parts of the book are used here: the relationship of the ethnic polity with its environment; the competition for political power, status, and influence within the community; the symbolic control exercised by the segment that has become politically ascendant in the community; and the intervention of external groups and organizations in the affairs of the ethnic community.

COMPONENTS OF COLLECTIVE IDENTITY

The content of collective representations can be classified in terms of three dimensions of community life: the character of the group ("who we are" and "who we are not"); the group's relationship with or position vis-a-vis other groups; and its place and role in the larger social environment, whether it be the local community, the region, the national society or the international system.[9]

The Character of the Group

The definition of the character of the group involves a selection of elements of history and culture that explains the group's origin, identity, and distinctiveness and justifies its existence (De Vos and Romanucci-Ross, 1975; Royce, 1982). The definition involves the designation of the values that are central to the group's identity. The core values "generally represent the heartland of the ideological system and act as identifying values which are symbolic of the group and its membership. . . . It is through core values that social groups can be identified as distinctive ethnic, religious, scientific or other cultural communities" (Smolicz, 1981:75). The core values are those that are defined by the group and its cultural elites as essential if the group is to continue to be itself.

In addition, the collective identity will usually contain components revealing the group's view of its past, its perceptions of the present, and its image of what its future is likely to be. The community's perspective on historical events "is not neutral or without purpose. It is the shared heritage of past events. It encourages group members to find common cause and reinforce loyalties. It bonds individuals to the group and gives the group a sense of continuity with the past and a shared stake in the future. It is built into our culture, its rituals and celebrations" (Troper and Weinfeld, 1988:xvi).

In his analysis of local urban cultures, Suttles (1984:288) identifies three sets of collective representations: (1) the community's founders or "discoverers"; (2) the "notable entrepreneurs and those political leaders who, by hook or crook, are thought to have added to the community's 'spirit' or 'greatness' "; and (3) "a host of catch phrases, songs, and physical artifacts which represent the 'character' of the place."

Collective representations defining the character of a group also include ideals, that is views as to what the group should be, the standards by which the group evaluates itself, its corporate actions, and its evolution as a community. Thus the collective identity does not consist only of self-perceptions and knowledge; it is also based on self-evaluations. These, of course, can be positive or negative. On the one hand, self-perceptions can be couched in a language of approval. They can serve to glorify the groups and its achievements. They can express a sense of superiority in relation to other groups, a self-conception frequently infused with a religiously inspired sense of a mission. For example, Berger (1970:99) observes that "the loyalist tradition began, as did all myths of national origins, with the assertion that the founders of British Canada were God's chosen people.... The original United Empire Loyalists were portrayed as a superior, cultured and elevated class of men.... One of the most distinctive features of the imperialist mind was the tendency to infuse religious emotion into secular purposes. The contention that the British Empire was a providential agency, the greatest secular instrument for good in the world, was a widely held conviction among imperialists" (217).

On the other hand, a group may be critical of itself. It may denigrate and reject certain of its cultural traits, parts of its history, or features of its socioeconomic performance. Outright self-rejection may be fairly rare, but groups frequently experience considerable ambivalence with regard to one or another aspect of the groups social organization or activities. A sense of inferiority (in some regards) is not an infrequent aspect of the self-conception of ethnic minorities and it can coexist with positive perceptions within the same collectivity. It has been suggested, for example, that one of the differences between Independentists and Federalists in Quebec during the 1960s and 1970s pertained to the factors to which they attributed the problems experienced by French Québécois. The ideology of the first tended to emphasize English dominance as the critical factor, while the other faction's ideology stressed the dominance of the clergy and negative features of the traditional culture and social structure.

Such negative representations, however, may be fairly rare or, if they exist, may be played down by group members and their elites. They may be articulated only by subgroups who are or feel marginal to the ongoing affairs of the community. This is not surprising: the mobilization of social, cultural, and political participation is possible only if the community is perceived as a positive object of identification.

Lopata (1964:122), for example, has observed that in American Polonia, the educational programs for the youth "stressed those aspects of the national or Polish-American culture which deal with literary and artistic achievements and especially with contributions to world or American culture. The purpose behind this selective education is to make the youth 'proud of their heritage.' " In the community studied by Tryggvason (1971:95), the ethnic language was among the main elements of culture selected by the leaders of community associations as "worthy of preservation in a formal setting." In the case of urban cultures, Suttles (1984:293) found that civic failure or unresolved class conflict were infrequent in the collective representations of cities. Rather, these drew attention to the fact that "some form of capitalism had succeeded" and had contributed positively to the quality of urban life.

Conceptions Pertaining to Relationships with Other Groups

The collective identity of a group is partly shaped in contrast with other groups. "We know who we are by knowing who we are not.... How one learns about oneself by contrasting oneself to other individuals and groups is important, for only in this way does one develop a strong sense of self" (De Vos and Romanucci-Ross, 1975:368). Of course, not all other ethnic groups are equally important in this social comparison process. In fact, some are even irrelevant for a particular ethnic collectivity while others play a central role in the identity definition of the collectivity. They are, so to speak, "significant others" or reference groups for a collectivity (Mead, 1934; Merton, 1957). As a result, certain similarities and differences with those target groups become part of the collective self-conception of the group.

Collective self-conceptions or representations frequently derive from the nature of a group's relationship with other groups and not only from intergroup comparison along cultural, political, economic, or other lines. For instance, a group can represent itself as being a friend or ally of particular groups. It can see itself as having common interests with them. On the other hand, it can perceive itself as threatened in its survival or in its economic and political interests by specific groups or by the social environment generally. It can sense itself as being dominated and oppressed by other groups or dependent on them.

In a conflictual relationship, the groups may give opposite value to historical events and actors. Troper and Weinfeld (1988:4–5) provide a vivid illustration in their observations on the seventeenth-century uprising— "events that remain part of the proximate history of both Ukranians and Jews." They write that "for some Ukranians and Jews the legacy of inherited mistrust continues—Jews were exploiters of the Ukranian people, forever allied with those suppressing the Ukranian national cause; Ukranians were anti-Semites needing little or no encouragement to turn on peaceful Jewish men, women and children in a frenzy of blood lust. Khmelnytsky was either a visionary Ukranian nationalist or a blackguard pogromist."

A group can see itself as a minority dominated by another group. Conversely, it can see itself as a majority—as the group that controls and ought to control the resources and institutions of the society, as the group others should accommodate.[10] Such groups sometimes have a Darwinist self-conception: they see themselves as culturally, economically, (if not biologically) the "fittest" and therefore, as having a legitimate right—indeed, even a responsibility—to rule (Hofstadter, 1955).

The process of defining the group's character and assessing its relationship with others implicitly or explicitly defines the criteria of membership and nonmembership. Through the identity formation processes, principles of inclusion and of exclusion are established. As noted earlier, the collective representations pertaining to a group's identity exist independently of any one individual. Thus individuals cannot arbitrarily decide to become part of an ethnic collectivity and be accepted as such. They must be able to demonstrate conformity to what is considered to be the core elements of the group's character, to show an authentic sharing of the group's symbols and ritualistic meanings, and to establish a legitimate claim to the group's name. It is also necessary for individuals to persuade members of the group that they are "on the right side of the fence" as far as the critical intergroup relationships are concerned. Failing this, they will be considered marginal to the group or outsiders.

Conception of the Group's Place and Role in Society

Collective self-conceptions tend to have a significant historical dimension as well as an orientation toward the future: the place occupied in the social order, on the one hand; the place and role aspired to, on the other. Suttles (1972:255–56) mentions that urban communities can "lay claim to a more or less rich historic legacy which is valued by some of its residents and incommensurate with the history of other communities." The potential for such claims vary among communities as they differ "in their historical impoverishment and their ability to lay claims to themselves as a cradle for important men, events, and accomplishments."

The potential provided by actual circumstances for the historical grounding of identity varies from one ethnic group to another. Indeed, communities vary in the length and richness of their history in the society. The time of their initial settlement in the country may not have allowed them to be present when critical nation-building events or crises were taking place. They also vary in demographic weight, which is far from being an insignificant factor in relation to a collectivity's conception of its place and role in society.

Historically based collective representations depend not only on past events and circumstances but on the process of selection and reconstitution that goes on in the community. The selection is usually such as to highlight the positive role of the group in the formation of the society. Attempts are made to have the group recognized as a "founding people," at least with regard to a particular region of the country. Similarly, the selection of events may be made to underscore the group's economic, cultural, artistic, scientific, technological, and political contribution.

Positive evaluations of one's group may be encouraged, but negative characterizations may be systematically rejected. Fernandez (1979) points out that arguments are put forward by members of the community rejecting the view that the Portuguese are newcomers in Canada by pointing to the explorations of eastern Canada by Portuguese before the French and the English. Other arguments emphasize that, with the exceptions of the native peoples, all are intruders in Canada, and therefore, all have an equal societal status.

The collective identity may also include ideas concerning the future place and role of the group in the society. Some groups may simply aspire toward the continuation of what has become historically established and accepted. Others may see their relationship with the society and its institutions as quite different from the existing one. Perhaps one of the most striking examples of such a change in Canada is to be found among native peoples, with their self-conception as nations that should have the institutional means to govern themselves. The self-government aspirations clearly indicate a new conception of their place in Canadian society (Little Bear et al., 1984; Watkins, 1977).

It is not only the national community that is relevant for a group's perception and evaluation of itself. The international community can also be quite significant for certain groups. The Solidarity movement in Poland seems to have had an impact on the members of Polonia and their conception of themselves. Several authors have noted the importance of Israel and of events in the Middle East for Jewish communities and their conception of their historical role.[11] Several other groups influenced by the international community could be noted: the Germans, Armenians, Japanese, Italians, and so on.

MANIFESTATIONS OF THE COLLECTIVE IDENTITY

There are different ways in which the elements of the collective identity manifest themselves or are expressed. By themselves, ideas, beliefs, and values are not sufficient to form an identity. In order to represent the group and its core features, they need to be embedded in and conveyed through social forms that will recurrently affirm, evoke, and reinforce them (Durkheim, 1912). Otherwise they weaken. They tend to become pure abstractions, dead letters that have no meaning in the life of individuals and institutions. They lose their inspirational value, thus depriving individuals and institutions of an important source of social energy. Klapp (1969:118) warns "against the assumption that most—perhaps any—institution can be stripped of ritual, streamlined to mechanical efficiency without doing harm both to the participants and society-at-large." It is indeed through symbols and rituals that "the society reaffirms the moral values which constitute it as a society and renews its devotion to those values" (Shils and Young, 1953:67). And because ethnic identities are, by their very nature, communal experiences, it is also through them "that one of these values, the virtue of social unity or solidarity, is acknowledged and strengthened" (Shils and Young, 1953:72).

Rituals and symbols have their impact in joining values and ideas with sentiments and emotions.[12] Rituals have an ideological and a sensory pole. "The norms, values, principles and rules at the ideological pole are abstract and remote and their mere perception by the person is not sufficient to induce him to action. It is only when the person is emotionally agitated by the sensory pole of the symbol that he will be moved to action" (Cohen, 1977:121).

Symbols, rituals, ceremonies, and explicit verbal statements are the main channels for the expression of collective representations. Religious festivals and rituals can be powerful expressions and, as Migliore (1988) shows, they can play an important role in the maintenance of the ethnic identity by bringing to consciousness images and meanings of the culture of origin.

"Names seem to be the simplest, most literal, and most obvious of all symbols of identity.... The matter of names keeps turning up in one form or another in all the ongoing rediscoveries, revisions, remakings, and reassertions of group identity now taking place all around us. It is clear that quite by itself the name of individual, of group, of nation, of race—carries a heavy freight of meaning" (Isaacs, 1975:46, 48). Changes in names illustrate very well the potency of that symbol to evoke a new identity: from French Canadian to Québécois, from Negro to black, from Eskimo to Inuit, from racial groups to visible minorities.

The lack of a subjectively adequate name for a group can be a source of "symbolic anxiety" or frustration. For example, the terms *other ethnic groups* or *the third force* are not a powerful symbol of group identification, to say the least. *Immigrant groups* is not suitable for groups that include a significant proportion of native Canadians. Another example of a name problem is the negative self-definition of the appellation "Francophone hors Québec." This is not an emotion-arousing name. The community finds it unsatisfactory and, occasionally, the association bearing that name expresses the need for a name with positive connotations (and has at one point undertaken a search for one).

In addition to names, various kinds of objects can be used as group emblems: flags, buildings, monuments, books and special documents, dress, flowers, and artifacts. Historical persons and events can be seen as incorporating core aspects of the group identity. Musical themes, songs, and anthems can also perform that function. Group identity is also expressed in rituals and ceremonies: celebration of national holidays, religious ceremonies, sports events, and annual festivals.

There are also verbal expressions of what the group is and aspires to be.

These can be at least as important, if not more so, than the various kinds of symbols. Smith (1969:188) notes that one of the major differences between modern and primitive society is not "the acceptance or rejection of symbols as sanctifying instruments in political life, but simply the forms of symbols commonly employed. Modern emphasis is on verbal symbols, written and spoken and usually organized into a sophisticated pattern of great complexity which we call a political philosophy or ideology." That is, the system of beliefs, ideas, and evaluations that a group holds about itself may be explicitly formulated in various propositions.These may even be systematically organized in a theory or doctrine about the group, its differences from and relationship with other groups, and its role in the national and/ or world society.[13] Zionism is an example of such a system of ideas as are most nationalistic ideologies or doctrines that formulate a group's particular mission in society or in relation to its country of origin.

From one group to another or from one period of time to another, collective representations can vary in their degree of development. They can be rich or poor in meanings. The repertoire of symbols and rituals available to a community may be more or less elaborate. Klapp (1964:317), among others, argues that contemporary Western societies show a certain degree of symbolic poverty that is not a lack of factual information but a lack of the "kinds of symbols which make a person's life meaningful." This poverty is at the basis of the "identity seeking movements of modern society." The source of identity problems is not the individual but the symbolic cultural system that, because of its inadequacies, "makes it harder for individuals to define themselves satisfactorily" (Klapp, 1964:140). Closely related to the notion of symbolic underdevelopment is the notion of symbolic confusion or disorganization. Such a condition in society generates "ambiguity in self-image, confusion in customary ways of living, and incapacity of inventing (collective) projects, all of which can be equated with anomic and social alienation" (Tremblay, 1984:9).

Variations can also be observed in the extent to which symbols, rituals, and ceremonies are used in the public life of the community. In Western society, if anything, symbols and rituals are underused. Shils and Young (1953) have attributed the underuse of and even resistance to rituals to an intellectual bias among elites. Bourdieu (1975) relates it to the *économisme* that pervades the private and public discourse. Klapp (1969) sees the source of this resistance in the bureaucratic and technological culture that pervades contemporary societies.

Ethnic communities are not immune to the impact of these society-wide phenomena. There are, however, other factors and processes bringing about variations in the content of ethnic collective identities and in the forms that express them, in the extent to which these forms are used. The remainder of this chapter explores some of these factors and processes.

SOCIAL FORCES SHAPING THE COLLECTIVE IDENTITY

Identity and the Sociopolitical Environment

A group's conception and evaluation of itself as a sociopolitical and cultural entity and of itself in relation to other significant groups and to the larger society can be seen as part of the adaptive or coping potential of the community in relation to its environment. It can be seen as one of the elements of the group's culture conceived "as a 'tool kit' of symbols, stories, rituals, and world-views, which people may use in varying configurations to solve different kinds of problems" (Swidler, 1986:273).There is a dynamic interaction between the environmental conditions and the problems a group has to cope with and the cultural elements and self-conceptions from which it constructs strategies of action. The group's self-conceptions shape its coping strategies, but, in turn, problems, especially enduring ones, shape the ways in which the group thinks of itself and of its place in society.

Also, changes in collective self-conceptions and evaluations should be analyzed in relation to the transformations taking place in the group's historical experience, which, in turn, are brought about by changes in its economic, political, or sociocultural context. In an interesting application of Berger's concepts of nomos-building and social construction of reality to ethnic groups in the prairies, Driedger (1980) focuses on the changes that groups (the native Indians, the Hutterites, and the Jews) had to undertake as their historical experience was transformed: "As food gathering people, the prairie Indians were faced with a complete reconstruction of their sacred canopy, when they were forced from the open plains into reserves. The Hutterites, as food producing agriculturalists literally transferred their communal society from Europe to the North American prairies with its ideology and structure intact. The Jews represent yet another form of change, when they transformed their east European shtetl ghettos into segregated urban communities" (1980:343).

A new world had to be constructed by these groups in order to give meaning to their new experience and social contexts. A socially constructed world is "an ordering of experience, onto a meaningful order, or *nomos*, which is imposed upon the discrete experiences and meanings of individuals" (Berger, 1967:19). The new arrangements that had to be created so as to generate "order for individuals and groups so that life makes sense" include ideology, community, culture, and territory (Driedger, 1980:353). In terms of the framework used in this chapter, the community is defined by a system of ideas concerning the bases on which the group is constituted, its distinctiveness, and its place in the larger social and historical order.

The impact of the environment on the collective identity occurs, in part, through spontaneous social processes and, in part, through the conscious, more or less systematic, interventions by particular individuals and groups in the community.

The collective identity is spontaneously generated through the interaction among individual members of a collectivity as they attempt to assure their survival and well-being and that of those to whom their own existence is tied. It is the outcome of the complex interaction of everyday life. It emerges from the sharing among members of a group of their ideas and feelings, their definitions of situations, and their perceptions and interpretations of various events. It also derives from the actions undertaken in relation to those situations.

Relevant circumstances and events are those that take place outside as well as within the collectivity. The shift among immigrants from Italy from an identity based primarily on the village or province to an Italian national view of themselves is the outcome of such processes. "Italian identity and inter-*paese* contact grew slowly as a result of proximity and shared experience in Canada" (Harney, 1981:44). The wider identity was promoted by merchants and newspaper editors who saw an advantage in attracting customers or readers beyond their hometown, a situation that consumers and readers themselves perceived as advantageous (Zucchi, 1980). It was also stimulated by the formation of national parishes and of formal associations organized by Italians generally, rather than by particular villages or *paese*. The formation of organizations encompassing subethnic groups was in part due to the fact that people from individual *paese* were not numerous enough to form their own.

Contacts with members of other ethnic groups and with societal institutions also fostered the emergence of a more-encompassing identity. Such contacts occurred directly through interactions with representatives or agents of those institutions or with other individuals or indirectly through the media. At a very fundamental level, people from different hometowns soon realized that they all faced the same conditions in the new country; intergroup differences were submerged by the common problems of acculturation: "Contact with the strange surroundings emphasized to the immigrant his kinship with those fellow-Italians in the new land who, regardless of their provincial origin, were in many ways like him" (Parenti, 1975:34).

Ware (1940:63) points out that the teaching of American patriotism and national consciousness has provided to immigrant groups such as the Italians "terms in which to think of national identifications and allegiances." She also observes that newcomers are constantly reminded of their national origin through the "many occasions in which persons are made to identify themselves by their national origin—as in filling out forms for social agencies or employment applications."

Among the important phenomena affecting the collective identity of a group are the changes in the composition of its own population due to factors such as the arrival of new waves of immigrants, the emergence and eventual predominance of second and subsequent generations, and the upward mobility of significant proportions of the members of the collectivity.

Kelebay (1980), for example, describes the first wave of Ukranian immigrants as concerned with social and economic injustices in their native land as well as in their society of adoption. It could be said that they thought of themselves primarily as constituting a social class. The second wave of immigrants was primarily nationalist in orientation: they were patriots aspiring to a sovereign Ukranian nation-state. They conceived of themselves in terms of the role they could play in relation to this national project. The third wave to arrive after World War II were also nationalists. Their views differed from those of the previous wave on specific points, such as strategies and tactics to be pursued with regard to the liberation of Ukraine.

Generational changes and the acculturation that almost inevitably comes with them are perhaps the most crucial factors in bringing about transformations in the group's collective identity (Reitz, 1974, 1980). First, the group ceases to be an "immigrant group"; its self-conception is that of a national ethnic group. Second, and most important, for the second generation, the ethnic background cannot mean the same thing as it does for the first since their life experiences differ in almost every respect.

The shift of identity has been described as one from a "behavioral" to a "symbolic" ethnicity (Gans, 1979; Driedger, 1977; Weinfeld, 1981). Successive generations become increasingly acculturated since their experience is almost totally within institutions and social contexts outside the boundaries of their own ethnic collectivity.[14] As a result, "People are less and less interested in their ethnic cultures and organizations—both sacred and secular—and are instead more concerned with maintaining their ethnic identity, with the feeling of being Jewish, or Italian, or Polish, and with finding ways of feeling and expressing that identity in suitable ways" (Gans, 1979:7).

In short, the group's conception of itself and of its social condition is, in a way, a sort of distillation of the members' experience in a particular environment. Through the interactions of an ongoing social life, conceptions concerning the group itself, its past and present experience, and its expected and/or desired future emerge as a shared mental production or cognitive baggage in the group.

Spontaneous processes of collective identity formation and evolution may predominate in fairly small groups. When the group is large, however, other processes may be more important. (It is a question of relative importance, not of mutual exclusiveness.) That is, the group's background and historical experience may not be automatically incorporated in the collective self-conceptions. A more deliberate and somewhat specialized reflection on the group and its experience is required. Thus, the ideas, beliefs, and evaluations that constitute the collective identity are the result of analyses carried out by social thinkers in the group. They are disseminated and used for collective mobilization by cultural entrepreneurs.[15]

Kordan (1985:27) suggests that the promotion of an ethnic collective identity becomes part of the political calculus of the intelligentsia when ethnic discrimination and conflict acquires a personal meaning for them. "As marginal men existing outside of the Canadian social structure—and here the reference is not to the intellectual as a political agent but as an ethnic himself—they soon came to recognize the restricted nature of their socio-historical role. They also came to appreciate that the fortune of the group, both past and present, was their history and likewise their future." Thus, a symbiotic relationship develops between the ethnic group and the intelligentsia: "The ethnic group was being given historical meaning and legitimacy, while the historical role and, to a certain extent, the social needs of the intelligentsia were being fulfilled" (Kordan, 1985:28).

The construction of a collective identity by the community's intelligentsia tends to include reconstitutions of the group's past experience, a definition of its distinctiveness, a diagnosis of its current predicaments, and the formulation of "theories" to explain both the positive and undesirable features of the current situation. The analysts select elements from the group's background and history and give them meaning in relation to its current situation. Certain elements are "primordialized" in relation to the circumstances perceived or defined as significant to the group. Nagata (1981:95) notes that it is in these circumstances "that we must seek the interests and issues that create, activate, sustain and perpetuate the loyalties and sentiments that are subsequently rationalized by a primordial charter. To this end, existing identities may be selected or resurrected, or new ones generated. The social category or group that is salient for a given interest will be identified by those primordial(ized) characteristics that most effectively differentiate them from the significant oppositional categories in connection with that particular issue.... The social situation is thus a critical variable that provides the setting in which primordiality is defined and is meaningful." The social thinkers of the community propose to the group interpretations of the social, economic, and political environment; identify significant issues; and define responses appropriate in terms of the group's survival, well-being, and position in society.

The relationship between identity and environment is a dialectical one: the identity is shaped by the group's experience in a particular social, economic, and political context but, at the same time, that experience includes attempts to fashion or modify the context in terms of the conceptions held by the group about itself and about its place in that context. It is useful, in this regard, to consider Geertz's (1966) distinction between models of and models for social reality. The process of collective identity formation and evolution include both of these dimensions of modeling. On the one hand, the identity is a model *of* the group's character and of its relations with the rest of society; but, on the other, it is a model *for* the group's character and the context in which it lives. Geertz (1966:78) points out that "unlike genes, and other non-symbolic information sources, which are only models *for*, not models *of*, culture patterns have an intrinsic double aspect: they give meaning, i.e. objective conceptual form, to social and psychological reality both by shaping themselves to it and by shaping it to themselves."

An analysis and interpretation of the group's internal social and historical life and of its relationship to other groups and societal institutions requires more or less explicit and systematic knowledge about the group itself and its experience. In concluding his analysis of Korean Americans, Hurh (1980:456–457) argues that the emergence of a Korean-American ethnic identity is the result of processes that "can be boiled down to the problem of the positive resolution of the immigrant's marginality." This, however, "requires intensive self-reflection. ... What immigrants need is objective knowledge about themselves. For instance, what are the positive aspects of the Korean national character in comparison to the Chinese and Japanese? How have Korean immigrants been presenting themselves to Americans? What would be a general image of Koreans for the average American?"

All ethnic groups do not devote the same attention and the same amount of resources to such self-reflection and to the accumulation of objective knowledge relevant for the definition of their collective identity and for the resolution of the identity problems posed by their marginality or other aspects of their relationship to the societal environment. As mentioned earlier, groups vary as to the amount of resources they devote to the collection of information on their history and culture (and other aspects of the group's life).

The sense that a group has of itself, however, is affected by several circumstances and events beyond the control of its leadership. For instance, one would expect the demographic situation of the group—its size, both in absolute terms and relative to the larger society, the extent of its geographic concentration or dispersion, the ratio of immigrants to earlier generations in the group, and its class composition—to have an impact on its identity as a group.

Equally, if not more important, is the experience both past and present of the group in the larger society. Whether in the economic, political, or sociocultural field, this experience is likely to shape a group's view of itself. Stereotyping and discrimination by members of the larger society were frequently the main forces underlying the emergence of an ethnic consciousness. Several researchers have observed that majority group bigotry is a major generator of minority group "consciousness of kind" and sense of a common fate. Much has indeed been written on the impact of discrimination on the self-images of members of ethnic minorities, especially the collective sense of efficacy—a critical dimension in connection with the capacity to deal with environmental circumstances and problems.

Parenti (1975) mentions discrimination as the most important factor in the rise of a collective identity among Italians. In the case of Ukranians, Kordan (1985:26–27) points out that, initially for the intelligentsia, the national question did not enter the political equation as an independent factor. It was there, but part of the broader issue of class struggle and social emancipation. "As long as it was seen to be on the periphery, the question of promoting a distinct collective identity as a means of achieving political consciousness was given secondary consideration. Ethnic mobilization, however, became necessary as growing nativism provided for its rationale."[16]

In addition to the experience in the society of adoption, the situation of the country of origin in the international arena also has an influence. In fact, the two can be closely related as the experience of groups such as the Chinese, Japanese, Germans, and Italians indicate. The experience of these groups also reveals that the international standing of the country of origin can have both positive and negative impacts at different points in time: the Japanese during World War II and in the contemporary period of great technological and economic achievements; the Italians in the first phase of the Mussolini era and after Italy attacked Britain in Ethiopia (Harney, 1979; Diggins, 1972; Nelli, 1970); the Chinese before and after their contribution to the war effort and China's own war against Japan (Wickberg, 1981).

Thus, the experience of a group in the society of adoption is not independent of what happens in the country of origin and of the relationship between the two countries. Kwong (1979), among others, has argued that there is a hierarchy among nations, and that there is a close correspondence between a group's treatment in the country of adoption and of its collective self-image and the international standing of the group's homeland.

Blumer's (1958:6) argument about the role of "big events" in shaping interethnic attitudes is also applicable to the development of collective conceptions in minority groups:

The happening that seems momentous, that touches deep sentiments, that seems to raise fundamental questions about relations, and that awakens strong feelings of identification with one's racial group is the kind of event that is central in the formation of the racial image. Here, again, we note the relative unimportance of the huge bulk of experiences coming from daily contact with individuals of the subordinate group. It is the events seemingly loaded with great collective significance that are the focal points of public discussion. The definition of these events is chiefly responsible for the development of a racial image and of the sense of group position.

Although Blumer's language is primarily in terms of the images of the subordinate group held by the dominant one, his notion of the "sense of group position" clearly implies that "big events" are important in relation to the images that both dominant and subordinate groups hold about themselves.

The degree and nature of social and political recognition given to a group by societal institutions and their authorities also communicate significant messages about its character and especially about its status and role in the society. It is in this regard that the Canadian government's multiculturalism policy has its main significance. It was an attempt to redefine the symbolic systems in such a way that public institutions would incorporate more than in the past the non-British, non-French element of the society. It was also an attempt to manage the allocation of public status and recognition among the various ethnocultural components of the population (Breton 1984). Because of a lack of evidence, it is impossible to assess the impact of the policy on the group's self-conceptions.

Variations in the amount of identity-relevant conditions also need to be taken into consideration in group identity formation. Social environments are not equally rich (or poor) in identity defining, sustaining, or transforming events and circumstances, whether these be positive or negative. Thus, some groups may be exposed to very few situations that incite or force them to assert certain aspects of their identity or to redefine their self-conceptions. The system of ideas or beliefs of a group may say little about its place or role in the larger society; but that may be because few or no events occur on the international, national, or local scene that raise identity-related questions for them. Thus no debate and collective soul-searching takes place in the community. Other groups, in contrast, are regularly exposed to events and circumstances that remind them of who they are and of their place in society.

In addition, the number of identity-related events of significance to a particular group may vary over time. There can be periods of "abundance" and periods of "scarcity" of such events. In short, some groups may almost never experience situations that trigger processes of self-evaluation, assertion, or redefinition; others are confronted with such circumstances on a regular basis; and others encounter them only sporadically. Classifying groups in terms of their exposure to identity-generating events and circumstances would be a very impressionistic endeavor. Yet, on the basis of casual observation, one senses that some groups are clearly more frequently confronted with conditions that remind them of aspects of their identity while others are rarely so confronted. For example, few people would object to the following ranking in this regard, at least as far as the last few decades are concerned (from the most to the least exposed): Jewish, West Indian, Chinese, Ukranian, Italian, Portuguese, and German.[17]

External Definition of the Collective Identity

Members of other ethnic groups, especially of the dominant group, may have an interest in the way particular ethnic groups conceive of themselves and of their place in society. Definitions and redefinitions by an ethnic group of its collective identity may have implications for other groups' self-images and self-evaluations. It may disturb their theories as to who they are and as to the position they and other groups ought to occupy in society. Institutional authorities will also be concerned with the collective representations of ethnocultural groups because they may have implications for the cultural management involved in the functioning of institutions. If an ethnic group, for example, significantly changes its ideas about itself and its place in society, societal institutions may be challenged in their own identities and ways of functioning.

There are at least three main ways in which external groups and agents can contribute to shaping the collective identity of an ethnic group. First, they can intervene in the identity formation or transformation process. Such intervention may be more or less deliberate, direct or indirect. Second, ethnic groups usually form their own conceptions and evaluations about the character of other groups and about their place in the society. Such conceptions and evaluations may be actively propagated through informal (interpersonal networks in neighborhoods, schools, workplace, and various associations) or formal channels (mass media, textbooks, speeches, public documents, and so on). Even if they are negative, those conceptions and evaluations may become progressively integrated in the system of ideas of the target group. Finally, external publics and institutions can accept or reject the conceptions and evaluations that ethnic groups have of themselves. By validating—or refusing to validate—a group's view of itself, external publics can have a considerable influence on the group's identity, sometimes reinforcing it, sometimes weakening it.

Intervention, propagation, and validation by external groups and organizations can occur through a wide range of social activities. Perhaps the most basic of these is the one that consists in the naming of the group (Isaacs, 1975) and its characterization through stereotypes, either positive or negative. As indicated earlier, groups name themselves, but they are also given names by other groups or in the official terminology of governments or other societal institutions. Names such as "anglophone," "francophone" and "visible minorities" become part of the common language largely because they have been integrated in the official terminology. With regard to Hispanics in the United States and whether they constitute "a discreet ethnic group that overarched earlier ethnic references such as Chicano, Puerto Rican, and Cuban," Enloe (1981:134) suggests that "if there is even a hint of such an ethnic group evaluation it is in no small part the result of state categorization practices."

Through public policy debates about ethnicity, race, and language in general, or about particular groups (or categories of groups), certain characteristics are usually identified and given social importance while others are not. Such debates are, for instance, about what really constitutes the essence of ethnicity: what is distinctive about particular groups, how essential language is to ethnicity, what the realistic possibilities of multiculturalism as policy are, and so on. The discourse of public authorities and of social analysts on these questions sends messages to the various groups about the kind of group they are and about what their place in society is or ought to be. Of course, the messages conveyed may not be accepted by the groups affected, and as a result some sort of confrontation and symbolic bargaining may take place.

There may be, on the other hand, concordance between the set of ideas promulgated by public authorities and those promoted by the political and cultural elite of ethnic communities. In such cases, the official position validates, so to speak, the views a group holds about itself (and vice versa) (Clammer, 1982). In Harney's analysis of the different definitions of the group's ethnicity competing for legitimacy in the Italian community, he observed that one view consisted in seeing immigrants as contributors to Canadian society and in terms of the aptitude with which they adjust to Canadian ways. This view, according to Harney, "derives ultimately from Canadian authorities, though its agents were and are often the children of immigrants themselves turned into cultural bureaucrats and school teachers" (1985:22).

The role that official languages minorities (i.e., the French outside of Quebec and the English in Quebec) were assigned by the federal government in the implementation of its policy objectives also had a significant impact on the conception these communities have of themselves and of the role they play in the Canadian polity at large. Giving communities a special role in the maintenance and strengthening of national unity changed the perception they traditionally had of their own social and political status. From purely local entities, they became communities whose existence and role had national significance.

Attempts on the part of a majority group to assimilate a minority are also likely to have an impact on the latter's collective identity. The impact may be in the opposite direction of what was intended, but it nevertheless contributes to shape the group's self-conceptions. Some assimilation strategies are aimed exclusively at individuals; but some are oriented to the group as a whole. In other words, the conceptions of the assimilationists transform the discourse that elites hold about the group because the elites either adopt or integrate those conceptions or reject them and reaffirm counterdefinitions of the group's identity. Ethnic elites become either co-opted by the assimilating groups and institutional authorities or they enter into a more or less intense conflict with them over the definition of the group's collective views of itself.

It should be noted that groups that are new to society may be particularly vulnerable to external assimilationist strategies. The reason for this vulnerability is that, being in a state of transition or social reconstruction, their own collective identity in the new context is also in the process of being formulated and crystallized. Being new to a societal context is not the only source of symbolic vulnerability of groups. The case of native peoples in North America illustrates in a striking way another source of vulnerability. As a result of geographical and social dislocation, their communities experienced severe disorganization that manifested itself at the symbolic as well as at other levels.

The strategies of social control of ethnic groups frequently entail attempts to affect their own self-conceptions. It is part of the "mobilization of bias" discussed earlier in relation to the strategies used by ethnic elites within their own communities. One of the main strategies available to external agents in this connection is the co-optation of minority group leaders. It is a sort of "symbolic indirect rule": elites of the dominant groups rely on minority elites to shape or reshape the system of ideas prevailing in the minority about itself and its place in society.

Finally, external groups and authorities that support the efforts of a group to mobilize and organize themselves in order to bring about change in their situation can also influence the content of the group's collective identity. Their symbolic role may be primarily in validating the new ideas emerging in the group about itself and its societal situation. But external groups may also be the source of new ideas that become adopted by the minority.

Identity and the Accommodation of Symbolic Interests

The processes of collective identity formation and evolution discussed in the previous section are those pertaining to the relationship between the collectivity and its social environment. Environmental conditions can be accepted by members of an ethnic group and progressively become part of their ethnic consciousness. In such situations, the symbolic system through which the individuals represent their community to themselves are simultaneously an indication of the community's integration and a means for building or reinforcing that integration. This may occur spontaneously, but usually it entails interpretations proposed by leaders either because they face the same circumstances as ordinary members or because they have their own interests in transforming certain components of ethnicity into political ideologies that serve their own power interests or both (Cohen, 1974; De Vos and Romanucci-Ross, 1975; Rothschild, 1981).

However, a consensus may not exist within the elite and among the various segments of the community. The implications for the group of environmental conditions may be ambiguous and, accordingly, subject to different interpretations. Or the implications may simply not be the same for different segments of the community. Or, no segment may be powerful enough to impose its conception of the group, its views of the community's place in the larger society, its selection of important historical events, or its ideas concerning the group's future on the rest of the group. Different systems of ideas may be used by leaders competing with each other for the loyalty of the members.

Subgroups competing over the definitions of the collective identity tend to be differentiated in terms of generation, political philosophy, source (institutional or other) of power, or some combination of these factors. They tend to have views of the world that not only differ but may also be in opposition to each other because of their background and/or their position in the sociopolitical structure. Lopata (1964:123), for example, notes a conflict in the American Polish community between "two segments interested in preserving different aspects of Polish culture: those who enjoy certain elements of the folk culture, such as dances, costumes, songs, and holiday observances, are frequently criticized by those who want to stress only the 'intellectual' national cultural achievements, such as the music of Chopin."

Harney's (1985:20–21) description of the elite of the Toronto Italian community provides an insightful illustration of the competing orientations and definitions of the situation that can exist in an ethnic community. He contends that the elite consists of four groups, "each with a view of, or definition of, the 'ethnie,' the meaning of the ethnonym Italian and an attitude toward the 'ethnic project' of Italians in Canada." One group viewed the immigrants as essentially *lavoratori* abroad, migrants or guest workers like those in western Europe. This was primarily the view of Italian government officials and the organic intelligentsia around them and of the immigrants who remained absorbed with Italian political parties. In this view, "the 'ethnie' is best understood as a 'colonia' and that leadership should come naturally from the consulate."

Others see immigrants as new Canadians. This perspective is essentially adopted from Canadian authorities whose agents were and are often the children of the immigrants. In this view, what is significant in the experience of immigrants is their contribution to the host country and their capacity to adjust to its ways. Ethnoculture and ethnic identity are seen as transient phenomena, whose main role is to assist in the process of gaining full-fledged participation in the host society.

The third group of the elite consists mainly of the leaders of ethnocultural organizations. For them, the hybrid identity acquired as a result of immigration in a new society constitutes a reality and a collective value that may persist indefinitely. "It is this group that now dominates what little history—in the sense of controlling the record of events and the writing of the narrative—exists in the 'ethnie.' This is so not least of all because this elite disposes of the funds or the political access routes to Canadian government funds upon which much of the immigrant or ethnoverted organic intelligentsia survives" (Harney, 1985:22).

The younger segment of leaders, educated in North America, have adopted a fourth interpretation of community: "The folk view common to the leadership of *paese* and regional clubs and to those who find cultural satisfaction in sub-national associations, dialect and the living vagaries of *Italiese* and change in the collectivity" (Harney, 1985:23).

An interesting description of competing conceptions of a collective identity is also provided by Wong (1977) in his analysis of the New York's Chinatown. The traditional and the new elites each claim to embody or represent the true identity of the community. The identity of the former has three components: "Overseas Chinese" when transacting business with the Taiwan government; the "real Chinese" in contrast to the second- and third-generation segment of the collectivity and especially in the context of their opposition to the new elite; and "Chinese American" when dealing with the American government (Wong, 1977). These conceptions are reflected in the types of activities the traditional elite engage in: regular cultural activities, such as festivals; membership and participation in traditional associations; and devotion to the traditional customs of China. Their ethnicity tends to be behavioral.

In contrast, the new elite promote the view that "every American who has full or part Chinese blood, irrespective of language and birthplace, is a Chinese-American" (Wong, 1977:6). They also define themselves as Asian Americans when useful in terms of the cause pursued (e.g., fighting discrimination) or in relation to more encompassing categories adopted in the larger society (e.g., Asians or Orientals). They "realize that the continual expression and validation of Chinese culture are necessary for ethnic solidarity" but in the context of securing more resources for the collectivity from societal institutions. Accordingly, they recall the "memories of the tragic history of the early Chinese immigrants in America" and use symbols that refer to "Chinese or Asian power." Their aim is consciousness-raising and "preparing the members of the Chinese ethnic group to participate in the larger society" (Wong, 1977:8).

The rise of the nationalist elite in the Ukranian community also involved serious symbolic competition with other segments of the community. As presented earlier, nativism in Canadian society was a determining factor in the rise of the nationalist elite. But processes internal to the community were also involved. For example, the elite articulating and promoting the nationalist identity rose in part through the organization of a new Ukranian church in Canada in opposition to the existing powerful Orthodox churches and the Roman Catholic church.

Resentful of the Uniate church's ties with the papacy, of celibacy, of property allotment; aware that parishioners had the democratic right to debate matters of parish policy and even to disagree with the priest; impatient with the refusal of the Russian Orthodox church to recognize Ukranian as a separate nationalism; . . . infuriated by the opposition of Greek Catholic Bishop Budka to secular residential schools or institutes that the Ukranian-Canadian intelligentsia were founding in the cities, the people were soon to demand an independent, democratically organized, Ukranian-nationalist church in Canada.... It was the petty intelligentsia—school teachers, newspaper editors, bookstore owners, progressive priests—who first brought the nationalist message.... They founded their own paper ... and drummed into their readers the need to use "Ukranian" as their ethnic designation. (Kostash, 1977:133–134)

The rising elite were also in conflict with the leftist groups who were promulgating a "radical populist" view of the Ukranian-Canadian reality. The symbolic opposition between them is well illustrated by the competing interpretations and meanings each gave to Taras Shevchenko, who is widely seen among Ukranians as one of their critical historical figures. However, those who attended events organized by the socialist groups "heard him spoken of as an international champion of the working classes, a man himself risen from the benighted serfdom who never compromised his hatred of the exploiter, be it the Polish regime, the Ukranian gentry, the priest, the tsar." But those who attended events organized by nationalist organizations "heard of Shevchenko as a great poet who associated with the intelligentsia and literati of St. Petersburg and Ukraine, who was admired by Charles Dickens and whose life represents the struggle against ignorance and enslavement and the achievement of genius and patriotist." They heard of him as one who denounced "the tyranny of communism over his people," as one who "wanted all Ukranians to be 'agreeable with each other and let neither borders, nor parties, nor social status, nor governments, nor wealth separate us' " (Kostash, 1977:264–265).[18]

Usually, the competition between groups in the community takes place not only with regard to the content of the collective representations but also over the means of symbolic production and dissemination in the community. These can include the press, radio and television, university chairs, research organizations, educational facilities, religious organizations, and cultural centers. All these are potentially powerful instruments for shaping the collective identity, and it is therefore not surprising that the groups with different views attempt to gain control over them.

Different subgroups or factions may also attempt to become recognized as the authentic bearers of the cultural heritage of the collectivity and the embodiment of its distinctive cultural traits. Each may claim that they are the most faithful followers of the group's traditions, that they are inspired and guided by the philosophies and achievements of historic figures, that they have grasped the true interests and deep aspirations of the community. In the process of having such claims recognized, the groups not only attempt to appropriate status and legitimacy for themselves, but, as will be seen later, contribute to the definition of the collective identity as well.

The competition for status and legitimacy and for the control of the means of symbolic production can also be carried out through strategies of degradation. These consist of attempts to discredit one's opponents by highlighting their weaknesses and errors, by pinning negative labels on them, and by demonstrating that they are unrepresentative of the community or, worse, that they are using the community for their own personal interests. Such status quarrels between subgroups and their organizations can also have a significant impact on the collective identity by imprinting in the public consciousness key elements that could define "who we are as a people" or "who we want to be."

The controversies underscore the lack of consensus; but even if this is so, it does not mean that they do not play a role in the crystallization of identities among members of the collectivity. Gerus (1982:195), for example, suggests that the competition among various subgroups has "stimulated a Ukranian national consciousness in many, without which the formation of the Ukranian Canadian Committee would have been impossible."

It should perhaps be noted, at least as a hypothesis, that if situations of complete or incomplete consensus are relatively rare, so are those of complete or almost complete lack of consensus. Partial consensus is probably the most frequent occurrence: disagreements concerning specific components of the collective indentity tend to exist within a consensus over a number of collective self-perceptions and self-definitions. The consensual layer is probably thicker in periods of social stability than in periods of economic, demographic, cultural, and political change.

Cohen (1974:32) points out that all struggles for power are segmentary: enemies at one level must be allies at a different level. One "is forced to be an enemy and an ally with the same set of people, and it is mainly through the 'mystification' generated by symbolism that these contradictions are repeatedly faced and temporarily resolved. . . . The degree of 'mystification,' and the potency of the dominant symbols that are employed to create it, mounts as the conflict, contradiction, or inequality between people who should identify in communion increases."

In many situations, each competing subgroup has enough of a power base to maintain itself as a proponent of a particular interpretation of the group's past and future, of a particular definition of the group's symbolic boundaries, of the elements of its cultural distinctiveness, and of its place in the larger society. In such instances, a description of the collective identity consists of a composite of elements promoted by the various factions. The subidentities may, on a day-to-day basis, be more important for members of the collectivity than any identity that may overarch them.

This coexistence is not due to the fact that each of the definitions of the collective identity has some inherent theoretical merit or validity. Rather, it results from the mobilizing potential of the social factions, that is, from their ability to gain support for the collective representations they favor and thus to assure their presence in the symbolic universe of the collectivity. As Berger and Luckmann (1966:120) point out, there is always

a social-structural base for competition between rival definitions of reality and... the outcome of the rivalry [is] affected, if not always determined outright, by the development of that base. It is quite possible for abstruse theoretical formulations to be concocted in near-total isolation from the broad movements in the social structure, and in such cases competition between rival experts may occur in a sort of societal vacuum.... As soon, however, as one or the other of those viewpoints gets a hearing in the surrounding society, it will be largely extra theoretical interests that will decide the outcome of the rivalry. Different social groups will have different affinities with the competing theories and will, subsequently, become "carriers" of the latter.... Rival definitions of reality are thus decided upon in the sphere of rival social interests whose rivalry is in turn "translated" into theoretical terms.

When each of the competing subgroups has a social-structural base, an accommodation tends to be worked out, even if only temporarily. The accommodation may come about tacitly or explicitly. It may be arrived at more or less reluctantly and thus may be more or less vulnerable to an upset as the opportunities available to each faction for symbolic initiatives change. The accommodation takes the form of a recognition, more or less grudgingly granted, of different subidentities, an acceptance of their coexistence. Two or more subethnicities are granted legitimacy within the encompassing ethnic collectivity.

Collective Identity and Political Ascendancy

The history of a group and its societal situations are very complex phenomena. Given this complexity, the system of ideas through which members represent to themselves their community and its relationship to the larger society consists in a selection from and interpretation of the realities of that history and societal situation. The features of the group's environment—opportunities, constraints, resources, and threats—are not equally critical to the group and, accordingly, influence the selections and interpretations that shape the group's conceptions of itself and of its position in the society.

But the selections and interpretations, as well as the resulting cognitive construction, are partly carried out by elites whose ideas and actions are influenced by the particular position they occupy in the community and in the larger society. They are not neutral conveyors of conceptions and evaluations. Their position in the sociopolitical structure affects the selections and interpretations they adopt and promote. Also, because of their position, members of the elite tend to have a greater interest in the maintenance of the community and in the particular definition of its identity than other categories of members.

Thus the collective identity as a system of ideas, beliefs, and evaluations can be shaped by an elite attempting to gain and/or maintain its political ascendancy in the community and to control the conduct of its public affairs. As Lukes (1975:301) pointed out, "Rituals can be seen as modes of exercising, or seeking to exercise, power along the cognitive dimension." The exercise and maintenance of power involves the manipulation of a system of ideas that renders "intelligible society and social relationships, serving to organize people's knowledge of the past and present and their capacity to imagine the future." It involves the authoritative definitions of certain ways of seeing society, specifying "what in society is of special significance, (drawing) people's attention to certain forms of relationships and activities— and at the same time, therefore, (deflecting) their attention from other forms, since every way of seeing is also a way of not seeing."[19]

The processes of spontaneous creation in the emergence of the collective identity and those of symbolic management are not mutually exclusive; one does not necessarily preclude the other, either theoretically or empirically. Both can exist simultaneously, although their relative importance can vary considerably with the sociopolitical context.[20] Symbolic management to mobilize the collectivity in relation to environmental threats, demands, or opportunities can occur at the same time as symbolic management for the sake of gaining and exercising power. Both can take place simultaneously and can be closely intertwined in the symbolic activities that are actually carried out by the governing elite. But, of course, the relative importance of these two purposes of symbolic management can vary considerably from group to group or from one historical period to another.

In order to understand how elite interests relate to the formulation of particular representations of the group, of its past and its future, it is necessary to examine the specific forms that these interests can take. Virtually all elite activities have a symbolic dimension (Edelman, 1964) and, as a consequence, are potentially relevant for the definition of the collective identity. But some appear to have a more direct and immediate relevance for the maintenance of political ascendancy. These have to do with the legitimation of the institutions of the community and of the elite's position of dominance in them, with the resistance or opposition offered by groups challenging the elite's positions and/or the institution itself, with the mobilization of support for particular objectives or projects, and with the selection of the means (e.g., symbols, rituals, monuments) for the expression and celebration of the group's identity.

All attempts to deal with these issues involve the use of arguments to explain and justify one's power position and its institutional basis. Facts are presented; theories are put forward; epithets, as evocative as possible, are used; images of good and evil are drawn; and ultimate values are invoked. Through this public discourse, a more or less precise conception of what the group is and what it stands for emerges or is reaffirmed. Orthodox views or representations of the collectivity are defined and validated; "heresies" are denounced. It is through such exercises of symbolic power that a system of ideas interpreting the group to itself becomes institutionalized; that a history of the collectivity becomes official; that what is essential about the group's identity is established; than an orthodoxy is established.

CONCLUSION

The boundaries and membership of ethnic polities are not defined legally or administratively. In this sense, membership has a voluntary character, although this does mean that one can enter and exit the ethnic polity arbitrarily, without going through social processes regulated by social norms.

The boundaries of a social entity have to do with networks of relations among individuals and organization. But they are perhaps more fundamentally symbolic. They involve the definition of the collective identity. Because of its voluntary character, the ethnic polity has boundaries that must be constantly redefined and/or maintained. Accordingly, the definition of the collective identity is a basic political task that ethnic polities and their elites must address. If the identity is not defined in at least some minimal fashion, there will not be any ethnic polity to govern.

Three components of the collective identity were discussed: the collective conceptions of the character of the group; those pertaining to its relationship with other groups, especially its "significant others"; and those related to the place and role of the group in the encapsulating society and in the international order.

Several sets of forces shape the collective identity. Collective identities are related to the four approaches considered in this work. First, a collective identity emerges from the individual and shared experiences of the members of the group in a particular sociopolitical environment. Thus, the features of that environment and the attitudes and behaviors that prevail in it can be a determinant for the views that an ethnic group holds of itself. But the composition of the group and the changes in its potential membership (i.e., generational changes, waves of immigrants) can also have a significant impact on the collective identity.

Second, groups outside the boundaries of the ethnic collectivity and institutional actors in particular can have an impact on the collective self-conceptions that prevail in a group or those that become secondary or are abandoned. External agents can intervene directly in the definition process (e.g., by assigning a role to the ethnic polity in their own policy initiatives). They can, in addition, have an influence through the promotion of particular ethnic ideologies and by validating or failing to validate particular elements of ethnic self-definitions.

The agents that actively pursue the definition and promotion of particular conceptions of the group, of its relations with other groups, and of its role in the larger context can also be found within the polity. The collective identity does not simply emerge from the experience of the group. It is also shaped by individuals who have particular symbolic (and associated power and material) interests. Accordingly, various segments of the polity may find themselves in competition with each other in their attempts to orient the system of ideas, values, and symbols that define and represent the group to itself and to others.

Finally, in situations in which one faction dominates the polity, this faction will attempt to promote a view of the world and of the place of the ethnic group in it that conforms to its ideological interests and to the maintenance of its position of power.

NOTES

1. Although it is not so if parents have different ethnic backgrounds.

2. This threefold distinction is quite similar to that made by McKay and Lewins (1978) between "ethnic category," "ethnic awareness" and "ethnic consciousness."

3. Ethnic boundaries are also voluntary in the sense that, at least in the Canadian context, they are not defined legally either in terms of territory or of social characteristics. They are social and symbolic, even if certain territories, such as urban neighborhoods, come to be associated with a particular ethnic group in the minds of both insiders and outsiders.

4. Empirical evidence of such variations are provided by the Ethnic Pluralism Study. See Breton et al. (1990).

5. Elazar (1976) makes a similar argument with regard to the Jewish community.

6. For analyses of ethnic identity at the individual level, see in particular Driedger (1977), Isajiw (in Breton et al. 1990), De Vos and Romanucci-Ross (1975), and Gordon (1964).

7. The structural tradition points to the social location of racial prejudice while the social psychological explanation locates it in the individual personality. But "both possess an essentially behaviorist understanding of racial processes, where different factors and situations predictably influence specific individual responses to racial differences." (Prager, 1982:106–107).

8. On the relationship between individual and collective identities, see Mannheim (1936:Ch. 1), Berger and Luckmann (1966), and McCombs (1985).

9. The three dimensions correspond to the principles of identity, opposition, and totality that Touraine (1965) identifies in relation to social movements.

10. The impact of the social environment on a group's collective identity is discussed further in a subsequent section of this chapter.

11. See, for example, Troper and Weinfeld on this question (1988:59–60).

12. Lukes (1975:291) defines ritual as a "rule-governed activity of a symbolic character which draws the attention of its participants to objects of thought and feeling which they hold to be of special significance."

13. Berger and Luckmann (1966) identify several levels of legitimation: incipient, theoretical propositions in a rudimentary form, explicit theories, and theoretical traditions that integrate different provinces of meaning.

14. Boldt (1980, 1985), for instance, argues and shows that in order to maintain a "behavioral ethnicity," the group must isolate itself from the larger society.

15. The expression *cultural entrepreneurs* is taken from Young (1976:45–46).

16. See also Marunchak (1970) and Makuch (1979).

17. These, it will be recalled, are the groups included in the Ethnic Pluralism Study.

18. Kostash's quote is from a Ukranian publication. On the symbolic conflicts between nationalist and socialists, see also Kolasky (1979:56–59).

19. See also Gusfield and Michalowicz (1984), Edelman (1964, 1971), Berger and Luckman (1966, especially pp. 120–124), and Prager (1982) on this question.

20. I share Lane's (1981: Ch. 1) position on this matter.

8

Conclusion

It is appropriate and fruitful to follow the course indicated by authors such as Elazar (1976), Harney (1981), Thompson (1979), Troper and Weinfeld (1988), and Waller (1974) and consider ethnic communities as polities (and not exclusively as cultural, social, or economic entities). Ethnic communities govern themselves in the sense that they have structures and carry out processes in relation to internal problems and goals or in relation to their sociopolitical environment. The extent to which and the ways in which governance takes place and the form and complexity of the structures through which it is carried out can, however, vary considerably from one ethnic group to another.

The structures of governance vary along several lines. The main variations are the following:

1. The degree of organizational differentiation, that is the extent to which various community functions are carried out by different organizations or organizational subsystems

2. The degree of interorganizational integration: the extent of relationships among the organizations operating in the community

3. The patterns of horizontal relationships such as coordinative (collaboration, pooling of resources, exchange) and oppositional (avoidance, competition, conflict)

4. The patterns of vertical relationships or of the distribution of power and authority in the system: dominance or centralization versus autonomy or decentralization in the interorganizational networks

5. The extent of formalization of relationships, that is the extent to which they take place through a set of formally established procedures and mechanisms

6. The extent of "pillorization" or factionalization or the existence of systems run for and by different segments of the collectivity

Like any political community, the ethnic polity is a complex reality. A large number of subgroups and organizations can be involved in its functioning and a multiplicity of processes can take place within it simultaneously and in interaction with each other. Four sets of processes were identified for analysis in this book. Each corresponds to a particular dimension of governance:

• Governance as the organizational capacity to cope with (adapt to or proactively change) environmental conditions
• Governance as "indirect rule" by external organizations or groups and their agents
• Governance as the accommodation of competing interests within the collectivity
• Governance as practice of dominance by a faction within the collectivity

Each of these possible dimensions has implications for the organizational apparatus within which governance takes place. Each also raises questions or issues with regard to leadership, policy-making, political participation, and the definition of collective identity (and other processes not examined in this book).

GOVERNANCE AS AN ORGANIZATIONAL CAPACITY TO DEAL WITH ENVIRONMENTAL CONDITIONS

There is no direct one-to-one relationship between features of the sociopolitical environment and the political structures and processes that are found in ethnic collectivities. However, the strategic choices that shape the governance institutions of a community are made within a context of possibilities and constraints and in relation to particular problems and opportunities. The environment is not necessarily the only determinant, but it is not irrelevant. For example, whether the environment is hostile or benign, simple or complex, and organized or coordinated in its relation to the ethnic community can make a difference. The environment can affect the degree of organizational differentiation in the polity, the occurrence and pattern of interorganizational coordination (i.e., horizontal or vertical), the existence of segmentation, and the extent of centralization or decentralization.

The central issue of governance as an organizational capacity is the mobilization, processing, and utilization of appropriate resources (Etzioni, 1967). Adequate policy-making is a matter of collecting and analyzing the necessary information and formulating theories of action: it is a matter of planning. It is a question of establishing linkages with individuals and organizations in the relevant settings within the collectivity, in the larger society, and even in the international sphere. Leadership is a role assigned to those who can mobilize resources, plan and coordinate action in such a way as to deal effectively with problems, or bring about results desired by community members.

The maintenance and strengthening of identification with the community and the mobilization of participation in its public affairs are perhaps the central problems that have to be addressed if the polity is to be effective. Membership in an ethnic category may not be voluntary, since individuals are necessarily born in one. Membership and participation in an ethnocultural community, however, is to a considerable extent a matter of choice, unless one is excluded through discrimination from participation in the larger society. This is one of the reasons why ethnic leaders frequently attempt, whenever possible, to sensitize members and potential members to the threats that confront the group. They may even exaggerate the threats or dangers or attempt to convince individuals that "they cannot make it alone" in order to encourage their involvement in the organized life of the ethnic community. Accordingly, the critical issues have to do with the conditions under which leaders can nurture and enrich the collective identity and increase or at least maintain the size of the polity and strengthen its cohesion.

GOVERNANCE AS "INDIRECT RULE" BY EXTERNAL AGENTS

The impact of the sociopolitical environment can be direct as well as indirect. As indicated, the sociopolitical environment is partly a set of resources, opportunities, problems, and constraints. But it also consists of a set of organizations and their agents or representatives. These may have an interest in the structures and policies and the selection of leaders in the ethnic polity and may attempt to intervene in its affairs, much like the government and corporations of a country can have an interest and try to influence the structures, decisions, and choice of leaders in other countries.

Resources controlled by ethnic communities and their members are potentially interesting to politicians and government functionaries. Among the main ones are legitimacy, support for the party in power or for a particular agency and its programs and moral validation of state policies in terms of the conformity to basic societal values (e.g., justice, equality of opportunity).

Other resources are organizational (means for service delivery, channels of communication). State agencies may need ethnic organizations or find the use of them very helpful in implementing their own policies and programs. This is particularly the case with regard to subgroups that are, for cultural and/or linguistic reasons, otherwise difficult to reach: new immigrants, the aged, and the children of immigrants. It may also be the case with subgroups who may offer resistance to government policies such as those pertaining to immigration and language. In addition, ethnic organizations may be necessary channels when state agencies deal with specifically ethnic interests, such ethnic/racial discrimination or the expression and maintenance of culture.

In addition to being a source of opportunities for government agencies and their officials, the ethnic community may also be a source of threats or dangers for them. A dissatisfied community may protest either the inaction of the state or the inadequacy of its existing policies or their implementation. The protest can take many forms such as violent outbreaks, disruptions, boycotts, orderly demonstrations, well-orchestrated campaigns through the media, or votes for another party at the next election. The fear of disorder, of a damaged public image, of trouble with bureaucratic superiors, of losing an election, and the like may prod politicians and functionaries to pay attention to the interests of the ethnic population. Also, the threats may be such as to lead them to establish mechanisms through which the situation of the ethnic population can be regularly monitored and taken into account in one way or another.

Thus, the interventions of external bodies can be supportive, obstructive, or directive. On the one hand, outside actors can intervene to assist ethnic organizations and their leaders to pursue the goals and implement the programs that are congruent with their own. On the other hand, they can attempt to prevent certain courses of action or the rise of certain persons to leadership positions. Also, in order to obtain conformity with their own organizational and political interests, they can intervene to structure the organizations of the ethnic polity, influence the content of its policies, shape the underlying system of ideas, and influence the extent and especially the modes of political participation.

Through these processes, the ethnic polity becomes more or less integrated in the apparatus of the administrative state. It becomes incorporated in policy communities and their interorganizational networks that correspond to the sectoral organization of governments (Pross, 1982; Laumann, Knoke, and Yong-Hak, 1985).

GOVERNANCE AS THE ACCOMMODATION OF COMPETING INTERESTS

Ethnic collectivities are socially differentiated along lines such as social class, region, generation, religion, and ideology much like the rest of society. When groupings are formed on the basis of these social cleavages, competition and conflict are likely to arise in the polity because the cleavages correspond to differences of interest (material, sociocultural, political, or symbolic).

Groups can compete for power and influence, prestige, and material resources. They can also compete over the very organization of the governance institutions since their structure can have serious implications for the distribution of power in the polity. Because of this, the form that governance institutions take is partly the outcome of political struggles among groups vying for their control.

If the groups or factions are relatively equal in power in the community, the forms that will emerge will tend to display accommodative features, such as coordinating agencies or federal arrangements. This will be the case if the competing leaders and their supporters are willing to make compromises. Otherwise, the polity will tend to split into two or more segments. Indeed, the central processes of accommodation are bargaining and compromise. Such processes will characterize decision-making in the community in attempts to represent the diversity of interests in policies and programs and in the symbolic representation of the community to itself and to the larger society.

GOVERNANCE AS POLITICAL DOMINANCE

If the competing subgroups in the collectivity have significantly unequal power bases, the more powerful group is likely to use its advantage to gain ascendancy in the community. It can attempt to achieve this by itself or in coalition with others. The structure of governance that will be put in place in such circumstances will tend to be based on unitary, hierarchical principles. Even if it displays some federal features, for example, the governance structure will tend to operate as a unitary, hierarchical system.

With time, if not from the start, the dominant elite will tend to become less concerned with the interests and problems of the collectivity and more concerned with its own interests, the main one being to maintain itself in power. It will tend to perceive political participation as a possible challenge to its position of ascendancy. Accordingly, it will be at best ambivalent about political apathy: not a problem and perhaps a good thing. It is with compliance that it is primarily concerned.

As already emphasized, these four dimensions of governance can occur simultaneously in a polity. Important aspects of the sociopolitical reality of ethnic polities are likely to be ignored and even distorted if the analysis focuses on one to the exclusion of the other dimensions. That is not to say, however, that they are all equally important at all points in time and in all types of historical circumstances. The conditions or factors that can give salience to one or to another set of processes could not be addressed in this book. Neither was it possible to analyze the interaction among the four dimensions of governance. These questions are important and in need of research.

A polity may not emerge in a particular ethnic collectivity. Or, one may exist during a period of time and then progressively weaken and disappear. The opposite may also be the case. In other words, ethnic polities can be established and disappear; they can expand and contract. The existence and dimension of an ethnic polity depends, among other things, on the importance of its public affairs. The scope and organizational complexity of its governance apparatus reflects the scope and complexity of its ongoing public affairs. Indeed, political organization on an ethnic basis supposes that there are events, issues, and societal conditions with ethnic significance.

The amount of significant events and activities taking place can vary considerably from one ethnic community to another and/or from one historical period to another. And there are many factors that affect the extent to which there are "ethnic public affairs." Such variations across groups and time periods are also in need of systematic research.

For instance, some circumstances constitute opportunities for the formation or expansion of a governance apparatus in ethnic communities: the multiculturalism policies of governments in fields such as education, culture, and recreation are an example. Others constitute problems to be dealt with or needs to attend to: economic well-being, discrimination, immigration policies, social services, housing conditions. Still others are objectives that members of groups may seek to attain: cultural maintenance and development, public recognition for the historical and contemporary role of the group in the larger society, increased representation and power in the political and administrative arms of government.

On the other hand, circumstances may offer a few or no possibilities for the formation of ethnic political organizations or at least none that potential founders and leaders perceive as realistic. These circumstances may be the result of extensive participation of members of the second and third generation in societal institutions, particularly economic; the accompanying acculturation and residential mobility; the role of governments in assuming functions previously carried out by ethnic communities; secularization trends; and the successful solution of problems of concern to ethnic minorities.

References

Aboud, Frances E.
  1981 "Ethnic Self-Identity." Pp. 37–56 in Robert C. Gardner & Rudolf Kalin
        (Eds.): *A Canadian Social Psychology of Ethnic Relations.* Toronto: Me-
        thuen.
Adam, Heribert, & Giliomee, Hermann
  1979 *Ethnic Power Mobilized: Can South Africa Change.* New Haven: Yale
        University Press.
Anderson, Grace, & Higgs, David
  1976 *A Future to Inherit: The Portuguese Communities of Canada.* Toronto:
        McClelland & Stewart.
Avery, Donald
  1979 *"Dangerous Foreigners." European Immigrant Workers and Labour Rad-
        icalism in Canada, 1896–1932.* Toronto: McClelland & Stewart.
Bacharach, Samuel B., & Lawler, Edsward J.
  1981 *Power and Politics in Organizations: Social Psychology of Conflict, Co-
        alitions and Bargaining.* San Francisco: Jossey-Bass.
Bailey, F. G.
  1970 *Stratagems and Spoils. A Social Anthropology of Politics.* Oxford: Basil
        Blackwell.
Balandier, Georges
  1969 *Anthropologie Politique.* Paris: Presses Universitaires de France.
Banfield, Edward, & Wilson, James Q.
  1963 *City Politics.* Cambridge: Harvard and M.I.T. Presses.
Barth, Fredrik
  1969 *Ethnic Groups and Boundaries.* Boston: Little, Brown & Co.
Baureiss, Gunter
  1980 "Chinese Organizational Development: A Comment." *Canadian Ethnic
        Studies* 12: 124–130.
Baureiss, Gunter
  1982 "Ethnic Resilience and Discrimination: Two Chinese Communities in Can-
        ada." *The Journal of Ethnic Studies* 10: 69–87.

Becker, Howard S. (Ed.)
   1967   *Social Problems: A Modern Approach.* New York: Wiley.
Ben-Tovim, Gideon, Gabriel, John, Law, Ian, & Stredder, Kathleen
   1986   "A Political Analysis of Local Struggles for Racial Equality." Pp. 132–52
           in John Rex & David Mason (Eds.): *Theories of Race and Ethnic Relations.*
           Cambridge: Cambridge University Press.
Benson, J. Kenneth
   1975   "The Interorganizational Network as a Political Economy." *Administra-
           tive Science Quarterly* 20: 229–249.
Berger, Carl
   1970   *The Sense of Power.* Toronto: University of Toronto Press.
Berger, Peter L.
   1967   *The Sacred Canopy.* New York: Doubleday.
Berger, Peter L., & Luckmann, Thomas
   1966   *The Social Construction of Reality.* New York: Doubleday.
Blumer, Herbert
   1958   "Race Prejudice as a Sense of Group Position." *Pacific Sociological Review*
           1: 3–7.
Boissevain, Jeremy
   1970   *The Italians of Montreal: Social Adjustment in a Plural Society.* Ottawa:
           Queen's Printer.
Boldt, Edward D.
   1980   "The Death of Hutterite Culture: An Alternative Interpretation." *Phylon*
           41: 390–395.
Boldt, Edward D.
   1980   "Maintaining Ethnic Boundaries: The Case of the Hutterites." Pp. 87–
           104 in Rita M. Bienvenue & Jay E. Goldstein (Eds.): *Ethnicity and Ethnic
           Relations in Canada.* 2nd Ed. Toronto: Butterworths.
Boudon, Raymond
   1977   *Effets Pervers et Ordre Social.* Paris: Presses Universitaires de France.
Bourdieu, Pierre
   1975   "Le Fétichisme de la langue." *Actes de la Recherche en Sciences sociales*
           4: 2–32.
Breton, Raymond
   1983   "La Communauté Ethnique, Communauté Politique." *Sociologie et So-
           ciétés* 15: 23–38.
Breton, Raymond
   1984   "The Production and Allocation of Symbolic Resources: An Analysis of
           the linguistic and Ethnocultural Fields in Canada." *Canadian Review of
           Sociology and Anthropology* 21: 123–144.
Breton, Raymond
   1988   "The Vesting of Ethnic Interests in State Institutions." Pp. 35–56 in James
           S. Frideres (Ed.): *Multiculturalism and Intergroup Relations.* New York:
           Greenwood.
Breton, Raymond, Isajiw, Wsevolod, Kalbach, Warren, & Reitz, Jeffrey, G.
   1990   *Ethnic Identity and Equality. Varieties of Experience in a Canadian City.*
           Toronto: University of Toronto Press.

Brettel, Caroline B.
1980 "Ethnicity and Entrepreneurs: Portuguese Immigrants in a Canadian City." Pp. 300–308 in Alexander Himelfarb & C. James Richardson (Eds.): *People, Power and Process*. Toronto: McGraw-Hill Ryerson, 1980.

Buchignani, Norman, & Indra, Doreen
1980 "Inter-Group Conflict and Community Solidarity: Sikhs and South Fijians in Vancouver." *Canadian Journal of Anthropology* 1: 149–157.

Buchignani, Norman, & Indra, Doreen
1981 "The Political Organization of South Asians in Canada." Pp. 202–232 in Jorgen Dahlie & Tissa Fernando (Eds.): *Ethnicity, Power and Politics in Canada*. Toronto: Methuen.

Cheetham, Juliet
1988 "Ethnic Associations in Britain." Pp. 107–154 in Shirley Jenkins (Ed.): *Ethnic Associations and the Welfare State. Services to Immigrants in Five Countries*. New York: Columbia University Press.

Child, John
1972 "Organizational Structure, Environment and Performance: The Role of Strategic Choice." *Sociology* 6: 1–22.

Clairmont, Donald H., & Magill, Dennis W.
1976 "The Changing Political Consciousness of Nova Scotia Blacks and the Influence of Africville." Pp. 73–96 in Frances Henry (Ed.): *Ethnicity in the Americas*. The Hague: Mouton.

Clammer, John
1982 "The Institutionalization of Ethnicity: The Culture of Ethnicity in Singapore." *Ethnic and Racial Studies* 5: 127–139.

Clark, Peter B., & Wilson, James Q.
1961 "Incentive Systems: A Theory of Organizations." *Administrative Science Quarterly* 6: 129–166.

Cohen, Abner
1974 *Two-Dimensional Man*. London: Routledge and Kegan Paul.

Cohen, Abner
1977 "Symbolic Action and the Structure of the Self." Pp. 117–128 in Ioan Lewis (Ed.): *Symbols and Sentiments*. New York: Academic.

Cohen, Anthony P.
1985 *The Symbolic Construction of Community*. London: Tavistock.

Coleman, James S.
1969 "Race Relations and Social Change." Pp. 274–341 in Irwin Katz & Patricia Gurin (Eds.): *Race and the Social Sciences*. New York: Basic Books.

Collins, Randall
1975 *Conflict Sociology: Toward an Explanatory Science*. New York: Academic.

Cornwell, Elmer E., Jr.
1964 "Bosses, Machines, and Ethnic Groups." *The Annals of the American Academy of Political and Social Science* 353: 27–39.

Cottrell, Leonard S., Jr.
1983 "The Competent Community." Pp. 410–412 in Roland Warren & Larry Lyon (Eds.): *New Perspectives on the American Community*. Homewood, Ill.: Dorsey.

Crenson, Matthew A.
   1983   *Neighborhood Politics.* Cambridge: Harvard University Press.
Crozier, Michel
   1963   *Le Phénomène Bureaucratique.* Paris: Editions du Seuil.
Daschko, Yuri
   1982   "The Ukranian Press in Canada." Pp. 263–280 in Manoly R. Lupul (Ed.):
          A Heritage in Transition: Essays in the History of Ukranians in Canada.
          Toronto: McClelland and Stewart.
Dasgupta, Satadal
   1974   "Associational Structure and Community Development: A Comparative
          Study of Two Communities." *International Review of Community De-
          velopment* 115: 213–226.
De Vos, George, & Romanucci-Ross, Lola (Eds.)
   1975   *Ethnic Pluralism: Conflict and Accommodation.* Palo Alto, Calif.: May-
          field.
Diggins, John P.
   1972   *Mussolini and Fascism: The View from America.* Princeton: Princeton
          University Press.
Driedger, Leo
   1977   "Toward a Perspective on Canadian Pluralism." *Canadian Journal of So-
          ciology* 2: 77–96.
Driedger, Leo
   1980   "Nomos-Building on the Prairies: Construction of Indian, Hutterite and
          Jewish Sacred Canopies." *The Canadian Journal of Sociology* 5: 341–358.
Driedger, Leo
   1988   *Mennonite Identity in Conflict.* Lewiston, N.Y.: Edwin Mellen Press.
Durkheim, Emile
   1898   "Individual and Collective Representations." Pp. 1–34 in *Sociology and
          Philosophy.* New York: Free Press.
Durkheim, Emile
   1912   *Les Formes Élémentaires de la Vie Religieuse.* Paris: Félix Alcan.
Edelman, Murray
   1964   *The Symbolic Uses of Politics.* Urbana, Ill.: University of Illinois Press.
Edelman, Murray
   1971   *Politics as Symbolic Action: Mass Arousal and Quiescence.* New York:
          Academic Press.
Elazar, Daniel J.
   1976   *Community and Polity: The Organizational Dynamics of American Jewry.*
          Philadelphia: Jewish Publication Society of America.
Enloe, Cynthia
   1973   *Ethnic Conflict and Political Development.* Boston: Little, Brown & Co.
Enloe, Cynthia
   1981   "The Growth of the State and Ethnic Mobilization: The American Ex-
          perience." *Ethnic and Racial Studies* 4: 123–136.
Epstein, A. L.
   1978   *Ethos and Identity.* London: Tavistock.
Etzioni, Amitai
   1967   "Toward a Theory of Societal Guidance." *American Journal of Sociology*
          73: 173–187.

Fernandez, Ronald L.
 1979   *The Social Meaning of Being Portuguese Canadian.* Toronto: Multicultural
        History Society of Ontario.
Frideres, James S.
 1974   *Canada's Indians: Contemporary Conflicts.* Scarborough, Ont.: Prentice-
        Hall.
Galaskiewicz, Joseph
 1979   *Exchange Networks and Community Politics.* Beverly Hills: Sage.
Gamson, William A.
 1968   *Power and Discontent.* Homewood, Ill.: Dorsey.
Gans, Herbert J.
 1979   "Symbolic Ethnicity." *Ethnic and Racial Studies* 2: 1–20.
Geertz, Clifford
 1966   "Religion as a Cultural System." Pp. 1–46 in Michael Banton (Ed.): *An-
        thropological Approaches to the Study of Religion.* London: Tavistock.
Gerus, Oleh W.
 1976   "Ethnic Politics in Canada: The Formation of the Ukranian Canadian
        Committee." Pp. 467–480 in Oleh W. Gerus, O. Baran, & I. A. Rozumny
        (Eds.): *The Jubilee Collection of the Ukranian Free Academy of Sciences.*
        Winnipeg: UVAN.
Gerus, Oleh W.
 1982   "The Ukranian Press in Canada." Pp. 263–280 in Manoly R. Lupul (Ed.):
        A Heritage in Transition: Essays in the History of Ukranians in Canada.
        Toronto: McClelland and Stewart.
Gilbert, Claire W.
 1968   "Community Power and Decision-Making: A Quantitative Examination
        of Previous Research." Pp. 139–156 in Terry N. Clark (Ed.): *Community
        Structure and Decision-Making: Comparative Analyses.* San Francisco:
        Chandler.
Glazer, Nathan, & Moynihan, Daniel P.
 1963   *Beyond the Melting Pot.* Cambridge, Mass.: M.I.T. Press.
Glickman, Yaacov
 1976   "Organizational Indicators and Social Correlates of Collective Jewish Iden-
        tity." Doctoral diss., University of Toronto.
Gordon, Milton M.
 1964   *Assimilation in American Life.* New York: Oxford University Press.
Gusfield, Joseph R., & Michalowicz, Jerzy
 1984   "Secular Symbolism: Studies of Ritual, Ceremony, and the Symbolic Order
        in Modern Life." *Annual Review of Sociology* 10: 417–435.
Harney, Robert F.
 1977   "The Commerce of Migration." *Canadian Ethnic Studies* 9: 42–53.
Harney, Robert F.
 1979   "Montreal's King of Italian Labour: A Case Study of Padronism." *Labour/
        Le Travailleur* 4: 57–84.
Harney, Robert F.
 1981   "Toronto's Little Italy, 1885–1945." Pp. 63–84 in Robert F. Harney &
        J. Vincenza Scarpaci (Eds.): *Little Italies in North America.* Toronto: Mul-
        ticultural History Society of Ontario.

Harney, Robert F.
  1985 "If One Were to Write a History of Postwar Toronto Italia." Toronto: Multicultural History Society of Ontario. Mimeo.
Harrison, Paul M.
  1959 *Authority and Power in the Free Church Tradition: A Social Case Study of the American Baptist Convention.* Princeton, N.J.: Princeton University Press.
Henry, Keith S.
  1981 *Black Politics in Toronto Since World War I.* Toronto: Multicultural History Society of Ontario.
Henshel, R. L.
  1976 *Reacting to Social Problems.* Don Mills, Ont.: Longman Canada.
Herbstein, Judith
  1983 "The Politicization of Puerto Rican Ethnicity in New York: 1955–1975." *Ethnic Groups* 5: 31–54.
Hickson, D. J., Hining, C. R., Lee, C. A., Schneck, R. E., & Pennings, J. M.
  1971 "A Strategic Contingencies' Theory of Intraorganizational Power." *Administrative Science Quarterly* 16: 216–229.
Hoe, Ban Seng
  1976 *Structural Changes of Two Chinese Communities in Alberta, Canada.* Ottawa: National Museums of Canada.
Hofstadter, Richard
  1955 *Social Darwinism in American Thought.* Boston: Beacon.
Huel, Raymond
  1986 "When a Minority Feels Threatened: The Impetus for French Catholic Organization in Saskatchewan." *Canadian Ethnic Studies* 18: 1–16.
Hurh, Won Moo
  1980 "Towards a Korean-American Ethnicity: Some Theoretical Models." *Ethnic and Racial Studies* 3: 444–464.
Isaacs, Harold R.
  1975 "Basic Group Identity: The Idols of the Tribe." Pp. 29–52 in Nathan Glazer & Daniel P. Moynihan (Eds.): *Ethnicity: Theory and Experience.* Cambridge, Mass.: Harvard University Press.
Isajiw, Wsevolod W.
  1974 "Definitions of Ethnicity." *Ethnicity* 1: 111–124.
Isajiw, Wsevolod W.
  1977 "Olga in Wonderland: Ethnicity in Technological Society." *Canadian Ethnic Studies* 9: 77–85.
Isajiw, Wsevolod W.
  1979 "Organizational Differentiation and Persistence of the Ethnic Community: Ukranians in the United States." Pp. 79–95 in Paul R. Magocsi (Ed.): *The Ukranian Experience in the United States.* Cambridge, Mass.: Harvard University.
Jabbra, Nancy W., & Jabbra, Joseph G.
  1984 *Voyageurs to a Rocky Shore: The Lebanese and Syrians of Nova Scotia.* Hailfax: Institute of Public Affairs, Dalhousie University.
Jackson, John D.
  1975 *Community and Conflict. A Study of French-English Relations in Ontario.* Toronto: Holt, Rinehart & Winston.

Janowitz, Morris
1976   *Social Control of the Welfare State.* New York: Elsevier.
Jansen, Clifford J.
1978   "Community Organization of Italians in Toronto." Pp. 310–326 in Leo Driedger (Ed.): *The Canadian Ethnic Mosaic: A Quest for Identity.* Toronto: McClelland & Stewart.
Jansen, Clifford J.
1981   *The Italians of Vancouver: A Case Study of Internal Differentiation of an Ethnic Group.* Toronto: York University.
Jedwab, Jack
1986   "Uniting Uptowners and Downtowners: The Jewish Electorate and Quebec Provincial Politics: 1927–39." *Canadian Ethnic Studies* 18: 7–19.
Jenkins, Shirley (Ed.)
1988   *Ethnic Associations and the Welfare State: Services to Immigrants in Five Countries.* New York: Columbia University Press.
John, DeWitt, Jr.
1969   *Indian Workers' Associations in Britain.* London: Oxford University Press.
Jurkovich, Ray
1974   "A Core Typology of Organizational Environments." *Administrative Science Quarterly* 19: 380–394.
Juteau-Lee, Danielle, & Lapointe, Jean
1983   "From French Canadians to Franco-Ontarians and Ontarois: New Boundaries, New Identities." Pp. 173–186 in Jean L. Elliott (Ed.): *Two Nations, Many Cultures.* Scarborough, Ont.: Prentice-Hall.
Kalbfleisch, Karl H.
1968   *The History of the Pioneer German Language Press in Ontario, 1835–1918.* Toronto: University of Toronto Press.
Kallen, Evelyn
1977   *Spanning the Generations: A Study of Jewish Identity.* Don Mills, Ont.: Longman Canada.
Kanter, Rosabeth M.
1977   *Men and Women of the Corporation.* New York: Basic Books.
Kapsis, Robert E.
1978   "Black Ghetto Diversity and Anomie: A Sociopolitical View." *American Journal of Sociology* 83: 1132–1153.
Katznelson, Ira
1973   *Black Men, White Cities.* Chicago: University of Chicago Press.
Kelebay, Yarema
1980   "Three Fragments of the Ukranian Community in Montreal, 1899–1970." *Canadian Ethnic Studies* 12: 74–87.
Kiefer, Christie W.
1974   *Changing Cultures, Changing Lives. An Ethnographic Study of Three Generations of Japanese Americans.* San Francisco: Jossey-Bass.
Klapp, O.
1964   *Symbolic Leaders, Public Dramas and Public Men.* Chicago: Aldine.
Klapp, O.
1969   *The Collective Search for Identity.* New York: Holt, Rinehart & Winston.

Knoke, David
   1981 "Commitment and Detachment in Voluntary Associations." *American Sociological Review* 46: 141–158.
Knoke, David.
   1988 "Incentives in Collective Action Organizations." *American Sociological Review* 53: 311–329.
Kolasky, John
   1979 *The Shattered Illusion: The History of Ukranian Pro-Communist Organizations in Canada*. Toronto: PMA Books.
Kordan, Bohdan S.
   1985 "The Intelligentsia and the Development of Ukranian Consciousness in Canada: A Prolegomenon to Research." *Canadian Ethnic Studies* 17: 22–23.
Kostash, Myrna
   1977 *All of Baba's Children*. Edmonton, Alta.: Hurtig.
Kotler, Milton
   1969 *Neighborhood Government: The Local Foundations of Political Life*. Indianapolis, Bobbs-Merrill.
Kriesberg, Louis
   1973 *The Sociology of Social Conflicts*. Englewood Cliffs, N.J.: Prentice-Hall.
Kwavnick, David
   1973 "Pressure-Group Demands and Organizational Objectives: The CNTU, the Lapalme Affair, and National Bargaining Units." *Canadian Journal of Political Science* 6: 582–601.
Kwavnick, David.
   1975 "Interest Group Demands and the Federal Political System: Two Canadian Case Studies." Pp. 70–86 in Paul Pross (Ed.): *Pressure Group Behaviour in Canadian Politics*. Toronto: McGraw-Hill Ryerson.
Kwong, Peter
   1979 *Chinatown, New York: Labour and Politics, 1930–1950*. New York: Monthly Review Press.
Lane, C.
   1981 *The Rites of Rulers*. New York: Columbia University Press.
Laumann, Edward, O., & Knoke, David
   1987 *The Organizational State: Social Choice in National Policy Domains*. Madison:University of Wisconsin Press.
Laumann, Edward O., Knoke, David, & Yong-Hak, Kim
   1985 "An Organizational Approach to State Policy Formation." *American Sociological Review* 50: 1–19.
Laumann, Edward O., & Marsden, Peter V.
   1979 "The Analysis of Oppositional Structures in Political Elites: Identifying Collective Actors." *American Sociological Review* 44: 713–732.
Laumann, Edward O., & Pappi, Franz U.
   1976 *Networks of Collective Action: A Perspective on Community Influence Systems*. New York: Academic.
Lavigne, Gilles
   1980 "Le Pouvoir Ethnique: Ses Assises et Ses Objets." Pp. 171–181 in Association canadienne des Sociologues et Anthropologues de Langue française

(Ed.): *Les Transformations du Pouvoir au Québec*. Montréal: Editions Coopératives Albert Saint-Martin.

Lewin, Kurt
1948   *Resolving Social Conflicts*. New York: Harper & Row.

Light, Ivan H.
1972   *Ethnic Enterprise in America*. Berkeley, Calif.: University of California Press.

Light, Ivan H., & Wong, Charles C.
1975   "Protest or Work: Dilemmas of the Tourist Industry in American Chinatowns." *American Journal of Sociology* 80: 1342–1368.

Lipset, Seymour M., Trow, Martin A., & Coleman, James S.
1956   *Union Democracy*. Glencoe, Ill.: Free Press.

Litwak, Eugene, & Hylton, Lydia F.
1962   "Interorganizational Analysis: A Hypothesis on Coordinating Agencies." *Administrative Science Quarterly* 1: 395–420.

Lopata, Helena Z.
1964   "The Function of Voluntary Associations in an Ethnic Community: 'Polonia.' " Pp. 117–137 in Ernest Burgess & Donald Bogue (Eds.): *Urban Sociology*. Chicago: University of Chicago Press.

Luebke, Frederick
1978   "The Germans." Pp. 64–90 in John Higham (Ed.): *Ethnic Leadership in America*. Baltimore: Johns Hopkins University Press.

Lukes, S.
1975   "Political Ritual and Social Integration." *Sociology* 9: 289–308.

Lyman, Stanford M.
1968   "Contrasts in the Community Organization of Chinese and Japanese in North America." *Canadian Review of Sociology and Anthropology* 5: 51–67.

Mackenzie, W. J. M.
1967   *Politics and Social Science*. Harmondsworth: Penguin.

Makuch, Nestor
1979   "The Influence of the Ukranian Revolution on Ukranians in Canada, 1917–22." *Journal of Ukranian Graduate Studies* 4: 42–61.

Mannheim, Karl
1936   *Ideology and Utopia: An Introduction to the Sociology of Knowledge*. London: K. Paul, Trench, Trubner.

Markides, Kyriacos C., & Cohn, Steven F.
1982   "External Conflict/Internal Cohesion: A Reevaluation of an Old Theory." *American Sociological Review* 47: 88–98.

Marunchak, Michael H.
1970   *The Ukranian Canadian: A History*. Winnipeg: Ukranian Free Academy of Sciences.

McCombs, Harriet G.
1985   "Black Self-Concept: An Individual/Collective Analysis." *International Journal of Intercultural Relations* 9: 1–17.

McKay, James, & Lewins, Frank
1978   "Ethnicity and Ethnic Group: A Conceptual Analysis and Reformulation." *Ethnic and Racial Studies* 1: 412–427.

Mead, George H.
1934 *Mind, Self, and Society*. Chicago: University of Chicago Press.
Meisel, John
1976 "Citizens Demands and Government Response." *Canadian Public Policy* 2: 564–572.
Merton, Robert K.
1957 *Social Theory and Social Structure*. Glencoe, Ill.: Free Press.
Michels, Robert
1962 *Political Parties: A Sociological Study of the Oligarchical Tendencies of Modern Democracy*. New York: Collier.
Migliore, Sam
1988 "Religious Symbols and Cultural Identity: A Sicilian-Canadian Example." *Canadian Ethnic Studies* 20: 78–94.
Miller, Michael V.
1975 "Chicano Community Control in South Texas: Problems and Prospects." *The Journal of Ethnic Studies* 3: 70–89.
Modell, John
1977 *The Economics and Politics of Racial Accommodation: The Japanese of Los Angeles, 1900–1942*. Urbana, Ill.: University of Illinois Press.
Moe, Terry M.
1980 *The Organization of Interests*. Chicago: University of Chicago Press.
Molotch, Harvey, & Lester, Marilyn
1974 "News as Purposive Behavior: On the Strategic Use of Routine Events, Accidents, and Scandals." *American Sociological Review* 39: 101–112.
Moore, Barrington
1958 *Political Power and Social Theory*. Cambridge, Mass.: Harvard University Press.
Morawska, Ewa
1985 *For Bread with Butter: The Life-Worlds of East Central Europeans In Johnstown, Penn., 1840–1940*. Cambridge: Cambridge University Press.
Nagata, Judith A.
1979 "One Vine, Many Branches: Internal Differentiation in Canadian Ethnic Groups." Pp. 173–181 in Jean Leonard Elliott (ed.): *Two Nations, Many Cultures. Ethnic Groups in Canada*. Scarborough, Ont.: Prentice-Hall.
Nagata, Judith A.
1981 "In Defense of Ethnic Boundaries: The Changing Myths and Charters of Malay Identity." Pp. 87–116 in Charles F. Keyes (Ed.): *Ethnic Change*. Seattle: University of Washington Press.
Nelli, Humbert S.
1970 *Italians in Chicago, 1880–1930: A Study in Ethnic Mobility*. New York: Oxford University Press.
Nix, Harold L.
1969 "Concepts of Community and Community Leadership." *Sociology and Social Research* 53: 500–510.
O'Brien, David J.
1975 *Neighborhood Organization and Interest-Group Processes*. Princeton, N.J.: Princeton University Press.

Oiwa, Keibo
  1986   "The Structure of Dispersal: The Japanese Canadian Community of Mon-
         treal, 1942–52." *Canadian Ethnic Studies* 18: 20–37.
Olson, Mancur, Jr.
  1965   *The Logic of Collective Action*. Cambridge, Mass.: Harvard University
         Press.
Painchaud, Claude, & Poulin, Richard
  1983   "Italianité, Conflit Linguistique et Structure du Pouvoir dans la Com-
         munauté Italo-Québécoise." *Sociologie et Sociétés* 15: 89–104.
Parenti, Michael J.
  1975   *Ethnic and Political Attitudes: A Depth Study of Italian Americans*. New
         York: Amo.
Paris, Edna
  1980   *Jews: An Account of Their Experience in Canada*. Toronto: Macmillan.
Patrias, Carmela
  1978   *The Kanadai Magyar Ujsaq & the Politics of the Hungarian Canadian
         Elite, 1928–1938*. Toronto: Multicultural History Society of Ontario.
Perrow, Charles
  1961   "Organizational Prestige: Some Functions and Dysfunctions." *American
         Journal of Sociology* 66: 335–341.
Perrucci, Robert, & Pilisuk, Marc
  1970   "Leaders and Ruling Elites: The Interorganizational Bases of Community
         Power." *American Sociological Review* 35: 1040–1056.
Petryshyn, W. Roman
  1980   "Changing Realities: Introduction." Pp. ix–xvii in W. Roman Petryshyn
         (Ed.): *Changing Realities: Social Trends Among Ukranian Canadians*. Ed-
         monton, Alta.: Canadian Institute of Ukranian Studies.
Pfeffer, Jeffrey
  1981   *Power in Organizations*. Boston: Pitman.
Pfeffer, Jeffrey, & Salancik, Gerald R.
  1978   *The External Control of Organizations: A Resource Dependence Per-
         spective*. New York: Harper & Row.
Phillips, Almarin
  1960   "A Theory of Interfirm Organization." *Quarterly Journal of Economics*
         74: 602–613.
Ponting, Rick J., & Gibbins, Roger
  1980   *Out of Irrelevance: A Socio-political Introduction to Indian Affairs in
         Canada*. Toronto: Butterworths.
Prager, Jeffrey
  1982   "American Racial Ideology as Collective Representation." *Ethnic and Ra-
         cial Studies* 5: 99–119.
Price, C. A.
  1959   "Immigration and Group Settlement." Pp. 267–287 in W. D. Borrie (Ed.):
         The Cultural Integration of Immigrants. Paris: Unesco.
Pross, Paul
  1982   "Space, Function, and Interest: The Problem of Legitimacy in the Canadian
         State." Pp. 107–130 in O. P. Dwivedi (Ed.): *The Administrative State in
         Canada*. Toronto: University of Toronto Press.

Pross, Paul
   1986   *Group Politics and Public Policy.* Toronto: Oxford University Press.
Radecki, Henry
   1979   *Ethnic Organizational Dynamics: The Polish Group in Canada.* Waterloo,
          Ont.: Wilfrid Laurier University Press.
Ramirez, Bruno, & Del Balzo, Michele
   1981   "The Italians of Montreal: From Sojourning to Settlement, 1900–1921."
          Pp. 63–84 in Robert F. Harney & J. Vincenza Scarpaci (Eds.): *Little Italies
          in North America.* Toronto: Multicultural History Society of Ontario.
Reitz, Jeffrey G.
   1974   "Language and Community Survival." *Canadian Review of Sociology and
          Anthropology.* Special Issue: 104–122.
Reitz, Jeffrey G.
   1980   *The Survival of Ethnic Groups.* Toronto: McGraw-Hill Ryerson.
Ridgeway, Cecilia L.
   1984   "Dominance, Performance, and Status in Groups: A Theoretical Analysis."
          Pp. 59–93 in Edward Lawler (Ed.): *Advances in Group Processes.* Vol. 1.
          JAI Press.
Rogler, Lloyd H.
   1974   "The Changing Role of a Political Boss in a Puerto Rican Migrant Com-
          munity." *American Sociological Review* 39: 57–67.
Roseman, Kenneth D.
   1974   "American Jewish Community Institutions in Their Historical Context."
          Jewish Journal of Sociology 16: 25–38.
Rosenberg, Stuart E.
   1971   *The Jewish Community in Canada.* Vol. 2 of *The Community Today.*
          Toronto: McClelland and Stewart.
Rothschild, Joseph
   1981   *Ethnopolitics: A Conceptual Framework.* New York: Columbia University
          Press.
Roy, William G.
   1981   "The Vesting of Interests and the Determinants of Political Power: Size,
          Network Structure, and Mobilization of American Industries, 1886–
          1905." *American Journal of Sociology* 86: 1287–1310.
Royce, Anya Peterson
   1982   *Ethnic Identity: Strategies of Diversity.* Bloomington: Indiana University
          Press.
Savas, Daniel J.
   1987   "Interest Group Leadership and Government Funding: The Federation des
          Franco-Colombiens—Community Organization or Government Policy
          Agent?" Ph.D. diss., University of British Columbia.
Segal, Morley
   1974   "Organization and Environment: A Typology of Adaptability and Struc-
          ture." *Public Administration Review* 34: 212–220.
Selznick, Philip
   1957   *Leadership in Administration.* New York: Harper & Row.
Shils, Edward, & Young, Michael
   1953   "The Meaning of the Coronation." *Sociological Review* 1: 63–81.

Siegel, Bernard J.
   1970 "Defensive Structuring and Environmental Stress." *American Journal of Sociology* 76: 11–32.
Sills, David L.
   1957 *The Volunteers: Means and Ends in a National Organization.* Glencoe, Ill.: Free Press.
Simmel, Georg
   1955 *Conflict.* Glencoe, Ill.: Free Press.
Skinner, G. W.
   1958 *Leadership and Power in the Chinese Community in Thailand.* Ithaca, N.Y.: Cornell University Press.
Skocpol, Theda, & Finegold, Kenneth
   1982 "State Capacity and Economic Intervention in the Early New Deal." *Political Science Quarterly* 97: 255–278.
Smith, Anthony D.
   1981 "War and Ethnicity: The Role of Warfare in the Formation, Self-Images and Cohesion of Ethnic Communities." *Ethnic and Racial Studies* 4: 375–397.
Smith, Whitney, Jr.
   1969 "The Study of Political Symbolism." Ph.D. diss., Boston University.
Smolicz, Jerzy
   1981 "Core Values and Cultural Identity." *Ethnic and Racial Studies* 4: 75–90.
Snyder, Peter Z.
   1976 "Neighborhood Gatekeepers in the Process of Urban Adaptation: Cross-Ethnic Commonalities." *Urban Anthropology* 5: 35–52.
Stasiulis, Daiva
   1980 "The Political Structuring of Ethnic Community Action: A Reformulation." *Canadian Ethnic Studies* 11: 19–44.
Stasiulis, Daiva
   1982 "Race, Ethnicity and the State: The Political Structuring of South Asian and West Indian Communal Action in Combatting Racism." Doctoral diss., University of Toronto.
Strauss, Anselm, Schatzman, L., Ehrlich, D., Bucher, R., & Sabshin, M.
   1973 "The Hospital and its Negotiated Order." Pp. 303–320 in Graeme Salaman & Kenneth Thompson (Eds.): *People and Organizations.* London: Longman.
Suttles, Gerald D.
   1972 *The Social Construction of Communities.* Chicago: University of Chicago Press.
Suttles, Gerald D.
   1984 "The Cumulative Texture of Local Urban Culture." *American Journal of Sociology* 90: 283–304.
Swartz, Marc J. (Ed.)
   1968 *Local-Level Politics: Social and Cultural Perspectives.* Chicago: Aldine.
Swidler, Ann
   1986 "Culture in Action: Symbols and Strategies." *American Sociological Review* 51: 273–286.

Tajfel, Henri
1974 "Intergroup Behaviour, Social Comparison and Social Change." University of Bristol. Mimeo.
Taub, Richard, Surgeon, George P., Lindholm, Sara, Otti, Phyllis B., & Bridges, Amy
1977 "Urban Voluntary Associations, Locality Based and Externally Induced." *American Journal of Sociology* 83: 425–442.
Taylor, Ronald L.
1979 "Black Ethnicity and the Persistence of Ethnogenesis." *American Journal of Sociology* 84: 1401–1423.
Tennant, Paul
1982 "Native Indian Political Organization in British Columbia, 1900–1969: A Response to Internal Colonialism." *BC Studies* 55: 3–49.
Tennant, Paul
1983 "Native Indian Political Activity in British Columbia, 1969–1983." *B.C. Studies* 57: 112–136.
Thompson, Daniel
1963 *The Negro Leadership Class*. Englewood Cliffs, N.J.: Prentice-Hall.
Thompson, James D.
1967 *Organizations in Action*. New York: McGraw-Hill.
Thompson, Richard
1979 "Ethnicity Versus Class: An Analysis of Conflict in a North American Chinese Community." *Ethnicity* 6: 306–326.
Tirado, Miguel David
1974 "Mexican American Community Political Organization: The 'Key to Chicano Political Power.' " Pp. 105–127 in Chris F. Garcia (Ed.): *La Causa Polvítica: A Chicano Politics Reader*. Notre Dame, Ind.: University of Notre Dame Press.
Tomasi, Sylvano M.
1975 *Piety and Power: The Role of the Italian Parishes in the New York Metropolitan Area*. Staten Island, N.Y.: Center for Migration Studies.
Touraine, Alain
1965 *Sociologie de l'Action*. Paris: Editions du Seuil.
Tremblay, Marc-Adélard
1984 "The Quebec Identity: Theoretical Perspectives and Trends." Quebec City: Laval University. Mimeo.
Troper, Harold, & Weinfeld, Morton
1988 *Old Wounds: Jews, Ukranians and the Hunt for Nazi War Criminals in Canada*. Markham, Ont.: Viking.
Tropman, John E.
1974 "Conceptual Approaches in Interorganizational Analysis." Pp. 144–158 in Fred M. Cox, John L. Erlich, Jack Rothman, & John E. Tropman (Eds.): *Strategies of Community Organization*. Itasca, Ill.: F. E. Peacock.
Tryggvason, Gustav
1971 "The Effect of Intragroup Conflict in an Ethnic Community." *Canadian Ethnic Studies* 3: 85–118.
Vecoli, Rudolph J.
1964–65 "Contadini in Chicago: A Critique of 'The Uprooted.' " *Journal of American History* 51: 404–417.

Waller, Harold M.
   1974   *The Governance of the Jewish Community of Montreal.* Philadelphia:
          Center for Jewish Community Studies.
Waller, Harold M.
   1981   "Power in the Jewish Community." Pp. 151–169 in Morton Weinfeld,
          William Skaffir & Irwin Cotler (Eds.): *The Canadian Jewish Mosaic.* To-
          ronto: John Wiley & Sons.
Ware, Caroline F.
   1940   "Cultural Groups in the United States." Pp. 62–73 in Caroline F. Ware
          (Ed.): *The Cultural Approach to History.* New York: Columbia University
          Press.
Ware, Caroline F.
   1958   "The Breakdown of Ethnic Solidarity: The Case of the Italian in Greenwich
          Village." Pp. 114–138 in Herman D. Stein & Richard A. Cloward (Eds.):
          Social Perspectives on Behavior. Glencoe, Ill.: Free Press.
Warren, Roland L.
   1963   *The Community in America.* Chicago: Rand McNally.
Warren, Roland L.
   1967   "The Interorganizational Field as a Focus for Investigation." *Administra-
          tive Science Quarterly* 12: 396–419.
Warren, Roland L., Rose, Stephen M., & Bergunder, Ann F.
   1974   *The Structure of Urban Reform.* Lexington, Mass.: Lexington Books.
Weber, Max
   1947   *The Theory of Social and Economic Organization.* New York: Oxford
          University Press.
Weick, K. E.
   1969   *The Social Psychology of Organizing.* Reading, Mass.: Addison-Wesley.
Weinfeld, Morton
   1981   "Myth and Reality in the Canadian Mosaic: Affective Ethnicity." *Cana-
          dian Ethnic Studies* 13: 80–100.
Weiss, Melford S.
   1974   *Valley City: A Chinese Community in America.* Cambridge, Mass.:
          Schenkman.
Welch, David
   1985   "Ethnic Minorities: A Conceptual Framework and Its Application to
          Franco-Ontarian Education." Unpublished manuscript.
Wellman, Barry
   1983   "Network Analysis: Some Basic Principles." Pp. 155–199 in Randall Col-
          lins (Ed.): *Sociological Theory.* San Francisco: Jossey-Bass.
Werbner, Pnina
   1985   "The Organization of Giving and Ethnic Elites: Voluntary Associations
          amongst Manchester Pakistanis." *Ethnic and Racial Studies* 8: 368–388.
Wickberg, Edgar
   1979   "Some Problems in Chinese Organizational Development in Canada,
          1923–1937." *Canadian Ethnic Studies* 11: 88–98.
Wickberg, Edgar
   1981   "Chinese Organizations and the Canadian Political Process: Two Case

Studies." Pp. 172–176 in Jorgen Dahlie & Tissa Fernando (Eds.): *Ethnicity, Power and Politics in Canada*. Toronto: Methuen.

Wilson, James Q.
1962   *Negro Politics*. New York: Free Press.

Wilson, James Q.
1973   *Political Organizations*. New York: Basic Books.

Wilson, Seymour, & Dwivedi, O. P.
1982   "Introduction." Pp. 3–16 in O. P. Dwivedi (Ed.): *The Administrative State in Canada*. Toronto: University of Toronto Press.

Wolf, Eric
1956   "Aspects of Group Relations in a Complex Society: Mexico." *American Anthropologist* 58: 1005–1078.

Wong, Bernard
1977   "Elites and Ethnic Boundary Maintenance: A Study of the Roles of Elites in Chinatown, New York City." *Urban Anthropology* 6: 1–22.

Woycenko, Ol'ha
1967   *The Ukrainians in Canada*. Winnipeg: Trident.

Yancey, William, Ericksen, Eugene, & Juliani, Richard
1976   "Emergent Ethnicity: A Review and Reformulation." *American Sociological Review* 41: 391–403.

Young, Charles H.
1931   *The Ukranian Canadians: A Study in Assimilation*. Toronto: Thomas Nelson & Sons.

Young, Crawford
1976   *The Politics of Cultural Pluralism*. Madison: University of Wisconsin Press.

Yusik, Paul
1953   *The Ukranians in Manitoba: A Social History*. Toronto: University of Toronto Press.

Zald, Mayer N.
1970   "Political Economy: A Framework for Comparative Analysis." Pp. 221–261 in Mayer N. Zald (Ed.): *Power in Organizations*. Nashville, Tenn.: Vanderbilt University Press.

Zucchi, John
1980   *The Italian Immigrants of the St. John's Ward, 1875–1915*. Toronto: Multicultural History Society of Ontario.

Index

ABOUT THE AUTHOR

RAYMOND BRETON is Professor of Sociology at the University of Toronto. He has co-authored *Cultural Boundaries and the Cohesion of Canada* and *Ethnic Identity and Equality: Varieties of Experience in a Canadian City*. His research interests are in the social structure and culture of Canadian society, with special attention to ethnicity, language, and intergroup relations. He is a Fellow of the Royal Society of Canada.

DATE DUE

DEMCO 38-297